ROBINS,
SCOTLAND AND THE SEA?

SCOTLAND AND THE SEA

SCOTLAND

and the *Sea*

The Scottish Dimension in Maritime History

NICK ROBINS

CITY OF EXETER
GLASGOW

Seaforth
PUBLISHING

Frontispiece: Ellerman's City Line *City of Exeter* (1914) proudly showing off her graceful cruiser stern and port of registry, Glasgow: a press photo, 'The specially chartered *City of Exeter* leaving Tilbury with the Anglo-French Mission for Moscow', August 1939. (Central Press Photos, London)

Copyright © Nick Robins 2014

First published in Great Britain in 2014 by
Seaforth Publishing,
Pen & Sword Books Ltd,
47 Church Street,
Barnsley S70 2AS

www.seaforthpublishing.com

British Library Cataloguing in Publication Data
A catalogue record for this book is available from the British Library

ISBN 978 1 84832 750 1

All illustrations, unless otherwise indicated in the credits, come from the author's collection.

Typeset and designed by JCS Publishing Services Ltd, www.jcs-publishing.co.uk
Printed and bound in Great Britain by CPI Group (UK) Ltd , Croydon, CR0 4YY

Contents

Preface

THE BRITISH MERCHANT NAVY was supreme from the close of the Napoleonic Wars until the era of cheaper operating costs that emerged under selected foreign flags some 150 years later. Scottish engineering, shipowning and operating, as well as business and entrepreneurial skills, all played a big part in the success of the Merchant Navy. Scottish emigrants took skills with them to the ends of Empire that promoted trade and wealth creation both overseas and at home. In terms of engineering, 'Clyde-built', was the one time 'Kitemark' for the shipbuilding industry the world over. Scottish shipowners included household names such as Allan, Anchor, Donaldson and Henderson, while Scotsmen were also instrumental in founding, and for much of the time managing, Cunard, British India, P&O, Orient, Glen and many other well known 'English' companies.

The story is traced from a variety of angles, even from the role of people such as David Livingstone in developing trade. The school of the 'Honest Scot' working in the City of London includes the iconic tale of the takeover 'merger' of P&O by British India.

This book aims to stir the memory and rekindle interest in this fascinating part of the history of the British Merchant Navy. The author is grateful to a number of people who have supported this endeavour; valuable discussion with Donald Meek helped to formulate the project, Ian Ramsay kindly provided detailed critical review of the text, while Iain Hope provided detail regarding a number of incidents including the sinking of *Athenia*. As always, the publisher, Julian Mannering, has provided valuable guidance during the preparation of the book.

Dr Nick Robins
Crowmarsh, Oxon

1

An Important Role in a National Service

It is surprising how often the historian seeking out the beginnings of famous British shipping companies discovers that the success which attended the pioneering work was largely due to the co-operation and harmonious relationship between brothers. Names which spring to mind are the Allan brothers – the five sons of Hugh Allan, founder of the Allan Line, the four Henderson brothers, linked with the origins of the Anchor Line, the brothers David and Charles MacIver who did so much to set Cunard on its feet … John and William F Donaldson, etc.

From an article which first appeared in *Sea Breezes*,
May 1967, by T E Hughes.

WHICH WAS THE LONGEST serving steamship company in the world? According to the Scots, it was the Clyde Shipping Company, while the English would have it that it was the General Steam Navigation Company of London. Neither company survives to this day, although they both traded vigorously for many decades; the Clyde Shipping Company was only deleted from the Companies Register in 1995. The foundation of the Clyde Shipping Company occurred at the very inception of steam power at sea, quickly following the successful trials of Henry Bell's pioneering little steamship *Comet*. Two early steamers, *Industry* and *Trusty*, entered the trade between the Broomielaw and Greenock in 1814, to form the nucleus of the new Clyde Shipping Company. This was ten years before Thomas Brockelbank floated the General Steam Navigation Company in London.

This Anglo/Scots argument demonstrates that the steamship was established commercially in the inshore trades early in the nineteenth century. The benefits of steam navigation greatly outweighed the vagaries of sail and oar on the river and estuary services, even though the early steamships were unreliable and prone to breakdown, and despite the hostility to the new technology vented by the watermen, most notably on the Thames. The steamer was here to stay, and Clydeside engineers readily took to building wooden-hulled paddle steamers – while the Thames shipbuilders remained steadfast in their commitment to yet more wooden-walled sailing ships for

Typical of the fleet of the Clyde Shipping Company was the coastal passenger liner
Rathlin (1905) which served her owners until 1933 when she was sold.

the Honourable East India Company. The birth of the steamship lay firmly at
the door of Scottish inventors, engineers, boilermakers and shipbuilders, and
the initial success of the steamship was keenly demonstrated by innovative
shipowning syndicates initially focused on Glasgow and Edinburgh. Or so
the Scots would have it – in reality the first commercial steamer service was
in America and the first paddle steamer to venture on the high seas was
American.

Steam-raising from coal was, of course, the driver behind the Industrial
Revolution ashore, and Scotsman Henry Bell took the new steam technology
to sea as a commercial venture aboard his *Comet*. The English engineer
Isambard Brunel wryly observed that 'Bell did what we engineers all failed
in – he gave us the sea steamer; his scheming was Britain's steaming'.

There are several good reasons why Scotland was the hub of maritime
industry in the nineteenth century, and why it exerted its dominance in
early marine engineering, in ship design, and even in the need to develop
international trade. The first was the opening up of the Glasgow Coalfield.
Shallow but rich seams of good-quality steam coal were extracted from
workings beneath what is now Glasgow city, and the mines worked
progressively eastwards into deeper reserves towards Monklands and
beyond. The second was a pool of intelligent and innovative men who had
been brought up on the technological race of the Industrial Revolution.
Collectively, these men maintained the vision that steamships would take
over from sail, and, unlike sailing ships, would run to an advertised timetable

at regular intervals. They were capable of applying their vision equally to the practicalities of timber and of iron castings, and to the business of economics and company management.

Equally important were the inventors and designers who so rapidly drove the evolution of the steamship. They were quick to recognise, for example, that the earliest marine steam engines were over-complicated and constantly in need of adjustment, and so set about simplifying their designs to make the engines less prone to breakdown. Another element was a determination to travel and to trade, complemented by a ready-made skills base which excelled in seamanship. The seamen were the islanders who relied on the sea for food and contact with the mainland; the Hebrideans and Shetlanders took the lead here, and taught the lowland men how to navigate. And the final element was an entrepreneurial will in men who were keen to take risks, but who were also able to manage the risk-taking. Of course, once these skills had been set to work, and steamers set out from the Forth and the Clyde, the momentum generated by the new industry drove it forward with increasing confidence. The developing British Empire provided an ideal global context in which the Scots and their inventions could reach the ends of the earth.

The early steamers arrived in heady days when the wealth of the Industrial Revolution engendered some grand and ambitious designs. When the celebrated English engineer John Smeaton was invited to work on the Forth

Dining saloon aboard the Carron Line steamer *Forth* (1887). (Linda Gowans collection)

& Clyde Canal in the 1780s, the forces driving the construction of the canal were primarily in the east of Scotland. The main impetus came from the merchants of Edinburgh and various innovative manufacturers, such as the Carron Company of Falkirk. They saw the canal as a means of accessing the Glasgow Coalfield, its energy, industry and wealth. In later years, of course, coal-mining spread east as the deeper Central and even deeper Lothian coalfields were successively exploited, with the Longannet Colliery in Fife one of the very last survivors. The merchants and industrialists in the west of Scotland were not so interested in the new canal, but the shipowners were. The Greenock shipowners could see that the canal would at last give them a short cut to Europe and the Baltic, to the extent that, following the opening of the canal, a number of Glasgow- and Greenock-owned schooners were based at Grangemouth where they transhipped cargoes via the canal.

The Carron Company, which was a shipowner in its own right for many years, is particularly significant in the development of the steam engine and of its going to sea. Owning iron ore and limestone quarries as well as coal mines, the company concentrated on iron castings as its main product. James Watt was a friend of Dr Roebuck, one of the founders of the Carron Company, and Roebuck agreed to oversee the making of the first castings for Watt's revolutionary new steam engine back in 1789. The castings were made at the Carron Iron Works in Falkirk. The newfangled engine was assembled at Dr Roebuck's home near Bo'ness and, following trials, was installed in a boat constructed by William Symington, which was then put to the test on the River Carron in 1790. The technology was revisited with sponsorship from Lord Dundas, which enabled the experimental stern wheeler *Charlotte Dundas* to be tried on the Forth & Clyde Canal between 1801 and 1803.

At that time the deep-sea merchant navy was essentially the Honourable East India Company, consolidated by Royal Charter in 1600. Big, heavy, and indeed heavily armed, sailing ships designed to trade to company outstations in the Far East were chartered by the company, although it also owned many ships in its own right. These outstations were themselves heavily defended by the East India Company's own army. Colonisation and the development of Empire was well advanced even before the nineteenth century when the Scots were already prominent in the East India Company.

In the nineteenth century private companies, owning ships on the 64th share principle, began to take up trade wherever perishable cargoes needed to be transhipped and lucrative returns could be earned. Much still depended on sail. The 'tea clippers' raced home with their precious cargoes, so as to receive

One of the Aberdeen Line's famous full-rigged ships, built by Walter Hood of Aberdeen, was *Thermopylae* (1868). In 1872 she beat *Cutty Sark* (1869) homeward to London from Shanghai.

the premium fee for the first ship of the season into port. *Thermopylae*, built by Hood of Aberdeen in 1868, conjures up a vision of racing against *Cutty Sark*, both with a thousand tons of tea in their holds. Nearer to home, the 'rantapike' (literally, 'a rakish young girl') or coastal schooner sailed between the Clyde and Liverpool, and with a fair wind did this in surprisingly little time. Of course, there were no railways in the early nineteenth century, and the 'fast' roads used by the stagecoaches were indifferent at best. The highwaymen too were plentiful, so the option of a quick passage by a fast sailing boat was attractive, especially in fair weather.

But the new maritime industry of the early nineteenth century only carried low-volume, high-value goods, but high-volume, low-value goods such as coal also needed transporting. Before large deadweight vessels were available to undertake this work and before coal wagons set out on the new railways, the availability of local coal dictated where industry could develop, as it could then only be transported in bulk by canal and the local tramroads. Lowland Scotland was set to benefit; the Scottish stage was indeed set for the steamship – bringing raw materials to the factories and mills and taking finished goods to market. One of the more attractive markets was London; it had no coal, and it had little industry, but its people were occupied in traditional trades, in which buying and selling, even to this day, have been the key to money-making. Scottish merchants were keenly aware of this potential, and helped to promote seagoing vessels that would help them lay out their stalls in monied London.

The greatest obstacle to speedy development was that the early seagoing paddle steamers were small and capable of carrying only a small consignment of passengers and perhaps mails. As the wooden hulls grew in size to match the development of more powerful engines, so an increasing load of goods could be conveyed. Crews' and owners' wages could always be enhanced by towage, and the steamship was very adept at helping becalmed sailing ships into port or assisting ships against adverse wind and tide. The steamer soon came to be recognised as a threat to the sailing ship, but it was not until the 1850s that sailing ships were ousted from the express coasting trade, and it was the outbreak of the Great War that caused the deep-sea sailing ships to give up against the superior economics of steam. The major development in the ultimate demise of the sailing ship was the screw propeller as this promoted the carriage of heavy, bulk cargoes such as coal or grain. The propeller, being fully immersed, was much less affected by a change in draught than the surface effective paddle wheel. The introduction of metal in shipbuilding also aided efficiency. The iron hull introduced in the late 1830s reduced a ship's weight by 50 per cent over an equivalent wooden hull, and mild steel, which was introduced in the 1870s, made a further reduction in weight of 10 per cent.

But what did the Scots contribute to this? In short, they designed and built the ships, engineered the propulsion systems, and put up the money to build and operate the steamship fleets. The Scots were not alone, of course, as merchants in Liverpool, Belfast and northeast England were soon to follow, but Scottish involvement with these maritime centres was all-pervading. Scottish-built ships, Scottish managers, Scottish crews and officers penetrated the south and eventually the entire global merchant navy. In the 1930s, for example, every passenger vessel on the Egyptian-owned Khedevial Mail Line's eastern Mediterranean routes was captained by a Scot.

Scotland's maritime industry owed much to the Scottish emigrants. First were the poor crofters displaced by the Clearances and later the skilled craftsmen and businessmen looking for a better life overseas. These men and women helped develop agriculture in numerous countries, they developed

Ben Line of Leith carried its archetypal, and to many unpronounceable, Scottish names around the world: *Bencleuch* (1949) is seen approaching Ocean Dock Southampton, 1 February 1969. (Author)

the transport system to get produce to port and they developed the port infrastructure to handle ships ready to bring primary goods back to the UK. Some trades were dominantly Scottish, the jute trade from Bengal to Dundee being just one example.

Scotland, with just one-tenth the population of England and Wales, represented over half the maritime expertise in Britain by the mid nineteenth century. Where would German-born Canadian national, Samuel Cunard, have been without the resources of George Burns and David MacIver, the latter a Scot exiled in Liverpool, and the engineering skills of Robert Napier working on the Clyde? There are many other great names: Aberdeen, Albion, Anchor Line and its founder Thomas Henderson, along with brothers David, John and William Donaldson (John and William Donaldson), Paddy Henderson – Patrick and brothers Thomas, Robert and George, Thompson's Ben Line of Edinburgh and tramp-shipowners such as 'Hungry' Hogarth of Ardrossan, Maclay & McIntyre of Glasgow, and the quaintly named Raeburn & Verel. Brothers in business were a common start to many early Scottish companies. G & J Burns of Glasgow, for example, was founded by the brothers George and James, although James was the driving force in shipowning. James and Donald Currie, another example, worked together in the established Hull & Leith Shipping Company in the 1850s, before Donald opened new routes, first to Calcutta and then to South Africa with his Castle Line, later amalgamated with the Union Steamship Company to create Union-Castle.

Scottish shipowners catered for the emigration of their own people, as Commander Vernon Gibbs described in his book *Western Ocean Passenger Lines and Liners*:

The prevailing theme of Scotland's story since pre-steamship days has been the outward drain of her people and the Anchor Line carried more Scots overseas than any other line. The main Anchor service was always between Glasgow and New York without likelihood of attracting English traffic, but the outflow of Scottish migrants seemed endless … Search for additional emigrant traffic took small Anchor steamships to Italian ports long before other British lines dreamed of entering the Mediterranean trade, and a Genoa–New York service commenced late in the 1860s. The Anchor Line became a public company, Anchor Line (Henderson Brothers) at the end of the century, and then reconstructed its Glasgow–New York fleet, but the size of the new ships illustrates the trade's limitations. The *Columbia* of 1902 and three later vessels averaged little over 9,000 tons, compared with the 18,000 to 24,000 of the Cunard and White Star intermediate steamers from Liverpool.

British India Steam Navigation Company was a London-based company but its roots were undeniably Scottish; *Kenya* (1920), a product of Alexander Stephen & Sons, was typical of the many proud passenger liners that once served the company.

There has been a succession of Scottish managers guiding otherwise English companies such as P&O, British India, a Scottish company to the core until its relocation to London, the Orient Line, and even London's own General Steam Navigation Company, the latter working on the Home Trade and Mediterranean runs. This penetration of the industry by Scots is paralleled to this day in the finance sector (now somewhat tarnished by the 2008 banking crisis), in which the City of London has always had its Scottish school, the honest and canny Scot being respected as a trusted broker. It is reflected also in modern-day television adverts for the same industry, which invariably feature a Scottish voice-over, and perhaps even a Scottish widow!

(*Above*) The Nelson Line of London imported meat from Argentina to London and strangely clad itself in tartan with its Highland fleet nomenclature; typical was *Highland Warrior* (1920); they were all fine-looking ships.

(*Below*) Tankers Limited, London, operated a tartan nomenclature: three of its ships are seen laid up in the Depression, from right to left, *Scottish Minstrel* (1922) and *Scottish Chief* (1928) and behind them *Scottish American* (1920). Elder Dempster Line's *New Brooklyn* (1920) is laid up to the right. (John Clarkson)

The honest Scot, or so it is perceived, has caused a number of English companies to masquerade under the Scottish banner. The Nelson Line of Liverpool had its distinctively Scottish 'Highland' ship nomenclature, even after its ships had been adsorbed into the Royal Mail Line in 1913. Tankers Limited, formed in London in 1920 to service the burgeoning oil tanker charter market, applied a distinctive 'Scottish' prefix to its twelve-ship fleet until it sold out to the Athel Line during the Second World War. Tankers Limited operated twelve 10,000-ton deadweight classic engines aft, bridge amidships vessels, a mix of twin-screw motor vessels and steamships.

James 'Paraffin' Young is yet another Scot to be celebrated, although a man of little maritime ambition. It was he who looked at the oil shale in Midlothian, and realised that something could be done with it that might even compete with the dominance of coal. He developed a low-flash liquid fuel, which, when pressed and refined into liquid paraffin, was suitable for lighting and heating when burned. It was also suitable for burning in a confined cylinder, in which the pressure of the burnt fuel pushed a piston away to create enough force to be harnessed in a circular motion – the internal combustion engine. Dr Diesel, a German, was the pioneer in the technology that led to the marine

Lochinvar (1908) was a pioneer paraffin-engined passenger ferry operated by David MacBrayne. Her prototype paraffin engines were replaced by diesels in 1926. (© National Maritime Museum, Greenwich, London)

oil engine, but early marine engines were fuelled by petrol, a fuel that was disliked at sea because of its high flashpoint, and later by paraffin. In the early twentieth century, the first passenger vessels powered by the internal combustion engine, and as it happens fuelled by paraffin, were *Comet*, *Scout* and *Lochinvar*, owned and operated by David MacBrayne & Company on a network of inter-island and island–mainland services within the Western Isles of Scotland.

The thread continues in many and diverse directions. The Scots pioneered the concept of the cruise ship, with early cruises to the Scottish Isles from 1827. Patrons included Queen Victoria, the artist J M W Turner, the poet William Wordsworth and the composer Felix Mendelssohn, who all visited Fingal's Cave on the island of Staffa in the late 1820s and early 1830s. Meanwhile, the first cruise round the Nore Light in the Thames estuary was offered to Londoners only in April 1830 – but what a tame venture that was, compared with the rigours of the Minches, even though the struggling and smoky steamer might be of the same genre!

Ships like David MacBrayne's *Iona* (there were three) and the *Columba* were unequalled on the Thames, the Bristol Channel, and the Mersey, or at any other population centre, and these fine ships served Glasgow and the Clyde towns and villages with an unparalleled service. Indeed, steamers such as the first *Lord of the Isles*, replaced on the Clyde by a new steamer of the same name, was 'retired' to the Thames to take over the prestigious tourist routes there, and went on to become the darling of Londoners, at the mature age of thirteen. Meanwhile, the Craigendoran fleet of paddle steamers, the former LNER, is remembered happily to this day in the form of the *Waverley*, which plies as a seasonal excursion ship round the coasts of Britain. Likewise on the Forth, the fleet of the Galloway Saloon Steam Packet took excursionists out of Leith and Newhaven to sleepy havens in Fife or down to New Berwick for a visit to the seaside.

The very foundation of Clyde and Forth excursions is based on a Scottish devotion to the sea. Sailings 'Doon the watter' from the Broomielaw, and away to Fife from Leith and Newhaven, became institutions, the Sabbath excepted, that Lowlanders enjoyed for generations. Although a trip from the pier round the bay 'weather and other circumstances permitting' was very much also an English day out, the Scottish version was accompanied by a piper, an accordion and any amount of drink, but above all by magnificent scenery! Galloway on the Forth, and the numerous competing companies on the Clyde, produced some majestic steamers to attract patronage, while Clyde steamers also maintained daily contact with otherwise remote communities.

David MacBrayne's *Columba* (1878) approaching Dunoon Pier on the Firth of Clyde. (Linda Gowans collection)

Trips further afield were offered in the west to the Hebrides, and in the east from Leith to Aberdeen and north to the Orkney and Shetland Islands. The excursionist was spoiled for choice. Bearing in mind that the *Columba* serving on the Clyde offered a post office, a barber, electric lighting and various other accoutrements, these ships were indeed the nation's market leaders.

Shipbuilding was synonymous with the Clyde, Forth, Aberdeen and Dundee. Scotland's shipbuilding industry produced some of the great ships, some still afloat today, as well as numerous types of coastal vessels. Survivors include two small Isle of Wight car ferries, built at Henry Robb's former Yard at Leith, the last-serving passenger cargo liner, *St Helena*, which was constructed at Aberdeen in 1990, Cunard's *Queen Elizabeth 2*, now languishing at Dubai, and the *Pride of York* which serves P&O Ferries' Hull to Zeebrugge overnight route. Although shipbuilding is largely a thing of the past in Scotland, due to competitive international labour costs in the global market, the legacy of 'Clyde-built' lives on. The tremendous skills base that the industry generated and sustained has been absorbed in other directions; the rivet squads, platers

The North Sea ferry *Pride of York* (1987), originally named *Norsea*, was the last major passenger unit to be built on the Clyde. (Author)

and other trades have now gone, as have the boilermakers in Paisley, and elsewhere, the engine manufacturers, large and small, and all the many and diverse industries throughout Britain that supplied the shipbuilder have ceased trading or diversified to other markets.

Although shipbuilding was essentially a British industry for much of the early nineteenth century, the label 'Clyde-built' evoked a prestige that has not been equalled. The 'Queens' were Clyde-built, while Clydeside craftsmen were renowned across the globe, notwithstanding the excellence of the yards along the Lagan and the Mersey, in northeast England and, at a later stage, at Barrow-in Furness.

Training was also very important. Leith Nautical College and other centres, such as James Watt College at Greenock, have been responsible for many a cadet's apprenticeship in navies across the world. Scottish-based shipping companies trained and promoted cadets for examinations towards engineering and deck officer appointments aboard their own ships, with many progressing to merchant fleets both at home and abroad. The distinction between cadet and apprentice was realised and many a shipping company preferred the apprentice who paid his own way to offer a form of cheap labour at sea.

By the Edwardian era almost every family in Scotland had at least one seaman in deep-sea trading. These men were not only working for Scottish-owned companies, but also supporting the many English shipowning companies, and providing officers and men for fleets flying the flags of diverse nations across the world. A disproportionate number of sailors were from the Hebrides and Shetlands, where frugal family incomes were commonly supplemented by money brought home from lengthy tours of duty back and forth across the Indian Ocean or trading between Australia and the Far East.

Others, of course, preferred the home and coastal trades, and were able to submit their pay packets to their wives on a more regular basis. Potential employers included Hutcheson/MacBrayne, Clyde Shipping, Carron, Dundee Perth & London, Aberdeen Steam Navigation, and London & Edinburgh in the passenger coasting trade, and Leith Hull & Hamburg, Gibson and Rankine with cargo and passengers within the Home Trade Limits – Brest to the Elbe. Even in the 1950s and early 1960s, during the twilight years of the Thames excursion steamers, the soft, gentle Hebridean brogue could be heard from the fo'c'sle of the *Queen of the Channel*, alongside the brash tones of cockney seamen, who were in the majority. Many a canny deep-sea Scot realised that working the Home Trade, and even on the Thames pleasure steamers of GSN, allowed a sight of their wives and children on at least a monthly basis. Experience with Shell Tankers and the like had shown them that home leave was at best yearly, and at worst much longer, with Dad meeting the baby for the first time on a second birthday!

The role of the Scots, however, lay in supporting the development and industry of the British Empire. As the badge of the greatest merchant fleet of all time, the Red Ensign dominated the waterfront of all major ports. It reminded any would-be tyrant that Britain ruled the waves, and that Britain was indeed in charge of the world.

Kathryn Moore, in a study on maritime Scotland in the period 1800 to 1914, summarised the influence of Scottish maritime enterprise on the Scottish people as follows:

> For those of us living at the beginning of the twenty-first century, the critical role played by maritime Scotland within the country's economy in the period from 1800 to 1914 is not easily understood. Nevertheless, the importance of the sea and ships to the lives of a large proportion of the population was, at that time,

generally accepted. Most communities of any size were located on the coast or on rivers making the arrival and departure of vessels a common occurrence. The sea provided jobs not only for those employed in manning ships but also for a wide range of allied trades and businesses on shore. For those with skill and ability, shipping and trade provided opportunities for advancement and prosperity. In many towns and villages investing in a vessel was a common occurrence even for people with relatively little finance at their disposal. It was a means of contributing to the economic life of their communities. To such people any loss at sea had not merely financial repercussions but meant that family members or friends frequently did not return.

The ports were critical to the rapid industrial and economic expansion of Scotland as most industries were export led. Even when the railway network was in place the shipping industry played a vital role in moving goods between maritime communities at home and abroad. And, without the essential food supplies brought in by sea it would have been impossible to meet the requirements of the expanding urban population. New technology transformed the shipbuilding industry and had an important part to play in port expansion. Economic success led to the construction of ever-larger harbours and docks at the main Scottish ports, in turn creating many jobs on shore. Maritime communities in the nineteenth century recognised the inter-dependence of the sea and land in a way that is far less common today but many of our present townscapes are a direct result of that relationship. The sea, and the shipping lines that were built up at this time, linked Scotland with the rest of Britain and with the world. Many chose to emigrate or to work abroad in order to make their own fortunes. But even for those at home, increased prosperity meant that by the early twentieth century the sea had also become a vehicle for recreation and holidays.

But where does Scotland stand today in terms of maritime dominance? The answer, sadly, is simply that it does not stand anywhere. The British Merchant Navy has been decimated, first, by the ending of the British Empire and empowerment of other nations, and second, and more recently, by the 'flag of convenience'. Today it is convenient to fly the flag of, for example, Panama or the Turks and Caicos Islands, to gain the advantage of tax concessions and laxer laws regarding crewing and general safety. With the exception of the ferries owned by Caledonian MacBrayne, which continue to be consistently registered at Glasgow, the names of Glasgow or Leith on the stern of a ship are now replaced by Nassau, Hamilton, and even Gibraltar. But step aboard and look at the crew list, which shows Poles, Bulgarians, and any nationality you like, but who is in charge of them? As often as not, it is a Scot.

The port of Aberdeen is an interesting and colourful harbour, with its blue-hulled NorthLink ferries to Orkney and Shetland and its numerous brightly-painted oil industry support craft. And who owns and operates most of the oily boats? They are very much multinational these days, but step aboard again, and the Scots brogue can be heard somewhere on the bridge or in the engineering department. Indeed, the problem today is persuading youngsters in Britain that there is still a good career to be had at sea, when British officers are in demand. Demand also prefers British hands on the bridges of anchor-handling ships and tugs, as the skills of these men are recognised the world over.

Of anecdotes there are many, and an entire book could be devoted to the stories passed down by each succeeding generation. One that was told on many a Saturday night with a broad Glaswegian accent by the landlord of a pub in Bevois Valley in Southampton related to his tenure as an engineer aboard BP tankers in the 1950s. On one voyage the entire engineering department came from the Glasgow area, and the boys were allowed ashore at Alexandria for just one night. At the end of the evening they found themselves slightly the worse for wear in a dockside warehouse. It appeared that a case of French perfume had 'accidentally' been unloaded from a ship bound from Marseilles to Australia. The collective wages of the engineering department were handed over and the consignment was heaved aboard the tanker, where it was hidden around the ship at leisure before arrival at Stanlow ten days later.

When the Mersey pilot came aboard off Anglesey, talk on the bridge soon turned to HM Customs who were reported to be searching all tanker arrivals from the Middle East. But by the time the ship had entered the Manchester Ship Canal and been brought safely alongside at Stanlow, the engineering department was beyond caring, glazed-eyed and slurred of speech. 'Well, we were no' going to waste the stuff, we paid good money for it, so we drank the lot double quick. But I ken we did smell a bit like a French brothel.'

It is interesting to reflect how the Merchant Navy would have evolved without the Scottish maritime influence. It is, however, noteworthy that throughout the nineteenth and much of the twentieth century Scotland took instruction and received policy from England, albeit often from London-based Scots; the agenda, of course, was set by Westminster. It is noteworthy also that the British Board of Trade aspired to the excellence of an English shipowner rather than accepting the label 'Clyde-built'. This, of course, was Liverpool-based Alfred Holt with its Blue Funnel and Glen Line brands, whose standards were indeed second to none.

Crossing to Orkney – from the Saturday Magazine Supplement *for*
June 1835 from Sketches of the Highlands and Islands of Scotland
by 'PSQR'

The alternative of crossing the Frith in an open boat was fortunately
prevented by the arrival of a small merchant vessel, the master of which
agreed to convey me … Between three and four the skipper summoned
me, excusing his not having done so before, as a gale had been blowing
… The weather had moderated, but it was still blowing hard. The hue of
the sky was inky black, and threatened squalls, and the Frith was boiling
and foaming beneath the dark horizon. … at half past four we bounded
forth with the rapidity of an arrow, for the vessel was light, unballasted,
and an excellent sailer. The crew consisted of the skipper, formerly in
the King's service, who had fought at Camperdown, another man, and
a wretched half-clad urchin … thirteen years of age, who was making
his first voyage, having spent just three weeks at sea. Heavy waves rolled
before a strong western breeze into the bays of Thurso and Dunnet,
which are separated by a narrow ridge, scaling and dashing against the
bold headland of Dunnet, which well merits the significant appellation
of Windy Knap, bestowed on it by seamen; we pass it at daybreak, and
bent our course across the Frith to Cantick Head. The shorter and more
direct passage to Stromness is by the Head and Sound of Hoy, and was
now rendered impracticable to our vessel by the sea setting upon the
island.

The principal headlands of Hoy, in Orkney, the farthest of which is the
Head, rose in fine perspective on our left. The waves were majestically
high and seemed to form a wall, traversing the Frith from coast to coast.
Excepting a fishing smack, off Dunnet Head, making for the harbour, and
a large three-masted merchant vessel, beating up the Frith to windward,
which passed close to us as she lay on one of her tacks, we saw no sail …

The ebb tide, rapid as a torrent, hurried us along; and as the water
was comparatively smooth, we sailed as along a broad majestic river. But
violent squalls now burst upon our unballasted vessel through the gullies
and inlets of the coast of Hoy, the severest of which befell us as passing
under the highest mountain of the island, called the Wart, or Ward Hill
of Hoy, we entered the sound which separates that island from Pomona,
a channel several miles in length, noted for the turbulence of its waters,

which even in calm weather is agitated at its western entrance, as if by a storm, by the mere conflict of the currents. The skipper, fearing lest the vessel should be laid on its beam ends, ran from the helm which he left in my charge, and lowered the fore-sail, while his help-mate was employed in taking in a second reef in the main-sail. Having thus provided for our safety, he lost no time in ordering the unfortunate boy to come on deck and hold to a rope, not that he could be in any degree useful, but that he might be accustomed to dangers to which his life was doomed. The little half-naked wretch obeyed; and after standing, shivering, and drenched with spray for a few minutes, slunk back into his hole. Rapidly crossing the Sound, between the small island of Gremsa and the mainland of Orkney, we approached every moment its formidable lee-shore, lying level beneath a heavy surf. The skipper, perceiving that our present sail was perfectly incapable of making head against the gale, and that wreck was inevitable unless every rag was spread, ordered the fore-sail to be unfurled, the main-sail to be loosed, and put about, having no alternative to face the tremendous swell of the Sound, and to beat up against it, making several tacks, whilst the vessel lay almost on her beam ends, and the waves rolled over her. At length, we were cheered with the sight of the masts of the vessels lying at Stromness Roads, and soon reached the harbour, which was filled by merchantmen detained by adverse winds, very thankful to Providence for our preservation, after a passage of about 35 miles. 'A very coarse day, Sir,' was the first greeting that reached my ear, as I stepped on shore, drenched with rain and spray; an expression to which it was impossible to refuse a hearty assent.

2

The Start of the Steamship Era

THE HISTORICAL BACKGROUND TO Britain's global dominance of the High Seas from 1815 onwards is summarised by Archibald Hurd in his book *The Triumph of the Tramp Ship*:

> The close of the Napoleonic wars in 1815 found Great Britain in an unchallengeable position at sea. Her maritime progress had been overshadowed in the fourteenth and fifteenth centuries by the great fleets of the Hanseatic merchants and those of the Italian republics; it had been outstripped in the sixteenth century by the immense maritime expansion of Portugal and Spain; it had secured, in the first place, independence and then definite ascendancy in the last decade or two before the opening of the seventeenth century; and this ascendancy it preserved first against the Dutch, and then against the French during the 150 years before Waterloo. There was no other navy in the world even remotely comparable with that of Great Britain, while in respect of her mercantile marine, this country emerged from the depredations of the French and American privateersmen stronger than ever in her history.

Hurd also underlines the important role of the American merchant fleet on the Atlantic until after the American Civil War. He describes the Americans as the only serious competitor to the British during the first half of the nineteenth century. From then on, iron and propeller replaced wood and sail. With only one yard in America then capable of working iron into frames and hulls, and with virtually no capability of rolling iron into plate, the Americans had a steep learning curve to rematch British maritime engineering technology.

Hurd also provides a less than glamorous account of life at home as the Napoleonic wars came to an end and the steamship voyage began:

> The country [UK] was still predominantly agricultural; its population since the days of Elizabeth had little more than doubled, and was still under 11 million. Most of what are now main roads were little better than earthen tracks, beaten more or less hard by traffic. The journey by coach from London to Edinburgh or Glasgow was still a matter of days. Though a beginning had been made on the construction of canals, the inland transport of goods was inefficiently carried

on in the main by rough wagons or pack horses. The principle of the steam engine had been discovered, and the enormous possibilities of the latent coal and iron resources of the country had begun to draw on Man's imagination, but the development of these, which the nineteenth century was still to witness, was still at the stage of infancy.

The Scottish coastal trades were maintained by cutter-rigged sailing packets and cargo smacks at the turn of the nineteenth century. The east coast packets were armed with carronades and pistols should they chance upon Napoleon's raiders. The packet routes included the prestigious Leith to London service and services north to Wick, calling at ports large and small, and there were numerous west coast routes from Greenock to Ayr or west to Campbeltown and beyond to the wild and isolated Western Isles. The sailing schedules were haphazard and depended entirely on wind and weather; the sailing packets could not compete with the incoming stage coaches even though sea travel offered an easier journey, unless, of course, the weather was really severe. If only the timetabling and scheduling of the sailing packets could be regularised then they would be better placed to compete with the new overland routes. This was accomplished to a certain degree on the more prestigious routes, such as the east coast packet service to London, by providing standby vessels should the arrival of the packet be delayed. But this was an expensive practice that the passenger fares inevitably reflected.

On the sheltered waters of the Upper Clyde were the fly-boats. These were wherry rigged boats with four oars that could carry about eight tons. They had benches along the sides for the passengers, and an awning, or fly, aft to protect the lucky few from the rain. The fly-boats could take up to ten or twelve hours for the journey between Greenock, via the winding and undredged channel of the Clyde, up to the Broomielaw, hardly a satisfactory journey time with few passenger comforts on offer. Andrew Rennie, the town drummer at Greenock, was part-owner of a fly-boat and decided that he might speed things up by equipping a new boat with experimental side paddles that could be driven by hand. The drivers of the paddle wheels, it would seem, were to be driven on to greater effort by the beat of his drum. It worked, but was stopped by the lack of volunteers to turn the paddles, once the blisters had burst and the novelty had worn off.

Although a number of attempts had been made by Scottish engineers and designers to put the land engine onto a boat in order to propel it, the first acknowledged commercially successful steamship in the UK was Henry Bell's *Comet*. Bell went to shipbuilder John Wood in Port Glasgow and together

Robert Fulton's *Steam Boat* or *Clermont* (1807), 'which poured forth volumes of smoke in the day and showers of sparks at night, filling the minds of onlookers with apprehensive calamities'.

they conceived *Comet* which was launched with steam up in early August 1812, her brick-lined furnace supporting the boiler. It appears that thirteen-year-old David Hutcheson was present at the launch, inspiring the boy with the romance of the steamship, and no doubt inspiring him towards his destiny of champion, if not hero (certainly of the islanders), of steamer services to the West Highlands. David Hutcheson, of course, preceded David MacBrayne in this same role.

The Americans were slightly ahead of the game at this stage as they already had *Steam Boat* (sometimes referred to as *Clermont*) running on the Hudson River above New York from 1807, and the French were not far behind them. Back at home, William Symington had tried his luck earlier on the newly opened and sheltered waters of the Forth and Clyde Canal. Had it not been for vested interests, he should, by all rights, have taken the prize for the first commercially successful steamship; and that before the likes of Robert Fulton, John Stevens and others had set to work in New York and Bell in Glasgow. It appears that the committee of management, chaired by Lord Dundas, which was funding Symington's experiments, recognised that its own towage fees and its herd of mighty horses that walked the towpaths were in serious jeopardy of being undercut on its own patch. But more seriously, there was also the issue of Symington spending the committee's money without prior request – by all accounts Symington was a committed inventor but a poor communicator.

Comet was placed in service almost immediately after her trials, running down from the Broomielaw to Greenock and Helensburgh in just three and a half to four hours. *Comet* was really too small even for the Greenock to Helensburgh run, so Wood lengthened the little ship by twenty feet. Bell then took her via the Forth and Clyde Canal to Grangemouth to be reboilered and after a brief sojourn in the east Bell next spread his wings to the West Highlands. The problem was that others had seen the potential that *Comet* purveyed, and larger steamships were being commissioned for competitive service both on the Clyde and on the Forth.

Bell's West Highland steamer service commenced in 1819 and was the pioneer coastal steamship service in Europe and it is this role for which Bell should rightly be remembered. When the little steamship was wrecked in December 1820 near Craignish, the larger steamer *Highland Chieftain* was brought in to take up the service.

The floating of the steam engine cured much of the uncertainty in sea travel and ensured greatly improved schedules for passenger and the mails. Geoffrey Body in his book *British Paddle Steamers* wrote:

> The *Comet* had been followed by the steamers *Elizabeth* and *Clyde* and *Glasgow* in 1813. In 1814 came the first signs of a boom, with nine steamers being added to the Clyde fleet ... The following year, 1815, *Dumbarton Castle* started on the Rothesay run and services were also extended from Dunoon to Inveraray. Between 1815 and 1819 a total of twenty-six vessels appeared on the Clyde waters while in the 1820s thirty-two steamers were built.

Meanwhile, just six steamers were registered in London during 1818, a further seven in 1819 and nine more in 1820. By the end of 1818 (all steamships had then to be registered) the aggregate tonnage of steamships on the Clyde amounted to some 3,000 tons burthen. There was a steamer service between Leith and Stirling by 1814, operated by *Stirling*, and the steamship service between Perth and Dundee commenced the following year. Even the Isle of Wight ferry out of Southampton remained subject to the vagaries of the weather until 1820, when the Solent's first steamer, which had been built in Lincolnshire in 1817, was set to work between Southampton and Cowes. Where the Clyde shipowners led, it seems those on the Thames and elsewhere followed.

Many of the established shipowning companies resisted the newfangled steam technology to let others experiment with the over-complicated and expensive single-cylinder expansion engines. Others did champion the smoky wooden-hulled paddle steamers and soon took their sooty sails beyond their sheltered estuaries to the rougher seas of coastal voyaging. In those early days the steamers were laid up in the worst of the winter weather, awaiting the calmer days of spring – once again the sailing smacks would reign supreme. But it was not long before improved and more powerful engines were developed, allowing larger hulls to carry them. These in turn reduced the risk of being overwhelmed in a heavy sea so that the steamers eventually became all-weather boats.

A steamer service was inaugurated from the Clyde to Belfast from 1818 by David Napier's *Rob Roy*. She was soon joined by the Clyde Shipping Company's steamer *Rapid*, which was later sold in 1825 to the General Steam Navigation Company for service between London and the Continent. The link between Dublin and the Clyde was started only in 1823, when the St George Steam Packet Company managed the *Emerald Isle* on the route, basing her at Greenock.

Within a short time, a host of coastal, rather than cross-channel, steam packet services developed. These included a stagecoach connection to the shallow riverside quay at Dumfries for the steamer to Liverpool and services such as the Leith & Aberdeen Steam Yacht Company, and its steamer *Tourist*, running twelve-hour voyages between Leith and up to eight intermediate ports of call to Aberdeen from 1821 onwards. The Aberdeen, Leith & Clyde company commissioned the steamer *Velocity* for the same service shortly afterwards. The fare between Leith and Aberdeen was an expensive 21s saloon and 12s steerage as there was little viable alternative, with river crossings making the overland route much longer in miles than the journey by sea.

City of Edinburgh started running between Leith and London in 1821. Owned by the London & Edinburgh Steam Packet Company which was established by a group of local merchants, she was soon joined by *Mountaineer*, and a direct competitor, the steamer *Brilliant*. The competition was resolved when the Steam Packet Company bought *Brilliant*, placing the ship on Leith to Dundee and Aberdeen duties for which, in fact, she had originally been designed.

As the reliability of the coastal steamers increased, so merchants and passengers transferred their allegiance to the steamship. The fruits of the recent industrial revolution provided cargoes aplenty, with many goods destined for onward transhipment at the port of destination. Sail remained in use alongside steam, and the London & Edinburgh Shipping Company (rather than its former competitor the Steam Packet Company) commissioned a series of sailing 'clippers', built in Aberdeen, as late as the 1840s. The so called 'Aberdeen Clippers' replaced the old schooners; they had wonderful names such as *Nonsuch*, *Rapid*, *Dart* and *Swift*. Indeed, these magnificent little sailing ships were the forebears of the larger full-rigged ships that later undertook the tea races from the Far East.

The Dundee & Perth Shipping Company and the competing Dundee & Perth Union Shipping Company had twelve smacks trading to London, offering four regular sailings per week from 1824 onwards. The smacks reigned supreme until 1832 when two Glasgow-owned paddle steamers, *Liverpool* and *Glasgow*, appeared on the scene. A belated decision was made by the board of the Dundee, Perth & London Company to go into steam, and more immediately, to charter the paddler *London Merchant* to face the rivals head to head immediately. In so doing, the passage time was reduced to just thirty-eight hours.

The new purpose-built ships, predictably named *Perth* and *Dundee*, were initially the fastest and best-appointed on the east coast, the Dundee owners taking delight in overtaking rivals from Edinburgh and Aberdeen (the inaugural steam sailing between Aberdeen and London was taken by *Queen of Scotland* in 1827). The *Perth*, with its figurehead of the Fair Maid of Perth, and *Dundee*, with Neptune on the prow, initially called at the fishing ports of Great Yarmouth and Scarborough, but speed was all-important and these calls were dropped after 1836. The pair were ordered from Robert Napier with hulls built by John Wood and the saloons decorated by the celebrated artist Sir Horatio McCulloch. Napier lost heavily on the contract – a fixed price of £36,000 was inadequate for the work undertaken. They took nearly two years to build and were delivered in 1834. But even then, the steamship service was still discontinued in the winter months when the vessels were laid up and sailing ships resumed duty.

Steamer services from the east coast to destinations across the North Sea did not develop for some time. The Leith & Hamburg Shipping Company was created in 1816 with a fleet of sailing brigs. The successors of this company, eventually to become the Currie Line, did eventually promote steamers on its service to Hamburg, but not until 1848. The Leith, Hamburg & Rotterdam Shipping Company, managed by George Gibson, remained true to sail until 1850. James Rankine & Sons worked the Glasgow to Amsterdam route with schooners, until the steamer *Therese* was introduced on a new route between Grangemouth and Amsterdam in 1854. The sailing ships ceased on the

Glasgow service in 1861, when a sharing arrangement was made with George Gibson on the Dutch sailings from Forth ports.

Further afield the concept of long-distance steamer voyages, or rather steam-assisted sail voyages, had been proven at a very early stage – not by the British but by the Americans. The first transatlantic crossing by a steamship took place in 1819 when Captain Moses Rogers sailed *Savannah* from New York to Liverpool and via various north European ports to St Petersburg and back to New York. Although designed as a sailing ship, she was bought on the stocks by the Savannah Steam Ship Company, inspired by the sight of pioneer paddle steamer, *Charleston*, steaming into port in 1817. *Savannah* took twenty-five days to cross the Atlantic. The little auxiliary steamer only used her engines for eight of them, as weather conditions prevented her from making better speed under sail with the paddles shipped inboard.

A second long-distance experiment followed in 1825 when the Honourable East India Company commissioned *Enterprise* for an experimental sailing from Falmouth to Calcutta. Their Lordships were not impressed by the 103-day passage time, hindered by gathering fuel on the way, which served only to reinforce their preference for the old-style wooden-walled sailing ships.

Scotland came back into the frame when Canadian Samuel Cunard visited the UK to articulate his vision of developing a regular transatlantic steamer

Samuel Cunard (1787–1865), founder of the British & North American Steam Packet Company.

George Burns (1795–1890), of G & J Burns, shipowners, a God-fearing man who was conferred a baronetcy a year before he died.

service. Robert Napier agreed to build three wooden-hulled paddle steamers for Cunard for a total of £90,000, although Napier soon realised that larger and more powerful vessels would be needed to maintain the reliability of service stipulated by Cunard's client, the Admiralty. Napier insisted that a four-ship service would be needed in order to satisfy the Admiralty requirements.

Introductions were made to George Burns and David MacIver in Glasgow who were soon able to guarantee Cunard 50 per cent of the enhanced capital outlay required for the four-ship service. £100 shares in units of £5,000 were offered to Glasgow businessmen, the first taker being Mr William Connal, who was persuaded by George Burns and responded simply by saying, 'I know nothing of steam navigation, but if you think well of it I'll join you'. A total of twenty-nine Glasgow businessmen invested in what became The Glasgow Proprietary in the British and North American Steam Packets. Samuel Cunard placed orders for the ships in May 1839 as specified and designed by Robert Napier, who in turn instructed four shipbuilders: Robert Duncan to build *Britannia*, John Wood, who had earlier built the hull of *Comet*, to build *Acadia*, Charles Wood, *Caledonia* and Robert Steele, *Columbia*.

The faith of Samuel Cunard and his client, the Admiralty, in the Scottish shipbuilders was rewarded by a reliable four-ship service to Halifax and Boston. The relationship between Cunard and its subsequent proprietors with

Glasgow and the Clyde remained amicable throughout the entire existence of the Cunard Line, with many of its subsequent mainline steamers being Clyde-built. Indeed, the entire Cunard fleet was registered in Glasgow until 1878, when its business forced it to adopt Liverpool as its home port, Liverpool having become the company's centre of operations.

Scottish shipowners did not enter the 'long-haul' steamer business until much later. For some it was the opening of the Suez Canal, which put steamships at an advantage over the sailing ships, that precipitated a move into steam, for others it was the increasing efficiency of steam propulsion which eroded the preference for sail. Examples of long-haul Scottish companies include the Donaldson Line, founded in 1855 by brothers William and John, with their straightforward vision of trading to South America with chartered sailing barques. Their first steamer was ordered in 1870, and shortly afterwards they changed allegiance to a new, more profitable service from the Clyde to Montreal and Quebec, although they retained an interest in the refrigerated meat trade from South America until the company's demise. Thereafter the North American route became the core business and was operated in direct competition with the Allan Line (see chapter 12).

Patrick Henderson, with his three brothers from Pittenweem in Fife, founded P Henderson & Company in 1834. Such was the energy of 'Paddy' that the business took his name, despite his early death at the age of thirty-three, just seven years after the foundation of the company in Glasgow. Like so many other Scottish companies it started by taking Scottish coal to Italy and importing Italian marble to Scotland. Venturing further afield, it eventually made Burma its main overseas destination, having earlier found difficulties with return cargoes from New Zealand, which had been its original target. Other famous west-coast companies include the Glen Line, established at Glasgow in 1867 by Alan Gow, becoming part of the London Scottish school (see chapter 5), and ultimately part of the Alfred Holt empire trading to the Far East, and even 'Hungry Hogarth', a firm noted for its tramp steamers registered at Ardrossan, and founded there in 1868 by Hugh Hogarth and James Goodwin.

In 1825 George Thompson of Aberdeen started to run sailing ships to Canada in the lumber trade. This became the famous Aberdeen Line, running passenger-cargo ships to Australia, and which eventually merged with an Australian company to become the Aberdeen & Commonwealth Lines. William and Alexander Thomson set up a company at Leith in 1839, specifically to import Italian marble, this time as the nucleus of the famous Ben Line of Steamships trading eventually to the Far East.

A host of new Scottish steamship companies were created to trade to all parts of the globe by the mid nineteenth century. But not all of the ships had Glasgow as their port of registry, as the merchants of Edinburgh, Dundee and Aberdeen were set for their share of the profits of shipowning as well. Besides, the east coast was the obvious location to develop trade both to Europe and along the shorter sea passage from Scottish ports to London.

By the late nineteenth century nearly all the ports on the globe that offered favourable trading conditions were served by a Scottish-owned liner company. The Donaldson Line traded to Canada from the Clyde and the Anchor Line to the United States. Andrew Weir set up farther afield in the Indian Ocean, and eventually focused on a round-the-world service. And although it became a company that based itself at Liverpool, Cunard always had a large proportion of Scots among its deck and engineering officers, a reflection of the respect held for the seafaring and engineering talents that these men offered. Masters of the two great Queen liners, it seems, were more often than not Scots seafarers – an indictment of Scouse talent, or rather a tartan compliment?

The Scottish legacy extends far wider than locally registered shipping companies. Both the Orient Line and Peninsular & Oriental Steam Navigation Company had distinctly Scottish roots, as also did the British India Steam Navigation Company. Shaw, Savill & Albion, of course, incorporated the Albion Line, formerly owned by Paddy Henderson and based at Glasgow.

But not all steamships flew the Red Ensign. The steamship slowly but surely populated the merchant navies the world over. As the steamers developed in size and power, so too higher-value parcels of cargo began to be carried. In due course, iron-hulled screw steamers with greater deadweight allowed bulk cargoes, such as coal and grain, to be transported on the high seas.

Scotland should take pride in the men who took up the development of infrastructure, not only in Scotland but on the wider front, prescribed by the massive incoming development of industry and international trade. Hurd again:

The names of two great Scottish engineers, Thomas Telford and John Rennie, emerge ... To Thomas Telford, the son of a shepherd, and himself in early life a herd boy, Great Britain owed the construction of the Caledonian Canal, the harbours of Dundee and Aberdeen, the construction of nearly 1,000 miles of road, as well as some 2,000 bridges ... The construction of St Katharine's Dock in London, finished in the year 1828, was also due to Telford. We trace to the engineering genius of John Rennie – the son of a farmer, and, like Telford, educated in a Parish school – the great system of the Kennet and Avon Canal, many bridges including Southwark and Waterloo bridges across the Thames, the construction of harbours at Grimsby, Hull, Holyhead and Kingston [Dun Laoghaire], as well as the improvement of Portsmouth, Plymouth, Chatham and Sheerness dockyards.

Currie Line of Leith – home trade, Baltic and Mediterranean

It is easy to overlook the unglamorous home trade and near-Continental services, despite their being an important part of the Merchant Navy. There are several compelling reasons for their importance. East-coast Scottish ports were strategically best placed for trade with Scandinavia, the Baltic, Germany and Denmark. Trade to southern Europe was promoted by the Victorian need for Italian marble with which to mark their wealth, and this led to a thriving trade with the Mediterranean. Additionally, there was a need for fine wine, port and sherry and this provided a nucleus for trade with Portugal and southern France.

A number of the famous long-haul shipping companies started in the European trade, notably P Henderson & Company working from Glasgow, and Arthur Anderson's Peninsular Steam Navigation Company in London, both initially focused on trade to the Mediterranean. Other companies evolved from coastal services and trade across the North Sea. The Currie Line was one such, going back to the days of sail when the Hull & Leith Shipping Company was established in 1800. Various mergers with other coasting companies took place until in 1848 the company became the Leith, Hull & Hamburgh Steam Packet Company [sic] on commencing a service to Hamburg. The new route was the outcome of an expanded fleet while the company was led by Thomas Barclay, shipbuilder of Glasgow, and Leith entrepreneur and businessman Robert Cook.

In 1862 James Currie joined the firm, providing a firm link with the Castle Line trading to South Africa under the direction of brother Donald Currie. James Currie maintained regular passenger and cargo sailings to Hamburg, Copenhagen and Stettin, with an extensive array of cargo services to the Baltic. James Currie soon needed extra capacity, and rather than replace his modern fleet of steamships he sent them to Granton one by one to be lengthened. Six of the fleet were so dealt with. All Currie's ships were, in any case, sturdily built to withstand the rigours of the North Sea. The rebuilding programme was followed in the 1870s by a progressive replacement of the engines with the new and more efficient compound system, while six brand new steamers were also commissioned. Business was indeed buoyant. The fleet survived the subsequent late-Victorian depression but twelve ships spent a lengthy sojourn in a backwater at Leith Docks for the duration, although the fleet had recovered by 1895 to a total of forty-one ships.

During the Great War the basic European trade of the company was suspended; three of its ships were detained in German ports at the start of hostilities. Post-war, Donald Currie's Liverpool-based Liverpool and Hamburg Line was absorbed into the Leith-based interests and the service suspended until conditions improved in the early 1920s. The important European emigrant trade, with connections in the UK for transatlantic routes, had virtually ended by the 1920s, but passenger berths were still on offer and were of an elegance that attracted the more discerning traveller away from the arduous Dover and Calais

Typical of the smaller traders in the Leith, Hull & Hamburgh Steam Packet Company fleet in the twentieth century was *Haarlem* (1917), one of a group of four steamers purchased from Dutch owners in 1922, seen at a frosty Danish port unloading a cargo of coke.

train links to Germany. Four Dutch cargo steamers, *Haarlem*, *Hague*, *Helder* and *Helmond*, were purchased to replace war losses, bringing their characteristic Dutch names into the fleet. In 1923 four ships were bought from the Khedivial Mail Steamship Company of Egypt. These were all given names ending in -land, eg *Sutherland*, *Finland*, and this nomenclature was preferred thereafter, except for the two new ships for the Copenhagen service delivered in 1928 which were given Viking names *Hengist* and *Horsa*. By 1930 the Leith, Hull & Hamburgh Steam Packet Company, James Currie's Currie Line, provided two departures a week from Leith to Hamburg, a weekly sailing to Copenhagen and Christiansand, and occasional services to other Continental ports.

The Hamburg service also received new tonnage when the twelve-passenger *Courland* and *Gothland* were commissioned in 1932. Sister ships, *Courland* built by Barclay Curle, and *Gothland* by Henry Robb of Leith, were then delivered for the Hamburg service. They were splendid examples of North Sea steamers built between the wars. Driven by one set of triple expansion engines with steam generated by twin oil-fired boilers at 185 psi (pounds per square inch), their service speed was a little under 14 knots. They were most attractive yet strong-looking ships, complete with modern cruiser sterns, gentle sheer and balanced profiles with central island accommodation. The all-riveted hull was ice-strengthened and built to a shelter deck design with a full length 'tween deck and a lower 'tween deck in the forward hold. There were four holds served by an array of derricks including a 10-ton heavy-lift derrick that plumbed no. 2 hold.

Accommodation was provided for twelve passengers in twin-berth cabins on the shelter deck and there were two single-berth cabins on the boat deck. The cabins were sold as staterooms and were comparable with the staterooms on offer aboard any of the crack transatlantic liners of the day. The dining saloon was panelled in mahogany and there was the obligatory stone fireplace complete, in winter, with an open fire. Above the saloon, and linked by an elegant staircase, was the oak-panelled smoke room which was adorned with leather armchairs in the style of a contemporary gentleman's club.

In 1933 the company bought M Isaacs & Sons of London and in so doing entered the Mediterranean trade. It rebranded itself as Currie Line in World War II when all its regular services were again suspended as it had suffered the ignominy of having correspondence opened by the authorities and censored! Twelve of its fleet of twenty-seven ships were lost in the Second World War, while one replacement was acquired in 1942, although this ship was lost to a torpedo a few months later. *Gothland* suffered bomb damage lying alongside at London in September 1940. Six months later *Courland*, under the command of Captain R Smith, was sunk by torpedo while in convoy approximately four hundred miles off Gibraltar. Three of the crew of thirty were lost; all the survivors were rescued by Currie's *Brandenburg* which was also in the convoy. Sadly, all but one man, a passenger, were lost the following day when *Brandenburg* was sunk under similar circumstances – a grim couple of days for the Currie Line.

Gothland was requisitioned in November 1941 for conversion at Plymouth into a Convoy Rescue Ship. The vessels selected for this role were all fast, low freeboard coastal ships with existing passenger accommodation. They attended to casualties in convoy so that the convoy escorts could concentrate on the attacker. This required good seamanship and adept use of the ship's boats. There was also a trawl boom and net that could sweep swimmers out of the water when the sea was too rough to launch a boat. *Gothland* was mainly employed on North Atlantic convoys to St John's, Newfoundland, and Halifax, Nova Scotia, but did attend occasional convoys down to Gibraltar. Between commissioning in February 1942 and the end of World War II Convoy Rescue Ship *Gothland* undertook twenty voyages and saved 149 persons from seven sinkings and one aircraft ditching.

Gothland resumed civilian duties post-war, this time on the Leith to Copenhagen route, but in the late 1950s her owners were beginning to concentrate on the bulk cargo trade and the North Sea services were run down; *Gothland* was sold for further service in 1958 and was scrapped three years later.

The first Currie Line motor ship was *Scotland* which ran from London to the Mediterranean from 1946 until she was sold in 1967. All passenger carrying ceased in 1958 but the cargo services persisted in partnership with foreign partners such that the Liverpool to Hamburg and Grangemouth to Finland services were entirely foreign flagged by 1964. Interestingly, the company ventured into the deep-sea tramp market in 1959, seeing an opportunity for the carriage of vegetable oils. Three ships

The first motor ship in the Currie Line was *Scotland* (1946) which, with sister ship *England*, maintained the Mediterranean sailings.

were commissioned, the oil carrier *Roland*, working to West Africa, the bulk carrier *Gothland* and the conventional break bulk cargo ship *Highland*, the latter chartered for much of her tenure with Leith registry to the Shaw Savill and Alfred Holt joint cargo service to Australia. She was sold to the Anchor line and renamed *Elysia* in 1968 when Walter Runciman & Company, then owners of Anchor (see chapter 12), bought the entire Currie Line holding and its goodwill. The Currie Line ships were replaced by chartered tonnage in the 1970s when the focus slowly changed to storage and road haulage.

3

The Emigrant – Fuel for Trade and Empire

In the evidence on the convicts in New South Wales a number of the colonists commented that Scottish emigrants were much preferred as settlers to any other nationality. The Scottish labourers were preferred because they were 'more skilful workmen, they are better agricultural servants, also better shepherds ...' and wherever skilled labour was needed employers preferred the Scottish emigrants. To help encourage Scottish emigration to New South Wales, Crown lands were being sold to pay for assisted passages and ... three ships having recently sailed from the United Kingdom, with several more being expected from the Western Highlands. He said that in the main the Scots were found to be keen to emigrate as they hoped one day to establish themselves as landowners. Because of this willingness on the part of the Scots the emigration officers were able to select those they wanted and usually picked married couples as near 30 years old as possible.

From *Transportation. Report from the Select Committee.*
Minutes of evidence, 1837, vol XIX (Sessional no. 518)

EMIGRATION IN THE EARLY nineteenth century was the result of both force and persuasion. Until the 1850s emigrants from the Highlands were forced to leave the land because of evictions whereas in the Lowlands the decision to emigrate was driven largely by the desire to improve living standards. Whatever the reason, Scotland lost between 10 per cent and 47 per cent of the natural population increase every decade. Those leaving Scotland during the period 1921–30 exceeded the entire natural increase despite the United States placing quotas on emigrant numbers in 1922. The scale of the emigration was exceeded only by Ireland and Norway.

The introduction of the US quota system was a severe blow to many passenger shipping companies on the Atlantic. The Anchor Line was forced to close its Mediterranean transatlantic passenger route which was heavily dependent on emigrant traffic from Italy (see chapter 12). Two new ships, *Caledonia* and *Transylvania*, had to be redesigned as a consequence, with greatly reduced steerage accommodation. It also meant that Anchor Line was overstocked with passenger liners leading to its inevitable collapse in the 1930s.

Transylvania (1925), with one smoking funnel and dummies to fore and aft, was too late for the Anchor Line Mediterranean to New York emigrant service and was reconfigured to work from the UK.

Emigrant traffic, both to the United States and Canada, as well as to South Africa and the Antipodes, was the mainstay of many shipping companies – Henderson's Albion Line, for example, was renowned for the carriage of migrants to New Zealand under the sponsorship of the Free Church of Scotland and enjoyed a near monopoly on the transit of passengers from the Clyde to Otago (see chapter 4). Only when the New Zealand government sponsored its own line of steamships did the Albion Line clippers get into financial difficulties, sail having become little match for steam by the 1890s.

The importance of the emigrant to the mother country cannot be overstated, the more so in the case of the skilled emigrants from Lowland Scotland who retained their links with Scottish business. The Scottish emigrant was a vital catalyst to the pre-eminence of Scotland as a maritime nation for much of the nineteenth and twentieth centuries. It is important to appreciate how the expatriate Scottish communities fuelled Empire and trade and underpinned Scottish maritime endeavour. The global impact of these emigrants is apparent to this day. The largest Highland gathering in the world is now held in Singapore – caber tossing, the lot – and in many Nova Scotian communities the older folk recount how Gaelic was their first language and the language used in school. Today there are few towns and cities in the world which do not have some kind of Caledonian Society or Club, even if only to celebrate Robbie Burns once a year in the local hostelry.

The Scottish emigrant took more with him than just his name. He also took experience and skills: the skill of the Highlander to survive on near barren land in a wild climate, and the Lowlander took his industrial skills and business acumen. In addition, they took pride in their homeland and their personal contacts with Scotland, people they could do business with and people they could trust as their agents. The Scottish business network was, and to a certain extent still is, a club whose membership depended simply on provenance. Membership was a bond that ensured trust and fair play. No other nation of people achieved this bond, not the expatriate English who invariably merged into the background of their overseas destination, not the Norwegians or the Irish, who for the most part were unskilled, nor any other European emigrant expatriate.

Scottish emigration took place in two phases. The notorious Land Clearances preparatory to the introduction of the four-legged Highlander, the sheep, produced a massive outgoing of crofters and farmers seeking a new start in North America and Australia. The exodus was accelerated with the decline of the hand loom and the decimation of herring stocks, which conspired to bring abject poverty to both Lowlander and Highlander. The stories of hardship on the long voyages with families cramped in poor accommodation with inadequate nourishment and poor sanitation are legion. Indeed, that so many families survived the journey is remarkable and the statistic that on many voyages new arrivals could equal the number of deaths was surprising.

One example of the conditions is reported in *Papers relative to emigration to the North American Colonies. Accounts and Papers*, 1852, vol XXXIII, p71 (sessional no. 1474):

The return includes information in the form of letters on the emigration of 1,681 destitute Highlanders from South Uist, and a further 986 from Lewis. The emigration agent in Quebec reported that immigrants had arrived from South Uist in a very poor condition. They had been existing on the island by eating shellfish and seaweed collected from the rocks at low water before being sent to Canada; their passage had been paid by the proprietor, Colonel Gordon. Upon arriving at Quebec it was found that they had insufficient funds or food for travelling across Canada to their final destination. On the voyage from Scotland, the wife of the captain had spent her time organising the making of clothes for the emigrants. One man leaving the ship was found to have no other clothes than a woman's petticoat. The Quebec Emigration Agent was very scathing concerning some of the proprietors for sending out tenants unable to fend for themselves, and at a time of the year when no employment existed for them.

The emigrants were packed in the 'tween decks, and life aboard the sailing ships could be tedious and uncomfortable. Deaths aboard ship were interspersed with new births, and life went on much as it could, despite the cramped conditions on board. More often than not a teacher was on hand to attend to the children's education, and a surgeon attended to the passengers' ills. A contemporary report by Captain J H Taylor of the Albion Line clipper *Timaru* described the emigrant's lot:

> The surgeon got £1 per head for every soul he landed. Many people in those days came to sea for their health, thinking that a long sea voyage would be beneficial. They generally gained strength in the tropics but after we got into the high southern latitudes the weather there was generally very cold and the

The Albion Line's *Timaru* (1874) was an iron-hulled full-rigged ship built by J E Scott at Greenock. (Oil painting by K A Griffin)

sudden fall in temperature was often too much for weakened bodies having only gained temporary strength in the tropics and they soon passed away ...

The first funeral aboard was always a very sad and serious event for the passengers, and generally tears were shed and everyone was present. As the time passed a similar event happened and fewer people were present, and when the third, fourth and fifth funerals took place it was noticed that many did not come and some did not even stop their games on deck to be present.

On the outward passage of the *Timaru* in 1877, south of Tasmania, there having been five deaths and four births, the surgeon naturally anxious to have his list of passengers back to the original number and he had evidence that a birth might take place before reaching our destination and, sure enough, three days before we arrived, at 1am the doctor called me up with great glee and said 'No. 5 has arrived' and the £1 per head was now secure.

The Clearances peaked in the 1840s and early 1850s. Knox (see reference section) wrote:

The landlord's course of action was based on the fact that the Highland economy had collapsed, while at the same time the population was still rising. As income from kelp production and black cattle dried up, the landlord saw sheep as a more profitable alternative. The introduction of sheep meant the removal of people. The crofting population was already relying on a potato diet and when the crop failed in the late 1830s and again in the late 1840s, emigration seemed the only alternative to mass starvation. The policy of the landlord was to clear the poorest Highlanders from the land and maintain those crofters who were capable of paying rent.

The Dukes of Argyll and Sutherland and other large landowners financed emigration schemes. Offers of funding were linked to eviction which left little choice to the crofter. However, the Emigration Act of 1851 made emigration more freely available to the poorest. The Highlands and Islands Emigration Society was set up to oversee the process of resettlement. Under the scheme a landlord could secure a passage to Australia for a nominee at the cost of £1. Between 1846 and 1857 around 16,533 people of the poorest types, comprising of mainly young men, were assisted to emigrate. The greatest loss occurred in the Islands, particularly Skye, Mull, the Long Island and the mainland parishes of the Inner Sound.

Subsequent to 1855 mass evictions ceased and emigration became a choice rather than a necessity. For the next forty years decline in the Highland population was less than in the rural Lowlands. The Highlands experienced a 9 per cent fall in population between 1851 and 1891 (Ireland in the same period faced a 28 per cent reduction). In addition the Crofters' Holding Act of 1886 provided security of tenure and in due course new crofts were developed so that by 1950 over 2,700 new tenant crofts had been created.

But people still chose to leave the Highlands with the promise of a better, perhaps even an affluent life, in a new country. By the 1930s the population of the Highlands was little over half that of a hundred years before. Many moved south into the Lowlands of Scotland and England but a substantial proportion, preferring to stay in contact with the land, left for permanent migration to Canada where the attractions of Ontario and Nova Scotia were compelling; the majority of nineteenth century settlers in Nova Scotia were of Scottish extraction. In Nova Scotia in the first half of the nineteenth century, 59 per cent of UK settlers were Scots-born.

As for the emigrant from Lowland Scotland, Knox wrote:

Keeping in touch with the land was not a consideration for the urban emigrant from the Scottish Lowlands. The decision to emigrate in this part of Scotland was purely voluntary. Indeed, emigration was seen by trade unions and other voluntary groups as a practical solution to unemployment and economic depression. Lowlanders were moved to leave their birthplace by a combination of low wages, poor housing conditions and unemployment. The high points in emigration statistics corresponded with years of severe economic depression. These occurred in the late 1840s and early 1850s, the mid-1880s, and the period 1906–13 … In fact in the economic depression of the 1920s emigration exceeded the natural increase in population. This was brought to a halt in the 1930s as the world trade depression saw emigrants return home. Indeed, the numbers leaving Scotland in the 1930s were at their lowest for a century.

The rise in emigration from urban areas saw a shift in the pattern of overseas settlement and the social status of emigrants. In the early 19th century it was the poorer members of society who chose to migrate. From the Highlands it was the landless peasants; from the Lowlands it was the unemployed craftsmen and labourers and small farmers. The country of settlement tended to be Canada. In fact, in the period 1825–1835 over 70% of emigrants from Scotland settled there.

The picture changed considerably in the twentieth century when skilled workers became the mainstay of the emigrant population. In 1912 and 1913, 47 per cent of adult male emigrants from Scotland were described as skilled, compared with just 36 per cent of the migrants leaving England and Wales, and only 29 per cent of the Scottish emigrants were described as labourers. Emigration progressively attracted the urban population, and ability and skills largely determined the destination of the emigrant. Unskilled labourers tended to go for Canada and Australia, while South Africa and the United States attracted craftsmen and other skilled workers.

Knox concluded:

The outflow of people was made easier by the revolution in transport. The steamship did not dramatically alter the cost of passage from Scotland to the USA, but it did reduce greatly the travelling time. In the 1850s it took around six weeks to cross the Atlantic; in 1914 it took only a week. The reduction in travelling time allowed for temporary migration as well as permanent; something unthinkable in the days of sailing ships. Also if things did not work out in the New World then the price of a steamship ticket brought you back to your native land in a week. Emigration seemed less risky in the age of the steamship.

The movement of Scots continued well into the 20th century. In fact, until 1989–1990 there had been only one year (1932–1933) in which Scotland experienced a greater inflow than outflow of people. Taking the twentieth century as a whole, Scotland … experienced a net loss through emigration of around 2 million people. During the 1920s and 1930s the principal aim of the emigrants was to find work and wages and escape mass unemployment at home. Age-wise this has generally most affected the age group 16–29; in terms of occupation, skilled rather than unskilled workers; and in terms of sex, men rather than women. Although most of the emigrants were able to make a better life for themselves and their families abroad, the impact on Scotland has been less favourable. Many of the most productive and talented Scots have left their birthplace to enrich, both economically and culturally, other countries at the expense of their own.

Scotland's loss, it seems, was the receiving countries' gain, but it was this gain that was so crucial to the development of trade and wealth creation. Chapter 8 describes the entrepreneurial, investment and creativity of the expatriate Scot, many of whom became leading merchants and businessmen in Liverpool and London as well as in Canada, Australia and New Zealand. But it was by no means all bad news for Scotland. The emigrants sailed from their homeland in Scottish-owned ships promoting Scotland as an important focus of shipowning, and once established overseas, the expatriate migrant promoted agriculture and developed trade and merchanting that required a maritime network to export and deliver produce back to the UK. Of course,

The Hong Kong & Whampoa Dock Company in February 1956 with British India Line's *Sangola* (1947) under refit. (P&O)

it was Scottish-owned and managed shipping companies that were preferred for this trade. The deep-sea fleet required servicing and maintaining whilst it was in foreign ports and it was often Scots' enterprise and know-how that developed the engineering facilities to provide these services.

One of the more remarkable examples of success in the engineering field is that of the Hong Kong & Whampoa Dock Company which illustrates how the skills of the Clyde, Aberdeen and other Scottish ports were propagated around the world. John Lamont was an early European settler in Hong Kong who was to become one of the foremost entrepreneurs of the new colony. He was a skilled carpenter and shipbuilder who had left Tiree in search of better reward for his services overseas and arrived in Hong Kong in his mid-thirties. The Chinese ceded Hong Kong Island to Britain in 1842 following their defeat in the Opium Wars. Within a year Lamont had set up a repair yard and slipway at East Point under the sponsorship of Jardine Matheson & Company to service that company's sailing barques (see chapter 4). Lamont often had a queue of ships awaiting attention, but still managed to build small vessels, including the first foreign ship to be constructed in Hong Kong, the 80-ton schooner *Celeste*, which he completed as early as February 1843. Ten years later, in 1853, John Lamont built Hong Kong's first steamship, the wooden-hulled *Queen*, which had been ordered by local businessman, and fellow Scot, Douglas Lapraik.

In 1859 John Lamont built Hong Kong's first dry dock, the Lamont Dock, at his yard in Aberdeen (a district on the south side of the colony, named after the British Secretary of State for War and the Colonies, the Earl of Aberdeen).

John Lamont placed the following advertisement for his dry dock in a local newspaper in April 1861:

> It is 335 feet long with a breadth inside the coping stone of 78 feet and a depth of 22 feet. At spring tides the depth of water at the sill of the dock is 18 to 18½ feet and at neap tides from 15 to 16 feet. Attached to the dock are engineering workshops with lathes of all sizes, planing, punching and shearing machines of the best description, a large foundry, saw mills with both vertical and circular saws, a powerful steam hammer, and every requisite and appliance for the repair of vessels both of wood and iron – the whole under the superintendence of European foremen. For particulars regarding docking and other charges, apply at East Point or at Aberdeen.

Lamont was also an innovator, and proposed lining dry docks with rubber, then a new product.

Encouraged by the success of Lamont Dock, he went into partnership with Douglas Lapraik, to construct a larger dock. The British government gave them a grant of £3,000, as there was then no facility in the region that could accommodate the larger British warships of the day. Lamont added yet another dry dock to his enterprise, the Hope Dock, but all this expansion was attracting the attention of the big boys, and in 1865 a consortium formed by P&O, Jardine Matheson and Douglas Lapraik purchased Lamont's interests to create the Hong Kong, Canton & Whampoa Dock Company.

The *Nautical Magazine and Journal of the Royal Naval Reserve*, 36, 1867, reported:

> On the 15 June, the new dock at Aberdeen belonging to the Hong Kong, Canton, and Whampoa Dock Company, was opened in the presence of the Governor and a large party of invited guests. The dock is, of course, constructed with the

intention of accommodating either the ironclad *Warrior* or *Black Prince* (for draught of water), or the Pacific Mail Company's steamer the *Great Republic* (for breadth of beam) … Under these circumstances, it would not be surprising if Her Majesty's huge ironclads be sent out to the China station, for the existence of this magnificent dock now opened in Aberdeen Bay, Hong Kong, removes what would otherwise be an insuperable objection to their presence – namely, the impossibility of dock repair in the event of an accident.

A contemporary report, quoted in the Tiree journal *Sil Eòlais*, 24, November 2011, described John Lamont:

Slim and bronzed, with humorous grey eyes, Lamont always wore at least one item of Scottish tartan, and spoke such broad Scot that no one understood him when he first arrived. He, like Douglas Lapraik, had settled in Hong Kong with a Chinese 'Protected Woman'. He was also one of those rare men who were able to move in any society and seemed equally at home whoever he happened to be with … One must admire such a man who could overcome all obstacles, get on with everybody and create for himself a happy home life with his two young boys and their Chinese mother.

Tiree Gaelic would have been Lamont's first language and he probably learnt most of his English at sea. He was proud of his Scottish identity, and despite the Dress Act which prohibited the personal wearing of tartan from 1746, Lamont sent out a strong message of its nonsense before it was repealed in 1782. Europeans were strongly discouraged from marrying local girls, but Lamont settled down with Awa Moy, and had two sons, Charles in 1847, and Archibald in 1851. The boys were both baptised in 1852 and were sent to a small private school in Peebles and later to Eton. They both settled in Scotland.

John Lamont also returned on a visit to Scotland, and died in Aberdeen in August 1866 at the age of sixty-two. He had certainly done well in his adopted country. He left £1,000 (the equivalent today of £80,000) to his eight Tiree nephews and nieces, and an allowance of £400 a year (the equivalent today of £30,000) to his sons until they reached the age of thirty, when they received their full inheritance. Matheson was his executor.

The Hong Kong and Whampoa Docks were heavily bombed by the Japanese before their invasion of Hong Kong in 1941, but remained operational. The assets of the yard were transferred to the Tsing Yi site of the Hong Kong United Dockyards in the 1970s. In 1985 the area was redeveloped and Lamont's docks now lie beneath the second largest private housing estate in Hong Kong.

The story of John Lamont was repeated around the globe. Scottish enterprise was able to support regional development and enhance the fortunes of Empire. Whether Empire encouraged emigration or emigration encouraged Empire is a question that is hard to answer. That the Scottish migrant had a specific and important role in Empire is indisputable. Liberal MP Sir Charles Dilke, writing in 1888, remarked that: 'In British settlements, from Canada to Ceylon, from Dunedin to Bombay, for every Englishman that you meet who has worked himself up to wealth from small beginnings without external aid, you find ten Scotchmen'.

Even in the nineteenth century expatriate Scots who had settled in North America dominated the tobacco trade in the south and fur-trapping in the north. In Canada, Scot Lord Mount Stephen was the driving force behind the creation of the Canadian Pacific Railway, and soon one-third of the country's business elite were of Scottish origin. India also became a hugely important trading partner. Most of its railway engines were built at Springburn, while Dundee became the centre of jute manufacture in the world.

Education and religion were other areas of cultural life where the Scottish influence was overwhelming. Religious motives were important also; the Otago settlement in South Island New Zealand and the Waipu settlement in the North Island were populated by Scottish emigrants sponsored by the church. Dunedin (Gaelic for Edinburgh) had its own university by 1869. In Waipu, Gaelic was the first language until the 1880s and was still widely used in the 1920s.

The post-World War II Scottish emigrant ships were *Captain Cook*, ex-troopship *Empire Brent* and formerly the Donaldson liner *Letitia*, *Captain Hobson*, formerly the Henderson liner *Amarapoora* and the Anchor Line steamer *Cameronia*. *Amarapoora* had served on behalf of the International Refugee Organisation until she was taken in hand by Alex Stephen & Sons yard for conversion for the emigrant run in time for her first voyage to Wellington in May 1952 as *Captain Hobson*. This voyage returned the Henderson company back to its original business, that started by the Albion Line to New Zealand almost a century previously.

The three emigrant ships were operated by the Ministry of Transport to satisfy the demand for assisted passages to the Dominions. *Captain Cook*, still under Donaldson management and *Captain Hobson*, under Henderson management and named after the first Governor of New Zealand, served emigrants travelling to New Zealand, while *Cameronia*, still under Anchor Line ownership, served the Australian emigrant. R S McLellan described her refit:

Captain Cook (1925), ex-*Empire Brent*, ex-*Letitia*.

The writing room aboard the New Zealand Government's emigrant ship *Captain Cook*. A postcard posted aboard ship in 1954 with a message which began 'Just a line of a reminder to let you know I have not forgotten you. There were pictures, dances, games of all sorts …'

The main lounge aboard *Captain Cook* reflecting her more glorious past on the North Atlantic.

The after dining room, not quite so glorious.

All the troop-carrying quarters and most of the original passenger accommodation had been dismantled and new accommodation built for the carrying of emigrants. Rooms with two, four and six berths, and hot and cold running water, had been built; the original six public rooms on the promenade deck had been retained, and one of the other public rooms had been fitted out as a nursery. The main engines had been completely overhauled and the boilers and most of the auxiliaries renewed. She sailed from Glasgow on 1 November [1948] with 1,276 emigrants bound for Fremantle, Melbourne and Sydney.

Cameronia was sold to the Ministry of Transport in January 1953 to become the troopship *Empire Clyde*, retaining an Anchor Line crew and Anchor Line management but operated by the Sea Transport Service out of Glasgow. *Captain Hobson* sailed under berth arrangements with Shaw Savill & Albion and was transferred to the New Zealand government in 1951, complete with her Henderson Line crew. She completed her final voyage to Wellington in May 1958 and was later sold for demolition. *Empire Clyde* was withdrawn and scrapped in 1957. In 1960 the government-sponsored service ceased and the last of the Scottish emigrant ships, *Captain Cook*, was laid up and withdrawn. Thereafter, the Italian-owned Sitmar Line offered cheap fares for emigrating families until the late 1960s, after which the emigrant service was operated by air. It is ironic that an Italian-owned company should provide a sea service for British emigrants, much as the Anchor Line had done earlier for Italian emigrants.

Empire Clyde (1921), formerly the Anchor Line's *Cameronia*, served on the post-World War II assisted passage to Australia for the Ministry of Transport

4

In the Service of Empire

THERE ARE TWO REMARKABLE aspects to Scotland's involvement in the Merchant Navy. The first is that the founders of the many important Scottish shipping companies all belonged to one great community. That they knew each other is not surprising, because the shipping company offices in Glasgow were mostly situated in and around Bothwell Street, and in Leith were focused on Leith Walk. These geographical clusters of like-minded companies not only reflected the respective industrial and port city foci, but also, like the numerous IT companies grouped in the Thames Valley today, stayed geographically close to each other in order to share experience and learn from each other. The other remarkable aspect is the breadth of Scottish shipping interests, with such 'English' companies as P&O, British India and, of course, Cunard being essentially Scottish in origin, and all heavily reliant on Scots managers and senior officers throughout their tenure.

The shipowners' cabal in Glasgow was so highly respected that it invited foreigners to aspire to its own standards. The most famous of these was Charles Cayzer, who brought his Clan Line of Steamships from Liverpool in 1881 under a refinancing package backed by Scottish merchants. Cayzer later became one of the most respected shipowners in Glasgow (see chapter 13). Other English shipping companies did not quite manage to forsake St George for St Andrew, but they adorned their companies in a distinctly tartan fashion – the Nelson Line, for instance, adopted its Highland fleet nomenclature, which clashed desperately with its corporate cockney accent.

So numerous were the Scottish shipping companies which maintained the trade routes with Empire that no single book could recount their histories adequately. A review of some of the companies and of their founding fathers will, however, illustrate the breadth of the industry and show how the family of Scottish shipowners actually worked.

Paddy Henderson was once a household name in Glasgow. The Henderson house flag not only flew on the High Seas, but in due course was seen the length and breadth of the mighty Irrawaddy and Chindwin rivers in Burma. The timeline for the various Henderson companies in the nineteenth century is complex, and is intertwined with other companies, both by marriage of family members and by a variety of business agreements:

1829 George Henderson bought 48/64th share in brig *Tom and Jessie*.

1834 Patrick Henderson & Company founded as import/export merchants in Glasgow.

1835 *Peter Senn* launched at Alloa.

1840 Henderson Brothers registered in Leghorn.

1841 Patrick Henderson died.

1848 Regular, but short-lived, service to Quebec, Montreal and New York advertised using chartered ships. James Galbraith appointed to Patrick Henderson & Company.

1852 George Henderson died.

1854 Robert Henderson died.

c1855 Patrick Henderson & Company renamed P Henderson & Company. Services to New Zealand started with chartered ships.

1855 European & Columbian Company charter new steamships to French government (hence company house flag of reversed Tricolour defaced by the Union Flag).

1856 First sailing of Henderson-owned ship (rather than chartered) to New Zealand (which had been colonised in 1840).

1857 European & Australian Royal Mail Company inaugurates an auxiliary steamship service to Melbourne and company is sold.

c1858 New Zealand sailing clippers marketed under Albion Line brand.

1858 Rival Shaw Savill & Company formed at London to trade between London and New Zealand.

c1858 Return cargoes for New Zealand ships sought in British Burma (Pegu Province) as Burma otherwise had no direct connection to UK.

1860 P Henderson & Company first advertised sailing to Burma.

1864 Albion Shipping Company registered at Glasgow.

1865 Irrawaddy Flotilla & Burmese Steam Navigation Company formed by Todd, Findlay & Company, Rangoon.

1868 Robert Henderson died.

1869 Suez Canal opens.

1870 First Henderson steamship sailings to Burma.

1873 Rival New Zealand Shipping Company formed.

1874 British & Burmese Steam Navigation Company formed, P Henderson & Company appointed as managing agents.

1876 Irrawaddy Flotilla Company formed.

1878 Devitt & Moore's steamer *Glenelg* trialled on UK–Suez–New Zealand route.

1881 Albion Line's clipper *Dunedin* arrived at London with first frozen meat cargo from New Zealand.

1882 Albion Line and Shaw Savill & Company sold to create Shaw Savill & Albion Company and registered at London.

1885 Second Burmese War – 'The 15 Day War'.

1886 La Platense Flotilla Company formed, P Henderson & Company appointed managing agents.

1889 Bibby Line enters Burmese trade and joint service agreement began with P Henderson & Company.

1890 La Platense Flotilla Company liquidated following Argentine Revolution.

1893 The Burma Steamship Company formed, P Henderson & Company, managers.

What this timeline does not reveal is the intriguing and sometimes romantic human forces behind the development of the various threads of the Henderson enterprises. There were five Henderson brothers who, along with their sisters, lived in the small fishing village of Pittenweem in Fife until their father died in 1824. The eldest of the boys was Thomas, who had been able to join Peter Senn & Company, General Merchants in Leghorn (later Livorno), Italy, through good fortune and help from various relatives. Thomas became fluent in Italian and later also in French and Spanish. The next eldest was George, a master mariner trading to the Mediterranean, who was often helped by his older brother in Leghorn to find return cargoes. The third eldest, John, became a steward at sea and took no part in the establishment of what was to become P Henderson & Company. Patrick was the fourth son, and he found employment in various trades, notably the weaving industry around Glasgow. The youngest son was Robert who left Scotland to join Thomas in Leghorn, taking his unmarried sister Nancy with him to keep house for the two brothers.

Patrick visited his brothers and sister in Italy and together they planned to develop the marble export trade from Italy to the Clyde with return cargoes of textile goods from the mills in the Clyde valley, so putting Patrick's knowledge of the weaving industry to best use. This arrangement was put on a firmer footing when Patrick was made the local Scottish agent for Peter Senn & Company. In December 1833 Thomas came home to Scotland to marry Jemima Thomson, formerly of Leith, whose brothers Alexander and William Thomson had started importing marble from Leghorn to Leith, a small step that ultimately would lead to the foundation of the Ben Line (see chapter 13). This friendship between the Hendersons and the Thomsons was to endure and became a bond between the Henderson and Ben lines well into the twentieth century.

Captain George Henderson led his family fortunes into shipowning with the purchase of a share of the brig *Tom and Jessie*. But George's pride and joy was the barque *Peter Senn*. He had overseen the construction of her at Alloa. She was funded 44/64th by the Henderson brothers and 20/64th by Alexander and William Thomson. Launched in September 1835, *Peter Senn* entered the Mediterranean trade with George in command. On her maiden voyage she carried Margaret and Jessie Thomson as passengers to Leghorn to visit Jemima. Patrick, for all his energy and drive, had never been strong and he died suddenly in 1841 at the tender age of thirty-three. His namesake company lived on, with George now holding the reins in Glasgow, and Robert and Thomas in Leghorn. The only noticeable difference was that George pushed the company increasingly towards shipping and shipowning at the expense of the merchant side of the business.

James Galbraith joined the company in 1848 and became a key figure in driving the Henderson fortunes forward. He was from Strathaven, and had worked variously in insurance for government, and, importantly, in the offices of Glasgow shipowner John Cree where promotion was blocked by the aspirations of Mr Cree's sons. When, in 1852, George Henderson died, Robert returned to Glasgow to take George's place, leaving Thomas in charge at Leghorn. Sadly, cholera and other epidemics in Leghorn took their toll and Thomas died two years later.

The formation of the Albion Line of full-rigged sailing ships by P Henderson & Company started in a small way with chartered vessels, but it soon became the benchmark brand in the emigrant trade. The Albion Line enjoyed a monopoly from the Clyde to Otago in New Zealand, with emigrants sponsored by the Free Church of Scotland. In those early days return cargoes were difficult and calls were made at Chinese and Burmese ports in search of business.

When the Suez Canal opened in 1869, the practicalities of running steamships to New Zealand were realised. But it was only the impatience of the New Zealand government, who championed the steamships of the New Zealand Shipping Company into competition with Henderson in 1873, that the demise of the Albion Line also became inevitable. The Albion Line had coped with competition from the English sailing ships of the Shaw Savill Company and these companies eventually joined forces to compete with the New Zealand company's steamships, as Dorothy Laird recounts in her history of P Henderson & Company:

... Walter Savill and James William Temple on behalf of Shaw Savill & Company agreed to sell the ships and goodwill of the Shaw Savill fleet to the new company [Shaw Savill & Albion Company] for £285,110 ... James Galbraith as Managing Director on behalf of the Albion Shipping Company to sell the ships of the Albion Line and its goodwill for £200,157 ... appointed P Henderson & Company as managers and loading brokers of the new company in Glasgow.

And so it was, that P Henderson & Company fell back on its trade with British Burma, developed first as a means of gaining return cargoes to the UK but later seen as the ideal route to place steamships via Suez. In collaboration with shipbuilder Peter Denny, the company was able to develop the inland waterways of Burma with specially designed steamers that were operated by associated company the Irrawaddy Flotilla Company. Interestingly, John Innes, head of P Henderson & Company, wrote a remarkable letter to Peter Denny in 1895 which included the paragraph:

Owing to continued troubles with our Scotch crews, I think it would be a judicious step to adopt Lascars. If anything it would mean economy in our wages bill, and for all the information I can gather, it also means increased efficiency, particularly in the Engineer departments. The P&O, British India, Bibby, Brocklebank, Clan, Smith's City and Anchor Lines have all adopted Lascar crews. Our Captains, I believe, are all in favour of Lascars, and while the change means a little preliminary trouble, we, like our neighbours, would quickly make up for it.

Arracan (1912), seen here, and sister to *Mandalay* (1911) were unique in the pre-Great War Henderson fleet as they did not accommodate passengers.

Burma (1914) was state-of-the-art on the Rangoon service at the eve of World War I.
(B & A Feilden)

The success of the Burma service was illustrated by the modern fleet list the company boasted at the start of World War I. A new ship had been commissioned every year since 1903 with the sole exception of 1907:

Irrawaddy (1903): cargo and passengers owned by The Burmah Steam Ship Company
Martaban (1904): cargo and passengers owned by British & Burmese Steam Navigation
Tenasserim (1905): cargo and passengers jointly owned
Ava (1906): cargo and passengers jointly owned
Bhamo (1908): cargo and passengers jointly owned
Henzada (1909): cargo and passengers jointly owned
Chindwin (1910): cargo and passengers jointly owned
Mandalay (1911): cargo only jointly owned
Arracan (1912): cargo only jointly owned
Pegu (1913): cargo and passengers jointly owned
Burma (1914): cargo and passengers jointly owned.

Possible competition with the Bibby family's service from Liverpool and London was overcome with an integrated timetable and berth sharing. P Henderson & Company then became a flourishing shipowner serving Empire and Scotland alike, a company that the young Patrick Henderson would have indeed been proud of. Intervention from Ellermans in 1915, who had bought heavily into Burmese rice mills, and subsequent agreement between Henderson, Bibby and Ellerman, allowed Ellerman ships to load at Rangoon for discharge at Colombo and Madras.

The distinctive Henderson fleet nomenclature was broken only in 1929 when a new ship built for the Panama and west coast of North America service was named after the Grand National winner Gregalia. This deviation in nomenclature was not, however, that odd because the racehorse was owned by a niece of the company's owners!

Ironically, success in the charter market eventually led Henderson Line to be taken over by Elder Dempster Line of Liverpool as Dorothy Laird explains:

By January 1952 six 'K' class diesel cargo vessels had been built and five were on order. The vessels in service were mainly employed on time charter to other liner companies. Among these charterers was the Elder Dempster Line, who had found these ships well suited to the requirements of their West African trade and this led to negotiations being opened whereby the whole of the Ordinary Capital of the British & Burmese Steam Navigation Company was acquired in January 1952 by Elder Dempster Line (Holdings).

Thereafter the 'K' class remained in Henderson management while the four ships on the Burma trade, *Prome*, *Salween*, *Martaban* and *Yoma*, remained in

Cargo liner *Yoma* (1948) on the joint Bibby and Henderson wharf at West Float Birkenhead in February 1963. (Author)

British and Burmese ownership. The passenger service was withdrawn in 1962 when *Prome* and *Salween* went to the breakers. Shortly afterwards most of the 'K' class were subsumed by Elder Dempster, and in 1965 Ocean Steamship Company (effectively Alfred Holt's Blue Funnel Line) acquired control of the group. In 1967 the Six Day War closed the Suez Canal and Henderson's service to Burma ceased. Its last three ships were transferred to Elder Dempster routes; the last Henderson ship was sold in 1970 and the company name fell into disuse.

Another great Glasgow enterprise was George Smith & Sons' famous City Line. George Smith started sending sailing ships to India in 1840. His first vessel was the Canadian-built barque *Constellation*, put on service between the Clyde and Calcutta. Within ten years George Smith & Sons was trading also to South America, the West Indies and Australasia. The famous City names were introduced in 1848 when Robert Barclay & Curle delivered the clipper *City of Glasgow*. The City Line was responsible for importing tea directly to Scotland, bypassing the London merchants and onward shipment costs, but it also brought tea from both India and Ceylon into London. But, as happened to other shipowners trading in the Indian Ocean, the opening of the Suez Canal caused a complete rethink and the first steamer for the Indian routes was delivered in 1870. This was *City of Oxford*. When spare vessels were available, the clippers took emigrants out to Australia and New Zealand. The last sailing ship was commissioned in 1882, when the sailing fleet numbered fifty-two vessels.

The City Line maintained a fortnightly cargo and passenger service to Calcutta from Liverpool and Glasgow, and a monthly cargo and passenger service to Bombay and Karachi. In 1900 the last of the sailing ships was sold, the youngest being *City of Madras*, built on the Clyde in 1882, the oldest a group of four sailing ships dating from 1867 which were sold for further service with a Norwegian company, although *City of Florence* was wrecked off California before delivery.

The success of the company was recognised by the English shipowner and entrepreneur John Reeves Ellerman. George Smith died at the age of just fifty-four in 1899. His son, also George, took over but showed no great enthusiasm for the task. This was Ellerman's opportunity and by August 1901 an offer, said to be about £1 million, was accepted by Smith junior. Negotiations were carried out in only ten days with Ellerman taking charge just three weeks later. Ellerman then went on to buy the City Line's main competitors, the Hall Line and Bucknall Steamship Line; John Ellerman was one of the most successful entrepreneurs in British shipping history. Earlier, in 1892, he led

City of Madras (1882), built by Barclay Curle, was the last sailing ship ordered by George Smith.

a consortium which purchased the interests of the late Frederick Richards Leyland, one of the largest shipowners in Britain. Ellerman then sold what had evolved into the London, Liverpool & Ocean Shipping Company to J P Morgan for £1.2 million, to become part of the American International Mercantile Marine Company. The proceeds of this sale funded the purchase of dominant holdings in the component parts of what became Ellerman Lines, including the City Line, which was retitled Ellerman's City Line.

At the start of the Great War, the City Line was delivering 500,000 chests of tea per year to London from ports in Ceylon and India. Some of the older City Line passenger and cargo steamers had been transferred to the Mediterranean routes operated by Ellerman & Papayanni Lines. But in the war many of the steamers were requisitioned and put to work as troopships and supply ships and some adopted a military role under the White Ensign. The Ellerman group of companies continued to operate as best it could with the ships it had available. After the war, the Ellerman Group's passenger and cargo services to Egypt, India, Ceylon, South Africa and the Far East were re-established as far as they could be with the tonnage available. A programme of rebuilding followed in the 1920s but like all shipping companies the City Line was hit by the Depression. The main passenger units were *City of Calcutta*, *City of London*, *City of Marseilles*, *City of Exeter*, *City of Nagpur*, *City of Paris*, *City*

City of Paris (1922) was typical of the City Line passenger ships built between the wars.
(B & A Feilden)

of Venice and *City of Lucknow*, formerly the German liner *Heluon* and a war
reparation vessel.

By way of celebrating the end of the Depression, and before shipbuilding
costs recovered, the City Line ordered its all-time flagship *City of Benares*.
This magnificent yacht-like two funnel liner was built by Barclay, Curle &
Company at Whiteinch on the Clyde, and equipped with single reduction
turbine engines which were built by Cammell Laird at Birkenhead. Her boilers
were coal-fired. She was launched in 1936, and was placed on her design route
between London and Bombay. She carried 219 first-class only passengers and
required a crew of 209. *City of Benares* was one of many ships lost in World
War II, but her loss was mourned by all, as she was carrying evacuees from
Liverpool, and there were many children who lost their lives (see chapter 11).

Post-war, the City Line, still based at 75 Bothwell Street, focused on twelve-
passenger cargo liners in a five-ship rebuilding programme which ended with
delivery of *City of Karachi* from William Denny at Dumbarton in 1951. Two
new ships were commissioned in the mid 1950s and the larger twins *City of
Oxford* and *City of Glasgow* were commissioned in 1962 and 1963. In October
1958 the two-ship Mossgiel Steamship Company, managed by John Bruce &
Company of Glasgow, was acquired by the Ellerman Group. Mossgiel was
incorporated as far back as 1894. Bruce had maintained the steamers *Alhama*

City of Karachi (1951) at anchor in the River Mersey on 2 November 1963. (Author)

Alhama (1948) traded between the Clyde and the Mediterranean, inward
the Barton Bridges in the Manchester Ship Canal in April 1962. (Author

and the Bauer Wach steamer *Alpera* on its Glasgow–Mediterranean liner service terminating at Alexandria and under Ellerman & Papayanni Lines management, now occasionally called at Liverpool and Manchester. The funnel colours were unique and comprised brown with a black top. Although retired for some years before the Ellerman takeover, John Bruce died in the 1960s aged sixty-nine.

In the early 1970s, the corporate branding of the Ellerman Group changed and the name Ellerman City Liners was adopted for the whole fleet, a fleet which declined rapidly from thirty-six ships in 1974 to just twenty-four ships four years later. Ellerman City Liners invested heavily in containerisation and in 1973 took delivery of the 2,687 TEU (twenty feet equivalent unit) *City of Edinburgh*, which was jointly owned with Ben Line of Leith, and sister to *Benalder* and *Benavon*. All three ships were built in Germany. They were twin screw, geared steam turbine ships fitted with co-axial condensers that had an available 88,000 shaft horsepower that could drive the ships at up to 30 knots. Economics dictated their service speed as more like 22 knots, but for a while they remained the most powerful container ships in the world. The ships were employed in the Trio Line consortium, working between ports in Europe and the Far East, and comprising British, German and Japanese shipowners. Ellerman also jointly owned the mighty 2,436 TEU *City of Durban* with the Harrison Line of Liverpool when she was delivered in 1978. Other interests included investment in Associated Container Transportation (ACT) alongside Ben Line, Blue Star Line, Harrison Line and Cunard's Port Line. George Smith's City Line had indeed come a long way from the days of its sailing ships to arrive at the container era.

The Henderson and Smith family stories are just two examples of shipowning entrepreneurs on Clydeside, trading to the colonies – there were many others. Nicol and Robert Handyside and Thomas Henderson (unrelated to P Henderson and family) were, for example, instrumental in developing the Anchor Line and its services to India and North America, culminating with the three splendid passenger liners *Circassia*, *Cilicia* and *Caledonia* carrying three hundred first-class passengers to Bombay until 1966 (see chapter 12).

Turnbull, Martin & Company was another Glasgow company of shipowners. It was founded in 1874, and in 1884 was a pioneer in the carriage of refrigerated meat imports from New Zealand. It started to carry passengers to New Zealand in 1893, when the name Scottish Shire Line was first used for the ships sailing to New Zealand via South Africa and Australian ports. The Federal–Houlder–Shire Line consortium was formed in 1904, and later in 1910 Clan Line acquired a controlling interest in Scottish Shire Line, although

Caledonia (1948) was the last of three sisters built for Anchor Line's Glasgow to Bombay service – seen here coming alongside Prince's Landing Stage, Liverpool, in 1963. (Author)

the company retained its identity and distinctive Shire nomenclature for its ships until the late 1960s.

Aitken, Lilburn & Company began operating a line of sailing ships to Australia in 1870, when it formed the Glasgow Shipping Company with a fleet of six 1,250-ton iron-hulled, fast, full-rigged sailing ships. The General Shipping Company was created shortly afterwards through a consortium of investors in Glasgow, but the two companies otherwise merged interests. Sailing from Glasgow, first to Adelaide, then on to Melbourne or Sydney, they returned with wool or grain for London, the round voyage lasting up to a year. The company only operated sailing ships. Prospective passengers increasingly preferred the speed and reliability of the steamships and the sailing ships became unprofitable as time went on. The companies finally closed their books in 1911 and the remaining ships were sold.

But the going was not all made on Clydeside. George Thompson was a key name in Aberdeen. George Thompson (known as George Thompson Junior to distinguish himself from his grandfather) went to Aberdeen Grammar School and then joined the Aberdeen office of the London Shipping Company. When he was twenty-one, he established himself as a ship and insurance broker in Aberdeen. In the same year, 1825, he was listed as a subscribing owner of his first ship, and thereafter his shipowning interests blossomed. In due course he operated a seasonal liner service to Canada, and built up a fleet of a dozen vessels with trades extending to Cuba, South America, the

Baltic, the Mediterranean, South Africa and the Far East. The first ship built specifically to George Thompson's order came from Walter Hood's yard in Aberdeen in 1840, and this yard built most of his ships up to 1881, including some of the world's finest and fastest sailing ships, when the yard was sold.

Thompson became established in the Australian trade by the mid 1840s. George Thompson first established the Aberdeen White Star Line (to distinguish it from Rennie's Aberdeen Line) on the Australian trade in his own right in 1856. Thompson's ships had green hulls, white masts and yards, and a red and blue house flag with a six-pointed white star.

George Thompson started to trade to China in 1848. An initial fleet of five steamers were built for the Aberdeen Line's Australia service: *Aberdeen*, *Australasian*, *Damascus*, a new *Thermopylae* and *Nineveh*. A regular voyage pattern was soon established: London to Australia with passengers and general cargo, onwards to China, Japan or Russia with coal, and then to China to load tea for home. *Thermopylae* broke the speed records for sailing from London to Melbourne, from Newcastle, Australia, to Shanghai, and from Foochow to London. *Miltiades* was a product of Walter Hood's Aberdeen yard and joined the fleet in 1871. She had accommodation for twenty-five passengers and about 150 emigrants in the 'tween decks. She had crossed double topgallant yards on all three masts and was heavily rigged. Her mainyard was an incredible 86ft long.

Thompson died in 1895 with an exemplary record for safety; he had never insured his ships against loss. Instead he invested the money he had saved in insurance premiums in the purchase of new ships and the maintenance of his existing ships. George Thompson was a supporter of the Free Church, and was one of Aberdeen's most generous benefactors. He promoted the extension of the Royal Infirmary and gave funds to the University for Medical Bursaries.

In 1905 the Aberdeen Line came under the joint control of White Star Line and Shaw, Savill & Albion Line. The Aberdeen Line commissioned two magnificent sisters in 1922, *Diogenes* and *Sophocles*, which were chartered to Shaw, Savill & Albion in 1926 as *Mataroa* and *Tamaroa*. White Star Line purchased the Australian government-owned Australian Commonwealth Line in 1928, but as Lord Kylsant's Royal Mail group which owned White Star Line collapsed, the Aberdeen Line was purchased by Shaw, Savill & Albion. In 1933 the fleet of the former Australian Commonwealth Line, which had not been fully paid for, was also acquired and the Aberdeen & Commonwealth Line formed. It had five near-identical passenger ships, all built in 1921 and 1922: *Esperance Bay* – renamed *Arawa* on transfer to Shaw Savill in 1936; *Hobsons Bay* – renamed *Esperance Bay* in 1936; *Jervis Bay*, which was sunk

Aberdeen & Commonwealth Line's *Esperance Bay* (1922) built as *Hobsons Bay* and scrapped in 1955. (Fotoflite incorporating Skyfotos)

by the German cruiser *Admiral Sheer* in 1940; *Largs Bay*; and *Moreton Bay*. In 1936 Furness Withy & Company took control of Shaw, Savill & Albion; in 1938 the Aberdeen name was dropped from the title, while the last of the 'Bay' ships were scrapped in 1955.

The Aberdeen Clipper Line of Packets was another important company. This was developed by the Rennie family, after brothers John and George Rennie bought their first ship, *Samson*, in 1845. John Rennie's ships initially traded to India, Australia and the Cape and from 1853 called also at Madagascar. John Rennie commissioned his first steamship in 1854. In 1869 a joint service with Natal-owned Bullard, King & Company, under the banner of the Aberdeen Clipper Line of Packets, was started between London and Natal. The company was eventually bought by the Harrison family of Liverpool, the older passenger steamships transferring from the Southern African service to the new owner's West Indian routes.

Another important firm, McIlwraith MacEacharn, was founded in London in 1875 by Scottish expatriates Andrew McIlwraith and Malcolm MacEacharn when they began business as shipping and insurance agents. They soon made an agreement with the state of Queensland for the emigrant trade from Britain to ports north of Maryborough in Queensland. Their first vessel, *Scottish Bard*, was completed in April 1876, and she was soon followed by *Scottish Hero* and *Scottish Knight*. The agreement ended in 1880 when British India took over the carriage of migrants. The sailing ships continued to trade to Australia, particularly in the carriage of wool and other produce as well as passengers to Britain, but they expanded operations to wherever cargoes were available.

In 1879 the chartered steamer *Strathleven* was fitted with the Bell-Coleman mechanical refrigeration plant. She loaded an experimental shipment of 30 tons of frozen beef and 2 tons of butter for London. New steamers joined the fleet in 1884 when the famous sisters *Cloncurry* and *New Guinea* were commissioned. McIlwraith MacEacharn developed other interests in Queensland and the London office operated an extensive export department. A branch of the company was established in Melbourne in 1887 and branches were subsequently opened in Newcastle, Sydney, Adelaide, Perth and Fremantle.

During 1893 the company began to dispose of its sailing ships. With the expansion of the company's interests in Australia, Malcolm MacEacharn settled in Melbourne when a branch was opened. He took a leading part in public affairs during his years in Australia, becoming Melbourne's second Lord Mayor. In 1900 he was knighted and in 1901 elected to the first federal parliament. All the steamships were registered in Melbourne and McIlwraith MacEacharn became a major operator in the Australian coastal passenger and cargo trade and between Australia and India.

Other Scots set up in business overseas and helped to found a number of successful businesses in the Far East, many of which contributed to the increasing corruption and illegal trading of the monopoly East India Company. William Jardine and James Matheson set up business in Canton in 1832. Their core business was trade between Canton and Calcutta and they were early experimenters with chartered steamships. Banker Nick Robins wrote in his book *The Corporation that Changed the World*:

Founded in July 1832, Jardine Matheson headed a new generation of aggressive enterprises that aimed to replace the [East India] Company in the Asia trade. William Jardine had been a doctor on the [East India] Company's ships, but left to pursue a business career in 1817 at the age of 33. Eight years his junior, James Matheson ... had gone straight into private trading in 1815. The two brought together a winning combination of commercial wisdom and political verve, which they deployed with great skill … Matheson was the Firm's propagandist, founding *The Canton Register* to act as a mouthpiece for his aggressive free trade views, urging the end to the [East India] Company's monopoly. When Parliament finally laid the China trade open to all in 1833, Jardine Matheson was well prepared, shipping out the first private consignments of tea to Britain the following year. Soon, the Firm, as the partnership was known, had the biggest share of a booming market, 'the safest and most gentlemanlike speculation I am aware of' Jardine told a friend interested in investing in the business. By the end of the decade, the company had a fleet of a dozen ships operating along the China coast, sending out tea and silk and importing thousands of chests of opium in return.

The Firm was quite frank about its trade. Writing to a potential business partner in 1831, Jardine stated 'we have no hesitation in stating to you openly that our principal reliance is on opium'. The Firm knew full well that the import of opium into China was illegal. But the reality of deeply porous borders and ever-present corruption meant that the tide of 'foreign mud' had grown steadily higher through the 1820s. While it is easy to criticise the ethics of the Firm's early business model, Jardine Matheson and other free traders did little more than intensify a poisonous exchange that had been progressing under [East India] Company guidance for half a century. For the private traders, the profits were high … This easy defiance of law did not appeal to everyone, and Dr Jardine was lampooned by the up-and-coming Benjamin Disraeli in his 1837 novel, *Sybil*, as 'a dreadful man! A Scotchman richer than Croesus, one McDruggy fresh from Canton, with a million of opium in each pocket, denouncing corruption and bellowing free trade.'

After the Opium Wars (1840–42) when foreign traders were banished from China, the base of the Firm, which was now no longer a drug runner, was moved to Hong Kong with a branch at Shanghai to give access to the Yangtze basin. In the mid 1850s steamships were introduced on the Bay of Bengal routes and occasional trips were made also to Japan. The China Coast Steam Navigation Company was formed in 1873 to develop the trade with Japan and the Indo-China Steam Navigation Company succeeded in 1881. This new company also took over the coastal services with links to Singapore, Calcutta and eventually Vladivostok. The company flourished and remained a key player in Chinese waters throughout much of the twentieth century.

James Matheson, later Sir James, who was a native of Stornoway, purchased a large part of the Isle of Lewis when he retired from business in the Far

East, and spent much of his retirement in a grandiose house that he built in Stornoway. He did much to alleviate the inherent poverty of the island by introducing and formalising commercial activities – like the introduction of a steamer service between Glasgow and Stornoway in 1846.

There were many other Scottish entrepreneurs and businessmen who took their skills to the colonies to help develop Empire (see chapter 8). The wealth creation to which they all contributed helped turn Britain into a global power. Some of the ethics of Empire are now questionable – opium for the Chinese, the slave trade, the appalling treatment of Lascar crews abandoned by their masters at London – but the Empire did open up trade routes which had previously not been possible. The many canny Scottish shipowners and Scotland's plethora of redoubtable seamen contributed heavily to this development. But what nobody realised at the time was that this was the start of what we now call globalisation. Ultimately, little by little, British enterprise would be undercut by cheap and poorly manned foreign shipping and later again undercut by the container revolution.

Clydeside Cameos, compiled by Ian Ramsay

These cameos are largely from a book called *Clydeside Cameos* which contains a series of character sketches of prominent Glasgow businessmen and was published in 1885 by the shipping magazine *Fairplay*. The book is a compendium of articles originally published in that magazine. Some of the sketches are quite scurrilous and, if they had been untrue, would surely have been libellous and could not have been published later in book form.

Captain Thomas Henderson of the Anchor Line

This is a little-known incident in Captain Thomas Henderson's earlier career when he, like his three brothers, was still employed at sea as a master. In 1850 Henderson was in the employ of G & J Burns as master of the paddle steamer *Orion* on the Glasgow, Greenock and Liverpool route and on the return passage from Liverpool on 17 June 1850, with a full complement of some 150 passengers, the ship struck in the early hours of a clear, calm morning, a rock near Portpatrick with the resultant loss of fifty passengers; many of whom were women and children.

At the time of striking the rock, Captain Henderson was below resting in his cabin and the vessel was in the charge of the second mate, but as soon as he was aware of the situation, Henderson rushed to the bridge and took charge but, despite all his efforts, *Orion* sank within seven minutes. At the subsequent trial it was stated that the ship was a mile too close inshore and it was averred that the second mate had been instructed to keep this inshore course to minimise the effect of a foul tide at the Mull of Galloway.

The brothers Burns were powerful shipowners in Glasgow but, as the *de facto* management of Cunard and the financial backers behind it, they were a power to be reckoned with and they wanted vengeance; especially as they had lost their brother, Professor Burns of Glasgow University, in the sinking. The result was that Captain Henderson and his second mate were arrested and charged with culpable neglect of duty and manslaughter and some months later they were put on trial at the High Court of Justiciary in Edinburgh. Captain Henderson was found guilty of carelessness, although not, like the mate, of reckless neglect, and was sentenced to eighteen months in prison whilst the hapless mate was sentenced to transportation for seven years.

After his enforced incarceration with time for deep thought and careful planning, Captain Henderson stepped forth on to the shipping scene again, and not without great difficulty, managed to re-establish himself and get financial backing from the Handyside Brothers for what was to become the Anchor Line of steamships. The formative years were difficult and many of the early ships were such poor affairs that the company gained a doubtful reputation because of some fearful losses. In time, however, the company prospered and new capital was attracted, both from within the Henderson family and beyond, and one is left wondering if his drive for success came from giving the Burns family 'one in the eye': especially when he carried his fight into the Port of Liverpool in direct competition with the great Cunard Steamship Company! One also wonders if the choice of ships' names ending in '-ia' was a calculated insult to Burns.

The company in the nineteenth century was very much family owned and the Anchor Line owned D & W Henderson brothers' shipyard in Partick was always locally known as 'the Anchor Line'. Indeed, up until the closure of the Henderson ship-repair business in the early 1960s, it was still known in Partick as such.

Sir William MacKinnon

Although a small, slight individual, he must have had a powerful personality and a totally ruthless business streak to achieve the business success that he did with his British India Steam Navigation Company. He was a native of Campbeltown, as was his original partner, and as stated in *Clydeside Cameos* in the 1880s, many of his original financial backers were from Kintyre, as were most of his senior managers and deck officers.

Prior to the move of BI's headquarters to London, MacKinnon played a very prominent part in the commercial affairs of the City of Glasgow and this was recognised by his appointment as chairman of the City of Glasgow Bank which was to fail spectacularly in 1878 – some time after he had resigned as chairman and sold his shares in the bank. The bank had unlimited liability and when it failed each shareholder was called to make up the deficit, their call being many times the value of the shareholding. Many businesses failed as a result and all the shareholders, whether large or small, were in effect ruined. The resultant hardship was so bad that a relief fund was set up throughout Scotland to alleviate the distress of the shareholders and others thrown out of work as a result of the bank's collapse.

Unlike the recent banking scandals, all the directors – mostly elderly men – were found guilty and sentenced to imprisonment with sentences ranging from eight to eighteen months (with hard labour). MacKinnon came in for much criticism in the Glasgow business community as he and his friends had all sold their shareholding a few years prior to the collapse and this was viewed with scepticism verging upon suspicion; especially as one of the Bank's liquidity problems stemmed from dubious loans to colonial developments, especially in India, which had been granted when MacKinnon was chairman and in some of which he had had an initial interest. This all proves that there is nothing new under the sun – as we have recently seen with sub-prime mortgages!

The one benefit of British India's large fleet was that there were always orders for new ships and, being a local man, MacKinnon placed his orders with Clyde yards. Denny, Barclay Curle, Stephen and Inglis all benefited from his order largesse. Inglis, who are remembered for building smaller ships and paddle steamers, built forty-two ships between 1863 and 1914 for BI and some of those built in the early 1890s were passenger ships of 5,500 gross tons which put them firmly in the ocean liner class of their day.

Charles Cayzer

Cayzer's success in building his fleet so quickly started with backing from a few very wealthy individuals but he ensured that although they had found the money, they were not going to get all the profit. In the early years when the company was flushed with success, Cayzer drew up a management agreement whereby he was constituted as absolute manager for a long number of years and in the heady early days of success he got all his co-owners to sign up to it: an action that his wealthy backers quickly came to regret as, by then, they were getting niggardly returns on their heavy investments.

With total control, Cayzer made his own contracts for steamers and freights and as each new ship was built the shipbuilder, engine builder, chandler, coal owner and every other supplier that he could coerce was impounded by the promise of more orders. It was averred that no captain or chief engineer was appointed unless he was willing to purchase shares.

Because of the competitive nature of Cayzer's approach to business, freight rates were driven down and routes established where there was little prospect of other than occasional cargo and this resulted in none of the ships showing any other than minimum profit. This, however, was of no real concern to Cayzer as he charged his management commission on the gross earnings of each ship and in 1885 it was stated that Clan Line was losing about £80,000 per annum whilst Cayzer was pocketing about £20,000 annually for his services. As the *Fairplay* article of 1885 put it 'He has built himself a magnificent house – drives his carriage and pair, and lords it with the best. Not bad for the store clerk of twelve and the ship chandler of eight years ago!'

George Smith (III)

From the early years of the nineteenth century, the Scottish mercantile class felt that they were being patronised by the old landowning classes and were being looked down upon as new moneyed, self-made men. This clash between the old and the new money was particularly evident in the Church of Scotland where patronage, in the form of the sole right of the local landowner to appoint the minister without any discussion with the congregation, resulted in 1843 in the Church of Scotland splitting into the established church and the new Free Church of Scotland.

The majority of the mercantile classes in Glasgow favoured the Free Church which was more evangelical and concerned itself with the plight of the poor and the need to curb excessive drinking. The Smiths of the City Line were very zealous in their pursuit of temperance, so much so, that no alcohol was ever served or could be purchased, on any of its ships. Their officers were expected to be total abstainers whilst at sea and moderate drinkers when ashore but it is doubtful if this could be applied to marine engineers on the Indian run! However, being a canny shipowner, George Smith knew he could not inflict his views indiscriminately on his fare-paying passengers without a resulting loss of business so in the passenger cabins of every City Line ship, or as it was popularly known – the Teetotal Line, there was provided a secure locker designed for the safe stowage of sufficient bottles of alcohol brought aboard by the passengers to sustain them on the voyage!

Abram Lyle

Abram Lyle was from the mid nineteenth century a successful sailing shipowner ('The Cape Clippers'), cask maker and sugar refiner in Greenock. In addition to his business success, he was reluctantly persuaded to take the provost's chair of Greenock Town Council at a very low state of the affairs of that municipality and by dint of sound management he carried through many important civic improvements and put the town's finances on a sound footing.

However, this public-spiritedness was not appreciated by the Greenock Harbour Trust when some years later Lyle sought permission to build a large sugar refinery on their James Watt Dock estate. This was refused, largely at the behest of other Greenock shipowners and sugar refiners, and Lyle turned his back on his native town and built his new, large refinery on the Thames at Silvertown, in London's East End, leaving only a small facility in Greenock which survived into the 1990s.

The Silvertown refinery prospered and expanded until it amalgamated with Tate & Company of Liverpool, then becoming the world-renowned Tate & Lyle. The shipping interest remained faithful to Greenock but it is doubtful if there was other than a tenuous family link latterly between sugar and shipping.

5

London Scottish

THE SCOTS HAVE ALWAYS been a fixture in London's city of finance and commerce. The perception (to the English) of the 'Honest Scot', has enabled generations of Scots to thrive and to contribute to the wealth of London and of the nation. Always a significant force in the banking and insurance industry, Scots have occupied top posts in all the service industries that London has to offer. Two such industries go hand in hand, import/export merchant and shipping, and the Scots featured heavily in both.

P&O is one example in which, almost without exception, its top executive was a Scot. Conceived by Shetlander Arthur Anderson in collaboration with Brodie McGhie Willcox, the Peninsular Steam Navigation Company (the '& Oriental' being added at later date) was founded by them in August 1837 to run the mails down to Portugal and Spain. The embryo company survived despite the maiden return voyage from Gibraltar ending in shipwreck. David and Stephen Howarth wrote in *The Story of P&O*:

Arthur Anderson (1792–1868), born in Shetland and rose to become first managing director and then chairman of P&O. (Oil painting by T F Dicksee, 1850)

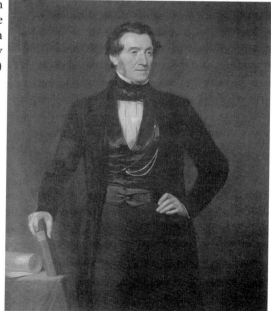

But the company's strength was that Anderson's practical genius was always balanced by Willcox's watchful bookkeeping. If Anderson's ideas ran too far ahead of reality, there was always Willcox to bring them back to earth, and Willcox would certainly have said that experimentation was not the company's job. Its job was solely to build reliable and comfortable ships and run them to the satisfaction of its passengers. This was what it was uniquely good at.

Young Arthur Anderson was first employed, when a child at Gremista in Shetland, to bring the fish ashore from the boats and to help to gut, bone, split, wash and salt the catch before it was laid out to dry. Despite being saved from the press gang by the local fish merchant, Anderson did join the Navy as a midshipman when he was sixteen. In 1815 he left the Navy to work as a clerk in London. Here he met Mary Hill, whom he was later to marry, and she introduced Anderson to shipbroker McGhie Willcox. It was their joint company that in 1840 was incorporated as P&O.

Anderson succeeded Willcox as managing director in 1854 and as chairman in 1862, following Willcox's sudden death caused by a falling tree. Anderson was a well-known benefactor. On Shetland he built a home for the widows of fishermen and his name is remembered by the school he built at Lerwick in 1862, the Anderson Educational Institute, now Anderson High School. Anderson died in 1868, just one year before the Suez Canal opened. The canal brought about an urgent need to rationalise P&O's business for through-traffic to the Far East without the need for an overland connection. Much of this change was championed by a young Aberdonian, Thomas Sutherland.

Sutherland had spent the greater part of his apprenticeship with P&O in Hong Kong and knew the business well. On his return to the UK in 1866, Anderson had appointed him as assistant manager, and Sutherland soon gained respect enough to be appointed managing director. He was just thirty-eight years old. Sutherland is remembered for having rationalised the company possessions, reducing staff numbers overseas and ensuring an even financial keel for the company. He also recognised the growing importance of freight revenues and moved his UK terminal from Southampton to London to be at the centre of commerce. He served the company for sixty years, stepping down as MD in 1914 and as chairman following the merger he personally engineered with chairman of British India, Lord Inchcape. Lord Inchcape, or James Mackay, had been born and brought up in Arbroath.

The British India Steam Navigation Company had its headquarters in Calcutta and its ships rarely came home to the UK. Its origins stemmed from the Calcutta & Burma Steam Navigation Company which was created in 1856,

Lord Inchcape (1852–1932), born in Arbroath, engineered the 'takeover' of P&O by British India Steam Navigation Company in 1913. (Oil painting by P A de Lazlo, 1931)

following an initiative by Scotsmen William Mackinnon and Robert Mackenzie who created Mackinnon, Mackenzie & Company, to carry the mail between Calcutta and Rangoon. William Mackinnon was born at Campbeltown in 1823 and moved to Glasgow at an early opportunity, where he worked in an Asian grocery. He travelled to India to join former schoolfriend Robert MacKenzie, who had gone to India in 1836 to set up an import and export agency. The pair were soon established in the coasting trade around the Bay of Bengal. Sadly, in 1853 Mackenzie was lost in a shipwreck off Queensland, while on a trip to Australia to explore for new opportunities for Mackinnon, Mackenzie.

In 1862 the British India Steam Navigation Company was formed out of Mackinnon, Mackenzie & Company, and it quickly became the natural successor to the East India Company as the vehicle of Empire in the Far East. In 1889 Mackinnon was made First Baronet of Strathaird and Loup; he founded the Free Church of Scotland East African Scottish Mission in 1891, but died in London two years later. Sir William Mackinnon was honoured in 1900 with the naming of a new steamer on Lake Victoria commissioned by the Uganda government in 1900. *William Mackinnon* was built and designed by Bow MacLachlan & Company at Paisley and reassembled on the lake. The honour recognised the part Mackinnon and his shipping

British India's *Uganda* (1952) fitting out at Barclay Curle's wharf.

line had played in opening up the interior of East Africa and his help in abolishing the slave traders.

The Scottish roots of British India were never overlooked. In 1913 Lord Inchcape was elected chairman and the following year he became chairman of the merged British India P&O group. Thereafter, although British India was always seen as a London-based company within the P&O group of companies, it retained a leaning to Scotland with regard to both senior officers and managers and also for its preferred shipbuilders.

It had clearly been apparent to Sutherland and Inchcape that the merger of interests would enable British India and P&O to better serve the interests of shippers and traders in the Far East, in Sutherland's words, 'in the interest of British commerce throughout our Eastern Empire'. Lord Inchcape, at the age of sixty-two, sixteen years younger than Sutherland, took up the reins of the P&O and British India companies, but any vision he may have had for the group was quickly overrun by the onset of the Great War. Inchcape was a masterful leader and was highly respected by all. His nineteen years in India led to the offer of his becoming Viceroy of India, an offer that had to be retracted because of his extensive business interests in the region. Inchape even oversaw the designs for the innovative turbo-electric liner *Viceroy of India* in the late 1920s, complete with interior design by Elsie Mackay, one of his daughters.

The magnificent baronial style first-class smoking room aboard P&O's *Viceroy of India* (1929) reflects the craftsmanship then available at her builders, Alexander Stephen & Sons.

Lord Inchcape died in 1932 and was succeeded by his son-in-law, Alexander Shaw, later Lord Craigmyle. At the same time William Crawford Currie, of Scottish extraction and born in India, came to P&O to be appointed deputy chairman. His early life was similar to that of Inchcape, working also with Mackinnon, Mackenzie, as British India's agent in Calcutta. He succeeded Lord Craigmyle who stood down after only six years as chairman in 1938. Although Craigmyle had done a wonderful job steering the group through the Depression, it was Currie who would deal with the Second World War.

With peace reigning once again, the granting of independence to India in 1947 did little for passenger numbers as fewer and fewer expatriate government officers left the UK for service in India with each passing year. Orient Line, which had been part of the P&O group since 1919, was finally bought outright in 1960 and it was its chairman who succeeded Sir William Currie. Currie stood down at the age of seventy-six, and Sir Donald Anderson, formerly of the Orient Line, and who had joined P&O in the 1930s, became the new chairman.

The grand and magnificent fleet of liners belonging to the Orient Steam Navigation Company was conceived in 1828 when seventeen-year-old James Anderson (of the same family as Sir Donald Anderson) left his home town of Peterhead for London. Turning his back on a career as a fisherman, Anderson's fortune had been moulded by his uncle Alexander Anderson. Alexander retired from the Navy in 1815, at the end of the Napoleonic wars, and bought a sailing ship which had been captured from the French. The new owner-captain traded successfully to the West Indies and appointed James Thompson & Company as his London agent, conditional on them finding a place for young James. Fourteen years later James Anderson was made a partner of James Thompson & Company. T E Hughes wrote in *Sea Breezes*, August 1970:

> ... in 1854 James Anderson, in turn, introduced a nephew into the firm – James George Skelton Anderson. He became a partner in 1863 when the title of the firm was changed to Anderson, Thompson & Company. By this time the company was operating as shipowners as well as shipbrokers, its sailing ships voyaging the world in search of cargoes – North America, India, Australia, the Far East, indeed any place that they could find employment. In particular a regular berth was established on the India–Australia trade routes, the company's ships being known as the Orient Line of Packets.

An advertisement in *The Times* in February 1874 advised a new development in collaboration with Frederick Green & Company of London. This was the move into steam with the sailing of the auxiliary steamship *Easby* to Port Phillip via the Cape in March, followed later by the screw barque *St Osyth* for Melbourne. The service proved popular and profitable, so, when in 1877 the mighty Pacific Steam Navigation Company found itself with a surplus of ships, Anderson and Green made a bid to charter four of them to cash in on the burgeoning emigrant route to Australia. *The Times*, March 1877, carried the advertisement:

> Steam to Melbourne and Sydney from London – Orient Line. The undermentioned magnificent full-powered steamships belonging to the Pacific Steam Navigation Company will be dispatched punctually for Melbourne and Sydney in accordance with the following arrangements:
> ss. *Lusitania*, 3,825 tons register, last shipping day for goods Friday 22 June. Will embark passengers at Gravesend 26 June and Plymouth 28 June.
> ss. *Chimborazo*, 3,847 tons register, last shipping day 8 August. This steamer will call at Glenelg for Adelaide if required.

ss. *Cuzco*, 3,845 tons register, last shipping day 21 September.

These steamers are of 3,000 horse power effective and are expected to make the passage in 40 days. The accommodation for passengers of all classes is unsurpassed and their appointment throughout are of the completest character. Passengers will be embarked by steam tender at Gravesend and Plymouth.

The service was later joined by *Garonne* and Anderson, Anderson & Company jointly with Frederick Green & Company exercised their right to buy the four PSNC steamers. So it was that the Orient Steam Navigation Company was registered with a capital of £44,642 in 1878. It soon operated a joint service to Australia with Pacific Steam giving a fortnightly departure from London. The first of the traditional 'O' names was the *Orient*, built, as also were the four original Pacific company ships, by John Elder on the Clyde. The Orient Line worked in collaboration with P&O from 1919.

Captain James Nourse was another Scot who moved his business to London. He started his famous Nourse Line from offices in Greenock in 1861, but realised that a move to London would enlarge his freight market and left Scotland in 1864. His initial trade was with India but this soon expanded; the successful company eventually became part of the P&O group in 1917.

One of the other famous London Scottish shipowners was Andrew Weir. Andrew Weir became a shipowner in 1885 in Glasgow when he purchased

Thornliebank (1896) was the last sailing ship to be built for Andrew Weir's Bank Line – she was wrecked on the Scilly Islands in 1913.

the barque *Willowbank*, and very rapidly developed one of the largest fleets of sailing ships under the British flag. In 1896 the company commissioned its first steamship, but it was 1913 before the last sailing ship in the fleet, *Thornliebank*, ceased trading when she was wrecked on the Scillies. In 1905 the company was registered as Bank Line and the head office was moved to London, although the ships continued to be registered at Glasgow. The Bank Line served the Empire in all regions, and latterly was famous for its round-the-world service offering passenger berths to just twelve discerning passengers. A large part of its income derived from tramping and charters to other liner companies.

Surprisingly, in the early 1930s, Andrew Weir decided to go into the passenger liner business, a high risk enterprise in the middle of the Depression when so many liners were set to cruising or were laid up. Andrew Weir spotted an opportunity that arose in the wake of the collapse of Lord Kylsant's Royal Mail Group. The Natal Line of Bullard King, then a subsidiary of Union-Castle, was forced to withdraw from the Cape Town–Colombo–Rangoon–Calcutta passenger link and Union-Castle sold it to Bank Line in order to generate cash to bolster other parts of Royal Mail. Known as the India Natal Line, three motor ships were ordered from Workman Clarke at Belfast. Bank Line had been at the forefront of dieselisation and by 1933 already had thirty-three motor ships at sea. The three new passenger liners, *Isipingo*, *Inchanga* and *Incomati*, were splendid-looking little liners. *Isipingo* was the first launch into the Lagan for seventeen months, so severe was the Depression. *Incomati*

Inchanga (1934) was one of three charming Bank Line motor liners ordered for the Cape Town to Calcutta route. (John Clarkson)

Two of the four engines from the brand-new Furness Bermuda Line's luxury liner
Bermuda (1927), destroyed by fire, were recycled aboard *Incomati* (1934).

received second-hand engines from the new Furness Bermuda Line's
Bermuda which had been destroyed at Belfast by fire following an earlier fire
at Bermuda; her engines were undamaged. The three sisters provided luxury
accommodation for five hundred first-class passengers and could carry an
additional five hundred deck passengers on coastal runs. Apart from linking
South Africa with Asia they provided the connection between the Union-
Castle mail ship arriving from the UK with P&O or Orient Line at Rangoon
for onward passage to Australia. The *Incomati* was lost in the Second World
War, but the other pair continued on their design route until 1964, when the
service was finally withdrawn and the two ships scrapped.

Andrew Weir was also instrumental in forming the United Baltic
Corporation in 1919 jointly with the Danish East Asiatic Company. The
purpose of the company was to create a cargo and passenger service between
London and the Baltic States bringing emigrants to London for connections to
America and Australasia. The company's last ship was the Korean-built *Baltic
Eider* which traded between Felixstowe, Hull and Finland in the Finncarriers
consortium until she was sold in 2005. For many years the ships traditionally
docked at Hays Wharf in the Pool of London.

Sir Donald Currie was another member of the London Scottish club. Currie
was born in Greenock but was sent to school at the Belfast Academy and
later at the Royal Belfast Academical Institution. At the age of eighteen he left
home for Liverpool and joined the staff of the Cunard Steamship Company.

United Baltic Corporation's last ship was *Baltic Eider* (1989), seen at Felixstowe on 23 April 2004. (Author)

Much of his time was spent at Le Havre as Cunard's French agent attracting freight for shipment to New York. He returned to Cunard's Liverpool office in the mid 1850s and then set up on his own. The Castle Shipping Line of sailing ships, the 'Calcutta Castle Line' operating between Liverpool and Calcutta, was the result. By 1864 Donald Currie, like others before him, saw the benefits of moving to London.

Once the Suez Canal was open, the sailing ships were quickly outmoded by steamships taking the shorter route through the Mediterranean. Donald Currie looked to the Cape Colony to develop a steamship service between Britain and what was to become South Africa. The Castle Mail Packet Company was hugely successful. Currie soon had a fleet of steamships running a regular passenger and cargo service to Cape Town and by 1876 shared the mail contract with the long established Union Line, trading under the banner Castle Mail Packets Company.

In 1890, *Dunottar Castle* took the British rugby team on a tour of South Africa on the ship's maiden voyage. Currie accompanied the team and presented the South African Rugby Board with a gold trophy to be used for

Fairfield-built *Dunottar Castle* (1890) took the British rugby team and Donald Currie to South Africa on her maiden voyage – the rugby tour was the first time that the Currie Cup was awarded.

internal competition. The Currie Cup was duly presented to Griqualand West at the end of the tour; the Currie Cup is contested to this day. The Castle Mail Packet Company merged with the rival Union Line in 1900 to form the mighty Union-Castle Line running to South and East Africa. Ultimately merged with Cayzer Irvine (Clan Line) in 1956, the Castle ships finally came home to their Scottish roots. Donald Currie died in Sidmouth in 1909.

The archetypically English and pompously named Royal Mail Line was also essentially Scottish to the core. James McQueen was born in Lanarkshire in 1778, but at the tender age of nineteen opted to work in the Caribbean as a sugar estate manager. He returned to Scotland and became part-owner of a Glasgow newspaper in which he aired a vision for a fleet of steamships serving the West Indies. Eventually, at the age of sixty, he prepared a 'General Plan for mail communication between Great Britain and the Eastern and Western parts of the world; also to Canton and Sydney westward by the Pacific'. He was able to canvass commercial backing, and obtained a Royal Charter for a fortnightly service to the West Indies commencing in December 1841, with branch services to the Spanish Main, New York and Halifax. Fourteen large wooden paddle steamers and three small sailing ships were ordered for the newly created Royal Mail Steam Packet Company. In February 1841, less than a year after placing the contracts, the first of the fleet, *Clyde*, was launched by Caird & Company at Greenock.

The first part of McQueen's vision commenced on 3 January 1842 when the steamers *Tay* and *Thames* shipped the mails out of Falmouth bound for the West Indies. *Forth* had already been dispatched westwards to provide the branch connection to New York, while the smaller sailing ships were waiting to provide a web of connections throughout the Caribbean. Despite a series of setbacks the company quickly became viable and grew in strength. However, day-to-day management of the business was slowly eased away from McQueen, who, it seems, was a vastly better visionary than he was as an operations manager.

The Glen Line was equally fascinating as it was moved south to London at an early stage of its development. Strangely, it almost ended up back home in Scotland when it became part of Ben Ocean in 1973. The Glen Line was founded by the McGregor and Gow families who had a brokers' business in Glasgow in the 1850s. Alan Gow bought the *Estelle de Chile* in 1866 and put her to work sailing from Glasgow and Liverpool to west coast South American ports. Two years later he put the *Glenavon* in the China tea trade, calling at Peru on the way out. When the third sailing ship, *Glenaray*, joined the service the trading name Glen Line was established and a direct eastward sailing to China was inaugurated. Two years after Suez was opened Gow took delivery of *Glengyle*, his first steamship, destined to compete in the China tea run against the market leaders P&O and Alfred Holt. *Glengyle* typically needed fifty days to get back from Shanghai via Suez against George Thompson's clipper *Thermopylae* which required ninety days round the Cape of Good Hope. Five sister-ships were ordered to support the trade and Alan Gow and James McGregor, realising that London and not Glasgow was the focus of the tea importing business, moved their ships and offices south. The home port of Glasgow was painted over on the sterns of the ships so that the word London could be applied.

By 1874 *Glenartney* reduced the voyage time from China to just forty-four days and that same year a new service commenced from New York to the Far East. John Swire of China Navigation Company worked alongside James McGregor to establish the Far East Conference. Until then freight rates bobbed up and down as a ship was loading, and the Conference ruled that the rate be fixed only as the ship was about to sail. Professor Francis Hyde explains the system in his book *Blue Funnel*; notice the similarity of the concept with the modern day retail loyalty card:

The shipping Conference which, under John Swire's leadership, came into existence in 1879, was one of the first of a series of such agreements lasting, with brief intermissions, from that time until the present day [written in 1956]. At their inception the Conferences applied to cargo liner shipments and were regional in character. Their primary purpose was to regulate competition in order to maintain rates of freight, all the shipping lines within a particular Conference agreeing to charge the same rate. In some cases the traffic was apportioned between the lines, by restrictions on the number of sailings or by division of the ports of sailing or by pooling some part of the freight earnings upon all or a portion of the cargo. A second purpose of such agreements was to concert measures to meet competition from shipowners outside the Conference. In this case the usual weapon employed was the deferred rebate. These rebates were paid only to shippers who used Conference vessels. At the end of a stated period (usually six months), they were credited with a sum equivalent to 10% of the aggregate freight earnings over that period. This, however, only applied if, for a further period of six months, they continued so to confine their shipments. As a means of stifling outside competition the idea behind the rebate system was to hold the shippers to the Conference by making the receipt of the rebates dependent on absolute 'loyalty' as far as shipments in the Conference area were concerned. It is true that the merchant was not forced to ship his goods in Conference vessels, but the prospect of losing a valuable rebate to his competitors was usually a sufficiently powerful inducement to make him conform to Conference terms.

By 1895 the London-based Glen Line offered a fortnightly service from London to the Far East with a passage time of just forty days. James McGregor died in 1896 and his son Allan became senior partner. His first task was to consolidate the fleet, as the China trade was suffering over-capacity, and he did this by gradually increasing the capacity of his ships while reducing the total fleet number. He also stopped carrying passengers although passenger carrying was later reinstated. But by 1905 Allan McGregor was in trouble and his financial problems made it almost impossible for him to maintain his Conference obligations. The great entrepreneur and businessman John Reeves Ellerman, on hearing of the difficulties stepped in, as James Taylor recounts in his book on Ellermans:

It is not clear whether Ellerman or McGregor made the opening gambit, but ... Ellerman found himself in the position of being able to provide financial aid in circumstances where, if the company he was assisting chose to sell, he would be in the very favourable position of heading any prospective buyers. At the end of 1905, however, sale of the company had not been mentioned or contemplated, and Ellerman's occupation was with a scheme that would satisfy McGregor's financial requirements and at the same time be profitable to himself. With McGregor he arranged for certain of his own ships to be transferred, officially to be sold, to Glen Line, though registered in the name of Ellerman Lines with McGregor Gow & Company as managers.

In due course Ellerman's *Netherby Hall* became *Glenearn* and *Branksome Hall* became *Glenavon*. Trade was poor on the Japan and Far East routes and profits were hard to make – Ellerman pulled out of the agreement in 1908.

Glen Line was acquired by Elder Dempster Line in 1911 making it an associate company within the Royal Mail Group. The ailing Shire Line (not to be confused with the Scottish Shire Line, chapter 4) also in the London to Far East trade, and founded by Exeter-born David Jenkins in 1860, was also acquired and amalgamated with Glen as Glen & Shire Lines. Royal Mail

Glengarry (1940) and sister *Glengyle* were typical units in the Glen Line and two of eight ships in the fleet with accommodation for eighteen passengers. (Fotoflite incorporating Skyfotos)

was deeply involved with Burmeister & Wain via its shipbuilding company Harland & Wolff, and the first motor ship in the Glen Line fleet, *Glenartney*, was completed as early as 1915, having been ordered by Elder Dempster as *Montezuma*.

Elder Dempster and Glen Line survived the collapse of Lord Kylsant's Royal Mail Group. Sir Richard Holt, chairman of Ocean Steamship Company (Blue Funnel), appointed to recover what could be recovered from the Kylsant mess, was encouraged to recapitalise the company by the accountants brought in by the Bank of England. The accountants, again recognising the role of the 'Honest Scot', were Thomson McLintock & Company of Glasgow. Holt was subsequently allowed to purchase a majority of the Glen & Shire Line shares. The Glen ships always kept their separate identity in the Holt group, the core of which was the Ocean Steam Ship Company or Blue Funnel Line. The Glen & Shire red funnel, instead of blue, and the *Glen-* prefix or the suffix *-shire* as opposed to the classical mythology nomenclature of the remainder of Alfred Holt's fleets kept the identities apart. Glen held forth at London and Holt at Liverpool and Birkenhead. When ships were transferred between services, as often they were, funnels were repainted and ships renamed. At times it almost seemed that one side of the ship's funnel was red, the other blue!

The operation of the mighty Glens was no trivial task. When the *Glengyle* sailed from King George V Dock on 4 July 1961, voyage number 45, for Penang, Singapore, Port Swettenham, Hong Kong, Yokohama and Kobe, she had a European crew list of twenty-seven, including a ship's surgeon (on a salary of £960 per year and usually employed on a short-term casual basis) and a Chinese crew list of fifty-nine. The Chinese comprised twenty-six members in the deck department, eighteen in the engineering department and fifteen in the stewards' department, each with a senior bosun. Their status included lamp trimmer, sailor, greaser, stores, fitter, steward, cook, painter and quartermaster. In addition, *Glengyle* called at Southampton to uplift eighteen passengers, making a total complement, for the ship's surgeon to look after, of 104.

So, just as the London Scottish rugby players never seem to play at home, so too the London Scottish champions of industry were always away. Their reputation was second to none, the respect they held, almost without exception, was high indeed. Collectively, their contribution to wealth creation for the whole nation was immense. Just why they commanded such respect among their English peers stems from the perception of the 'Honest Scot', but they were hard-working, visionary, no-nonsense men who knew, unquestionably, how to steer the ship.

Glengyle (1940): a photographic record of Voyage Number 45 by ship's surgeon Dr David Mason:

(*Above*) King George V Dock, London, departure 4 July 1961.

(*Opposite, top left*) At sea, forward view port side.

(*Opposite, top right*) At sea, forward view starboard side.

(*Opposite, bottom*) Ship's dog on the boat deck.

(*Left*) In the tropics with deck awnings in place.

6

Wood to Iron, Iron to Steel, Sail to Steam: The Shipbuilders and Engineers

IF YOU THINK OF all the ships that were built, from the smallest Clyde puffer to the largest Queen, and when you think of all the fine joinery and fittings that Clyde men put into the many magnificent ships they built, you cannot help but wonder where it all is now. Where are the chandeliers, where is all the fine wood panelling and where did the carved staircases go? The puffer skipper would laugh at such finery but even so, where did the puffer go? Where are the great steel hulls that were put together by Scottish shipbuilders, and what have we got to show for it today?

While the Thames shipbuilders were still building wooden walls for the East India Company, the Scottish engineers were designing and building steamships. Wooden-hulled and paddle-wheeled they may have been, but from the outset the steamship was set to overtake the wooden sailing ship and one day chase it off the high seas. That day was not going to dawn just yet, but when it did, it was to a large extent the consequence of inventiveness, engineering skills and know-how pooled in the shipyards along the Clyde and elsewhere in northern Britain. As the steamship-building industry grew in the 1820s and 1830s, a parallel industry of suppliers developed, notably boilermaking, deck and engine room auxiliaries, iron and later steel factoring and stockholding, chainmaking, and a whole new chandlery industry for the supply of the myriad of items that ships required.

The key to the success of the steamship was its engine, and the engine in the early days was built, not by the shipbuilder, but by an engine builder using castings provided by the Carron Company at Falkirk or other specialist iron foundries. Scotland was favoured by plentiful raw materials required to support iron foundries: coal, limestone and, of course, iron ore, plus a keen and intelligent workforce that was prepared to learn new skills.

Demand for ships was increasing in the early nineteenth century. But in those days most of the tonnage was built on the east coast, with only one in five Scottish-built ships coming from the Clyde. The east-coast shipyards were to be found in almost all the coastal towns and villages. Yards came and went, depending on the local appetite for new ships. But it was not easy for a shipwright to set up his own business or to take over a disused yard. Kathryn Moore reports in her treatise on maritime Scotland:

The size of vessel built at such yards varied from under twenty tons to several hundred tons. In the early part of the century many coasting craft were less than 50 tons in size but later on the 50 to 150 ton range was most popular as they could be used for coastal or short sea trades. Vessels several hundred tons in size were used for long-distance trade. Nevertheless, even a shipbuilding firm such as Alexander Hall and Sons of Aberdeen (which built ships of 300 to over 500 tons in size) found that their main clients in the early decades of the century remained local shipowners ordering smaller craft. By the middle of the century yards in relatively small towns were also capable of producing the occasional large vessel for clients taking the opportunities offered by world trade. From the 1840s, however, the success of the clipper hull made Halls (and other Aberdeen yards) famous. Their production shifted to much larger vessels for cargo and passenger use. Dundee, too, had several shipbuilding yards at this time with wood also remaining the preferred material there because of the town's jute and whaling industries. Wooden hulls were more flexible than metal ones if caught in Arctic ice and, as the Indian sub-continent was the main source of the bulky (but low-value) jute required for the Dundee mills, wooden sailing ships such as those commissioned by the Dundee Clipper Line were long preferred to steamships. One shipbuilder in the town, Alexander Stephen and Sons (a firm that began in Burghead and spent periods at Aberdeen, Arbroath and Dundee before relocating to the Clyde) launched, like the Aberdeen yards, vessels over 1,000 tons. Leith was less fortunate. A major shipbuilding centre for centuries, the shipyards there lost ground to Aberdeen and the innovations on the Clyde although ship repairing remained important.

Moore again:

The massive contribution made by Clyde engineers and shipbuilders, not merely to Scottish but to world shipbuilding, lay in three areas – the commercial application of steam to power vessels, the technical development of compound expansion engines, and the steady improvement in boiler design. The highly innovative Napier family trained many men who became noted engineers and shipbuilders later in the century.

By the early 1830s, David Napier, who was still only in his forties, decided to move to London and by 1835 had disposed of his interests in Glasgow and moved south. He had been discredited by a series of boiler explosions and sought a new start. David Napier offered Lancefield Foundry to two of his most trusted employees, David Tod and John Macgregor. He wrote subsequently, 'During the latter part of my career, I was very much assisted by two excellent workmen, David Tod and John Macgregor'. However, his offer was not taken up, Tod and Macgregor preferring to start independently at a more modest level. In 1839 David Napier, now a member of the 'London Scottish' club, acquired a new shipyard on the River Thames at Millwall, London. The yard was run by his two sons, while Napier experimented with improving the efficiency of the steam engine. In 1854 the yard was sold to Messrs J Scott Russell & Company where *Great Eastern*, the leviathan of her day, was later built.

The relationship between Napier and his two most trusted employees is illustrated by the story of the inception of the steeple engine, an invention that came to Napier while lying in his bed one night. Napier ran to his dining room, clearing it of furniture and ripping up the carpet to expose the bare boards which he used as a chalkboard. A servant was dispatched to Tod's house asking him to come quickly, which, of course, he did, fearing that his master was ill. By morning the pair had the drawings transposed ready to take to the patternmakers. The engine was a variation of the American crosshead design, save that the cylinder was placed below the crank with the crosshead guides on top to make a very compact but tall engine assembly. This was Napier's steeple engine, first tested in the steamer *Clyde* in the early 1830s, *Clyde* being owned by his friends James and George Burns (G & J Burns after 1842). The installation and testing of the engine was the charge of engineer John Macgregor.

Tod & Macgregor started their own engineering business in 1833, in Carrick Street which ran northwards from the Broomielaw. Their reputation from the earlier Napier days guaranteed orders and the new company was soon busy. In January 1834 *Benledi* was launched at the Robert Barclay yard and towed up to Stobcross quay to receive her 100-horsepower engine built by Tod and Macgregor, marine engineers 'whose experience and ability ensure her speed to be of the very first class'. The second engine Tod and Macgregor built was a steeple engine for *Rob Roy*, an engine which 'is on a new construction and stands in a very small space'.

The Clyde shipbuilders concentrated more on passenger and cargo ships, both sailing ships and steamers, rather than on cargo carriers for the tramp or 'cargo seeker' trades. For the moment the shipbuilders of the Tyne, Wear and the Hartlepools were the premier builders of iron-hulled cargo steamers, as Archibald Hurd reported:

It was not, indeed, until the 1880s that the Clyde shipbuilders began to appreciate the advantages of steam as applied to tramps ... Towards the end of the 1890s, however, the pendulum began to swing from the east coast to the west. For reasons a little obscure Newcastle and Hartlepool ceased to compete with the sailing shipowners of the Clyde, who were now beginning to build a very high-class type of tramp steamer.

Why there should have been this geographical change with regard to the ownership and production of tramp steamers it is a little hard to say. Possibly the long voyage trade, so familiar to Glasgow owners in sailing ship days, did not seem to them at first so profitable a field for the introduction of steam power, while to the east coast owners, with the pre-eminent experience in the Baltic, Black Sea and east coast American trades, the advantages of steam may have appeared more manifest.

Nevertheless, one of the first iron-hulled steamers to be built to Lloyd's new rules for the construction of iron ships was *Azof*, launched after dark at Port Glasgow in July 1855 as the daytime tides provided insufficient water. The *Illustrated London News* for 11 August 1855 described *Azof*:

First ship built to Lloyd's new iron hull regulations on the Clyde was *Azof* (1855), launched after dark from J Bourne's yard at port Glasgow as the daytime tides were unsuitable. (Linda Gowans collection)

She has been built under the immediate inspection of Lloyd's surveyor, will have a high class on Lloyd's books, and is admitted to be the strongest steam vessel of her size yet built in [*sic*] the Clyde. She is to be propelled by an engine of 180 horse power; and, as the model of the vessel is a very fine one, a speed of 11 knots per hour [*sic*] is expected. *Azof* will carry 1,000 tons of cargo, 250 tons of coal, and 8,000 gallons of water in tanks. She has, besides a spacious cabin, accommodation for forty first class passengers.

She was built for P&O director James Hartley and his partner D Hoyle. Their company was registered at Greenock, but it was not long before *Azof* found her way into the P&O fleet working out of Aden along the African coast. 'Strongest steam vessel of her size' or not, she sprang a leak in 1867 on passage from Aden to Suez and was sold four years later only to be lost at sea after just a few months working for her new owners.

The dominance of the Clyde shipbuilders was clear by the 1860s, when 20,000 people were already employed locally in the industry. Clyde shipbuilders led the way with the revolutionary iron-hulled steamers that rapidly overtook the traditional wooden construction. Indeed, any sailing craft completed on the Clyde with wooden hulls were of composite fabrication, with the wooden shell built onto an iron frame. By the early 1870s, 90 per cent of ships built on the Clyde were iron-framed and iron-plated steamships. Just 2 per cent were wooden-hulled sailing ships and 9 per cent iron-hulled sailing ships, many of which were fast vessels at the pinnacle of sailing ship design that were built for the tea and wool trades to the Far East. Meanwhile, the old established east-coast shipyards in Scotland had tended to stick with wood and sail.

The introduction of steel led to lighter construction and greater deadweight capacity, but early mild steel was susceptible to corrosion and some shipowners preferred to stay with iron. In the early 1880s, however, improved boiler design, the ubiquitous Scotch boiler, coupled with the successful introduction of the triple expansion steam engine, collectively provided both reliability and reduced fuel consumption so enabling steamships to make longer voyages between coaling ports. This finally removed the last remaining advantage of the sailing ship – the ability to make long, non-stop, ocean passages.

On the east coast, shipbuilding began to concentrate at Aberdeen, Dundee and Leith, and finally turned away from wood and sail to steam and iron. Steam drifters were in great demand in the 1880s to support the burgeoning fishing industry, and vessels both large and small came from these yards at that time. But at the turn of the century less than 10 per cent of Scottish building capacity remained on the east coast.

Potomac (1893) was one of the initial group of innovatively designed steam-driven oil tankers completed on the Clyde for the Anglo-American Oil Company. She was wrecked off Andros Islands in the Bahamas during a hurricane in September 1929.

The first dedicated oil tankers were designed and built on the Clyde for individual one-ship companies that merged in 1900 into the fleet of the Anglo-American Oil Company registered at London. The first was *Bayonne*, delivered by A & J Inglis in 1889 and *Manhattan* which was delivered by D J Dunlop & Company a few months later. Each had a deadweight capacity of 4,000 tons, arranged in nine pairs of tanks that could be discharged at Purfleet on arrival from Ohio by twin onboard cargo pumps in about ten hours. The pair was so successful that orders followed for similar steamers with *Weehauken* completed on the Tyne in 1891, *Delaware* from D J Dunlop & Company at Port Glasgow in 1893, *Potomac* from A & J Inglis in 1893, and *Lackawanna* and *Chesapeake* from D J Dunlop in 1894 and 1895 respectively. The bridge amidships, engines aft arrangement, with a raised walkway over the well decks forward and aft, remained essentially unchanged in tanker design until the 1980s. Meanwhile, the deadweight capacity increased by almost two orders of magnitude! The Anglo-American Oil Company took delivery of *Narragansett* in 1903, then the world's largest oil tanker with a gross tonnage of just 9,196, from Scott & Company at Greenock.

But it was the large, fast and luxurious passenger liners that the Clyde shipyards produced routinely by the end of the nineteenth century for which the yards had acquired most acclaim. Ships such as the sisters *City of New*

(*Above*) J & G Thompson built the fabulous *City of Paris* (1888) for the Inman Line. She won the Blue Riband on her second crossing of the Atlantic. She is seen here as a two-funnel steamer in later life as the *Philadelphia*.

(*Below*) *Umbria* (1884), along with sister *Etruria* (1884), were both built at Govan and both were Blue Riband holders.

York and *City of Paris* delivered by J & G Thompson to the Inman Line in 1888 were built to the highest standards, as also were the numerous passenger liners delivered by various yards to the Cunard Line. These included *Umbria* and *Etruria* built by John Elder & Company at Govan and completed in 1884, and *Campania* and *Lucania* completed in 1893 by Fairfield, all of which set new standards on the North Atlantic. William Denny & Son produced a succession of fine liners for P&O including the magnificent *Australia* and *Himalaya* in 1892 and numerous passenger liners also for British India.

But there was yet to be the final flowering of the Clyde-built sailing ship, the four-masted barque. The sleek-hulled full-rigged ships of the nineteenth century were an American invention. Designed for speed rather than optimum cargo capacity, the typical three-masted vessel could carry low volume, high value goods including, for example, contraband, like no other type of ship before her. Early American vessels include the famous *Ann McKim* delivered from a Baltimore shipyard in 1832, and *Rainbow* completed at New York in 1845. The emigrant trade to America coupled with the repeal of the British Navigation Laws brought the American sailing ships to Europe, and it was not long before British yards, notably on the Clyde and the Tyne, as well as at Aberdeen, started to copy the design. The ships were perfect for the China tea trade and the British vessels reigned supreme when the American fleet retrenched to assist in the American Civil War. The opening of the Suez Canal in 1869 put steamers on a competitive fast track to the Far East and once coaling stations had been established the fast sailing ships were transferred to the Australian wool trade. By about 1880 the tonnage of deep-sea shipping was divided roughly equally between sail and steam. But the day of the commercial sailing ship was far from over.

Although the development of the Suez Canal hastened the demise of the sailing ship, severe competition from steamships in the late nineteenth and early twentieth centuries led to ever more efficient design of sailing ships and significant technological advances. The sailing ship at this time was by no means the outdated backwater that romantic maritime novels about this era would have the reader believe. In addition four masts rather than three, sail for sail, allowed shorter masts, better stability, fewer crew and greater tonnage – all factors increasing the competitiveness of the commercial sailing ship in an age, that by right, should have been the age of steam. Frank Scott wrote in *The Mariner's Mirror* (November 2012):

> In the mid-1870s sailing ship construction turned towards a more industrial product, where the ability to carry a large quantity of cargo at a low cost had become a higher priority than speed. It was also realised that if ships were to become larger, and more economic, spreading their sail area over four rather than three masts allowed the mast height to be reduced, thus making the rig much stronger. The logical first move was to produce a four-masted ship, and the first of these, the *County of Peebles*, came down one of Barclay Curle's Upper Clyde slipways in 1875. Much to many people's surprise, and to the delight of canny shipowners, subsequent experience was to show that the four-masted barque was no slower than the four-masted full rigged ship [of which a few 'one-offs' had been built], though obviously a good deal cheaper to build and maintain, and much simpler and less labour intensive for ship handling.

Elginshire (1889), typical of the many four-masted barques to come from Scottish yards. She was scrapped in 1923.

The concept proved such a success that a boom in orders for four-masted barques only peaked in 1892 when sixty-seven of them were launched. While the Americans also built four-masted barques they stuck with tried and tested all-wood construction, whereas British builders tended increasingly towards iron and steel frames, and eventually steel-ribbed and -plated hulls. Even the masts and yards were steel. The first iron- and steel-hulled vessel of this type was *Tweedsdale* completed in 1877, again by Barclay Curle. She was small, of just 1,043 tons gross, but she paved the way for larger vessels, such as *Elginshire* completed in 1889 by Birrel Stenhouse & Company at Dumbarton with royals over double topsails and single topgallant sails. She was some 2,160 registered tons gross and entered the Australian and New Zealand service of T Law & Company, Glasgow. The largest of the barques were about 3,100 gross tons, and included the famous German 'Flying P-liners' owned by Ferdinand Laeisz and operating in the Chilean nitrate trade, with names such as *Peking*, *Passat* and *Padua*. These three vessels are preserved to this day, *Padua* now the Russian-flagged training ship *Kruzenshtern*. Many of Laeisz's barques were built on the Clyde although the sisters *Peking* and *Passat* were built in Germany in 1911 and *Padua*, the last commercial four-masted barque to be built, was completed in 1926 at Bremerhaven.

Passat (1911), looking forward showing the array of winches and capstans available on deck.

The sail plan and rigging was much simpler than the traditional square-rigged ship. Gone were the deep single topsails and topgallants, and the royals became wider than they were high. Even the rigging moved from natural fibre rope to hard-wearing flexible steel hawsers providing strength and durability. One problem was that should the vessel become dismasted and reach some distant haven, it would be almost certainly uneconomic to repair her and the vessel, no matter her age, would be abandoned. This is the reason why so many steel-hulled hulks lie in places such as the Falkland Islands. Safety was greatly improved; the steel yards were fitted with two jackstays rather than one, so that men could indeed have 'one hand for the ship and one for himself'. Sail stowage was also made safer with the introduction of the Jarvis short gasket, rather than men having to cope with the traditional but cumbersome 'four-fathom gasket'.

Captain John Charles Barron Jarvis was a Scot, a master mariner and an inventor. He first went to sea on the barque *Grecian* under command of his father Captain David Jarvis and was given his first command at the age of just twent-three. The Jarvis winch was a labour-saving device first tested on the Flying P-Line's *Preussen* in 1897. So successful was it that the entire Laeisz fleet was quickly equipped with the winches. The Bullivant Company of London, and F C W Wetzel (later Wetzel & Freytag) in Germany, manufactured and sold the winches under licence, but sadly few dues were ever paid to Captain Jarvis, whose skills as a sailor and inventor far exceeded those as a businessman.

Steel rigging required better equipment to handle sails, and sophisticated conical drum halyard winches were introduced. Numerous capstans were also in place on deck to assist with heavy wire tacks, and separate winches were available for handling headsail sheets. Many of the winches were steam-driven and some ships even had diesel donkey engines of the primitive and noisy hot-bulb type. Geared steering mechanisms were a great improvement, although they still did not altogether prevent backlash in heavy weather. One neglected area was the rudder itself, which still retained a gap between the sternpost and the leading edge of the rudder which allowed cross flow and excess weather helm. This is not a problem on steamships as the wash from the propeller maintains the sensitivity of the rudder.

The Clyde shipbuilders mainly responsible for the development of the new breed of four-masted barque were Robert Steele & Company, Alexander Stephen & Sons, and J Reid at Whiteinch; and Russell & Company, Robert Duncan & Company and William Hamilton & Company at Port Glasgow. The role of the Clyde shipbuilders in the development of the technically sophisticated four-masted barque is summed up by Scott, with not a little frustration over the lack of uptake by British owners:

> Of course, by no means all vessels took advantage of all of these features, and British and American owners were particularly resistant to change. For example, R W Leyland & Company ordered two full rigged ships in 1891, the *Speke* and *Ditton*, which at 2,875 and 2,901 gross registered tons respectively were considerably larger than most of the four-masted barques built that year, and they compounded this by giving them single topgallants ... The irony for the British was that shipyards on the Clyde did turn out excellent examples of advanced sailing ship design, but these were mostly for German owners. Such a vessel was the bald-headed four-masted barque *Pommern*, which was built as the *Mneme* for B Wencke Söhne of Hamburg by J Reid & Company at Whiteinch in 1903.

But as the Germans were fond of pointing out, only one of their Flying P-Line ships was ever dismasted, and she was, of course, British- and not German-built! This was *Pitlochry*, in an incident that occurred in her eleventh year of trading from when she was delivered from her Dundee builders in 1905.

Barrie's legendary four-master *Lawhill* (1892) was finally laid up as unserviceable in 1948 and scrapped several years later.

Perhaps the most famous British four-masters were the sisters *Juteopolis* and *Lawhill* built for Charles Barrie to serve the Dundee jute trade. They were of all-steel construction built by W B Thompson in Dundee and delivered in 1891 and 1892 respectively. Given the competition from steamers on the Bengal route, Barrie opted to sell them in order to develop his own steamer fleet. The two barques were then used firstly in the Chilean nitrate trade and latterly for the Anglo-American Oil Company carrying boxed oil. *Juteopolis* was later renamed *Garthpool* under the ownership of the Marine Navigation Company of Canada but she was registered at Glasgow. Company chairman Sir William Garthwaite vowed to keep the ship in service under the Red Ensign as long as he could, but she was wrecked in 1929 on passage from Hull to Adelaide. *Lawhill* remained in service under various national flags and different owners until finally broken up in the late 1950s.

Glasgow port

From the seventeenth century onwards the shallowness of the channel from Dumbarton upstream fourteen miles to Glasgow was of increasing concern to the merchants of Glasgow. Attempts at deepening it by hand and through the construction of training walls brought only modest returns, and it was only the introduction of the steam dredger that allowed significant progress. The hand-powered and horse-powered bucket ladder dredger had been tried with limited success. The first steam-powered bucket ladder was applied by John Grimshaw at Sunderland in 1796 but it was not until 1824 that the Trustees of the Clyde Navigation decided to buy a powered bucket ladder system. The result was the excitingly named *No. 1*, a 59ft by 20ft dumb wooden pontoon with a single central well for the bucket ladder and a small side-lever engine to turn the bucket ladder drive wheel. The design dredging depth was just 10ft 6in, increased as time went on to 14ft.

Over the next thirty years *No. 1* was joined by *No. 2* and so on to *No. 6*, the design dredging depth having increased to 28ft. The dredging spoils were initially dumped behind bankside revetments to reclaim land and, more importantly, to make the various small islands part of the whole riverbank. When the reclamation of all the low-lying land in the Upper

Clyde had been completed, the dredging spoil was taken by steam-powered hopper barges to be dumped in Loch Long, but after 1892 it was taken to the Outer Firth of Clyde (the first hopper barge, of course, was named *Hopper No. 1*).

'QSPR' wrote in the *Saturday Magazine Supplement*, no. 160 for December 1834:

The author ... quitted Glasgow in a steam-vessel, in company with some friends, on 19 July 1827. The channel of the Clyde, for several miles below Glasgow, is narrow, and of little depth; but the want of water has been gradually remedied by the indefatigable efforts of the dredging-machine, which, by deepening the channel, facilitates the approach of larger vessels to Glasgow, which formerly received or discharged their cargoes at Greenock or Port Glasgow. Hence this instrument is significantly designated the 'Terror of Greenock' or 'Greenock's Lament'. The vessels are towed up the river by steam, which originally rendered the operation of the dredging-machine important.

In 1858 the great engineer John Ure, having completed the deepening and straightening of the Clyde approaches, left his tenure at the Clyde Navigation Trustees to join the Tyne Improvement Commissioners where he successfully continued his work of harbour and river improvement. In 1869, on the death of his brother-in-law, John Elder, he joined his sister, Elder's widow, as a managing partner of the John Elder & Company's Fairfield shipyard.

Glasgow Harbour in 1802. (*Illustrated London News*)

MacLehose on his work at Glasgow wrote:

... the quayage of Glasgow Harbour extended from Victoria Bridge to Stobcross Ferry on the north side, and from Glasgow Bridge to 200 yards west of Stobcross Ferry on the south side of the river, together 4,376 lineal yards, or not quite 2½ miles; the water area of the harbour was 70 acres and the annual revenue £78,783, while as to docks they were only on paper.

The quayage on the north side now extends [1885] from Victoria Bridge to the River Kelvin, and on the south side from Glasgow Bridge to 900 yards west of Stobcross Ferry; and in addition Kingston Dock, with its 5⅓ acres of water area and 930 lineal yards of quayage, was opened in 1867, and Queen's Dock, having 33¾ acres of water area and 3,334 lineal yards of quayage, was completed in 1882. The total quayage of Glasgow Harbour, including the two docks, is now 10,623 lineal yards, or 6 miles 63 yards, the water area is 153¾ acres, and the revenue last year was £291,638 – truly gigantic growths in 27 years. The Clyde Trustees' first public graving dock, 560 feet long, with nearly 23 feet depth at high water, was opened in 1875, and a second of equal size is nearly completed.

The nearest dock to the city centre was the small Kingston Dock which opened on the south bank in 1867 on the site of Windmill Croft. It survived until the Kingston Bridge was under construction in 1966 when the dock was infilled, making way for the new bridge foundations. Next down river was the Queen's Dock at Stobcross on the north bank which offered nearly two miles of quayside from its opening in 1880. This dock was home to the Clan Line, City Line and Donaldson Line. Immediately downstream of Queens Dock was Yorkhill Quay, and across the River Kelvin was Merklands Quay and lairage which opened in 1907, and Meadowside Quay which opened in 1912 for the importation of bulk grain cargoes from Canada and the USA. On the other side of the river was the Prince's Dock which was completed in 1897 with another two miles of wharves which became home to Anchor Line and Allan Line ships. In 1907 Rothesay Dock was constructed at Clydebank for the coal trade, while Yorkhill Quay and Basin was completed in 1910, providing berths for the Anchor Line for its New York passenger liners. The Yorkhill development was somewhat protracted as Shearer's small shipyard outside the Queen's Dock had to be relocated to Scotstoun before the construction of the quay could start. King George V Dock at Shieldhall was built opposite Connell's shipyard at Whiteinch. It is a single elongated dock, although originally two were authorised, connected directly to the river. It was completed in 1931 to service the larger vessels then using Glasgow and was home to Clan and Blue Funnel lines until they ceased to use the port. It remains operational and currently handles dry bulk cargoes, including animal feeds, grains, and chemicals.

Rowing boats served as cross-river ferries until the Broomielaw ferry accident in November 1864. Twenty-seven men were killed when one of these boats was overturned in the wash of a passing steamer, the tiller in the hands of passengers while the helmsman collected the fares! The subsequent public outcry led to the introduction of steam ferries in 1865. From 1884 until 1903, twelve small steam passenger vessels, or 'Cluthas', provided a very financially remunerative service for the three miles between Victoria Bridge and Whiteinch Ferry until Glasgow Corporation decided to electrify the city's tramway system and effectively killed the river service. The Finnieston, Govan and Whiteinch vehicle ferries were almost unique as their vehicle decks were able to be raised or lowered to suit the tidal condition at their loading points. They were double ended, twin-screw vessels but had no rudders, all steering being done by manipulating the engines ahead and astern to achieve the desired directional progress across the river. In addition there were two vehicle-carrying chain ferries, one at Renfrew and one at Erskine.

7

Clyde-Built

THE DOMINANCE OF THE Clyde shipbuilding fraternity was globally acknowledged. The term 'Clyde-built' became a mark of quality and respect,
a standard for another shipbuilder to aspire to. Scott's yard at Greenock,
founded in 1711, was by far the oldest shipbuilding firm in the world, but many
other famous names were also founded on the Clyde. Many of them focused
on a particular niche area, be it at one end of the scale the mighty commercial
passenger liners and naval battleships that graced the seas, or at the other, the
humble dredger and tugboat so essential to the maintenance of harbours and
their approaches. Names such as William Denny & Brothers at Dumbarton
immediately evoke the image of fast cross-channel steam turbine passenger
ferries, but this same company also specialised in building bulk refrigerated
meat carriers, pulp and paper carriers and many other specialist cargo vessels.

The Denny family, like any good shipbuilding family, was not averse to a
bit of wheeling and dealing. The Union Steam Ship Company or Union Line
was founded in Dunedin, New Zealand, in 1875 by James Mills, formerly a
shipping clerk to a local company. Mills floated the Union Company with
backing from Peter Denny, with the proviso that Mills order his ships from
Denny at Dumbarton. The Union Company eventually attained a near-
monopoly on trans-Tasman shipping, and was known affectionately as the
'Southern Octopus'. The company was sold in 1917 to P&O; perhaps Peter
Denny recognised that Mills was onto a winner in the first place.

Denny as a company was particularly innovative. The Denny Test Tank
was the world's first commercial ship-model experimental test tank. William
Froude had earlier established the very first test tank at Torquay for the
British Admiralty in 1871, with the objective of examining ship resistance and
the effective horsepower needed to overcome it by correlating a full-size ship
to its scale model. Froude discovered that the resistance of a ship to motion
through water was made up of two components, surface friction and wave-
making. This initial work was indeed seminal; a much larger, better-equipped
and more sophisticated facility was built at Haslar, near Portsmouth. The
Denny tank was commissioned in 1882 by senior personnel seconded from
Haslar and adopted the best practices then in use at Haslar. Denny was able
to use the tank to streamline hulls of fast paddle steamers on the Dover Strait

and elsewhere, and to develop efficient hull shapes for fast deep-sea passenger and cargo ships. Denny was also an acknowledged builder of fast, shallow river craft, and again the Denny Test Tank was fundamental to the design of them. The tank is now part of the Scottish Maritime Museum and is still in operation at Dumbarton.

A remarkable partnership was established by William Denny & Brothers at Dumbarton with the inventor of the turbine engine, Sir Charles Parsons, who was working out of Wallsend. This partnership was set to revolutionise the mercantile marine. Denny was an established and world-renowned builder of fine ships for the British registry, as much as for any other seafaring nation. The company foresaw the potential of the turbine, and approached Parsons who was keen to demonstrate his engine to merchant shipowners. A day-excursion steamer, conceived in Denny's design office, was to be the test-bed for the turbine concept for commercial use. The steamer was *King Edward*, launched at Dumbarton on 16 May 1901 to the order of the Turbine Steamer Syndicate, and placed under the management of Turbine Steamers Limited. Denny put up £24,200, with Parsons providing a further £8,000

King Edward (1901) was the first commercial turbine steamer in the world. (From a painting by John Nicholson)

and Williamson, the registered shipowner and manager, a further £800 as an operational fund.

King Edward had three direct-drive turbines working on the compound principle and built by the Parsons company at Wallsend-on-Tyne. The higher pressure turbine was connected to the central propeller and the two lower pressure turbines, of equal power, took the exhaust steam from the centre turbine and were connected to the port and starboard wing propellers. The central propeller was 4ft 7in in diameter, and the port and starboard shafts each had two sets of 3ft-diameter propellers with the after one set 10ft behind the forward one. This arrangement was found to give rise to excessive cavitation at speed and they were removed and replaced by larger single propellers in 1905. Steam was provided at a pressure of 150 psi (according to Captain James Williamson). The reverse turbines were incorporated in the low pressure casings. This arrangement produced 3,500 horsepower and gave a speed of 20.5 knots on trials with a noticeable absence of vibration. The design speed of the wing propellers was 755 revolutions per minute. The efficiency of the new machinery was illustrated by the ship's ability to steam at 18 knots on one ton of coal for nine miles whereas the contemporary paddle steamer *Duchess of Hamilton*, which was of almost identical dimensions to the *King Edward*, then only managed eight and a half miles at 16 knots using the same quantity of fuel.

King Edward was placed on the long Greenock to Campbeltown day excursion route, and was an immediate success with the travelling public. A consort, *Queen Alexandra*, was commissioned in 1902. She was placed on Ardrishaig and later Inveraray duties, in competition with the established paddler *Lord of the Isles*. After ten years sharing the route with the turbine ships, Turbine Steamers bought the paddle steamer and put her onto a new subsidiary service. *Queen Alexandra* was partly destroyed by fire in 1911 whilst alongside at Greenock, and was later renovated and sold to Canadian Pacific Railways for use out of Vancouver. A replacement turbine steamer of the same name was delivered in 1912. This ship was later recast as MacBrayne's three-funnelled *Saint Columba* in 1936.

The obvious success of the first day-excursion turbine ships led almost immediately to fast shallow draught cross-channel ferry services. Denny and Parsons made appropriate overtures to the main Dover Strait operator, the South Eastern & Chatham Railway. Its newest steamer was the 1899-built paddle-driven *Mabel Grace*, but four years later the SE & C's first turbine steamer, *The Queen*, was delivered by Denny, and without any intermediate transition via compound or triple expansion engined screw steamers, a

Typical of the Denny/Parsons fast turbine passenger ferries was *Biarritz* (1914) – single reduction gearing and capable of 24 knots, seen at Valletta during World War II.

succession of new Denny-built turbine steamers saw the company's paddlers off the Dover Strait by 1910.

The Queen was the first cross-channel turbine steamer in the world. She was offered at a cost of £83,000 with the proviso that if she failed to perform to the required standard, the builders would buy her back. As it was she set the standard for the next decade. She initially had five screws but the outer pair, designed to reduce cavitation on the middle set, were discarded during trials. During her first season she maintained an operating speed of 20 knots with ease. Her propeller speed was 800 revolutions per minute – these were the days of direct drive turbines with reduction gearing yet a distant dream. At this stage, there was one early Scottish example of the direct drive cross-channel steamer, *Princess Maud*, delivered by Denny to the Portpatrick & Wigtownshire Joint Railway in May 1904 for service between Stranraer and Larne. She had to wait until 1912 before a consort, *Princess Victoria*, joined her, also from the Denny fold.

The first transatlantic liners to be commissioned with turbine drive were the 15,000-ton sisters *Victorian*, commissioned by the Allan Line from the Belfast shipbuilder Workman Clarke & Company, and *Virginian*, ordered from Alexander Stephen & Sons on the Clyde. In 1905, the Cunard Line contracted John Brown & Company at Clydebank to build the twins *Carmania* and *Caronia*, identical save for their machinery. *Carmania* was equipped with Parsons turbines and three shafts, with two low-pressure turbines on the wing shafts and one high-pressure turbine on the central shaft. *Caronia* had conventional steam reciprocating engines. Under similar operating conditions the turbine ship could attain over 20 knots, whereas *Caronia* could only make 19 knots.

Thereafter the turbine became accepted not only for fast cross-channel ships and passenger liners but also for the world's fast cargo liners. It remained the supreme motive power until the price of fuel oil forced owners to turn to the more economical internal combustion engine and the era of the motor ship.

The Clyde shipbuilders were also very active at winning contracts from the Admiralty. Fairfield delivered the battleship HMS *Howe* at the height of World War II, representing the largest and most ambitious single military project to date. But she was just one of many mighty fighting ships large and small that were delivered by Clyde men to the Royal Navy as well as to numerous foreign navies the world over.

But Clydeside shipbuilding is synonymous to this day with John Brown's yard and the construction of various Cunarders, including the famous *Aquitania* completed just before the Great War and, of course, *Queen Mary* and *Queen Elizabeth*. Few of us remember the host of magnificent ships built

HMS *Howe* ready for sea trials on completion by Fairfield Shipbuilding & Engineering in 1942. Steel & Bennie's tugs *Campaigner* (1911), *Empire Palm* (1942) and *Chieftain* (1930) are in attendance.

Aquitania (1914) on the stocks at Clydebank.

on the Clyde, but all of us remember this pair of majestic North Atlantic liners that were the pinnacle of design and engineering in shipbuilding. The lead article on the front page of the *Daily Mirror*, Thursday, 27 September 1934, reported excitedly:

'I name this ship *Queen Mary*.' In a clear, calm voice the Queen spoke these words before a microphone at Clydebank yesterday when, in the presence of the King, the Prince of Wales and huge crowds, she named and launched the new Cunarder, the world's largest ship, which, it is hoped, will win back for Britain the Blue Riband of the North Atlantic.

As Her Majesty revealed the closely-kept secret of the new liner, which till then had been only a number, 534, some 200,000 spectators burst into tumultuous cheering. Then came a tremendous moment as the Queen touched with her gloved hand a gold button and the mammoth ship began to glide forwards. Cheer after cheer went up as she took the water, after going down the slipway in under sixty seconds.

Sir Percy Bates, Chairman of the Cunard White Star Line, announced that a second great ship – a sister to *Queen Mary* – is to be built as soon as pressure of work on the first has been eased.

(*Above*) *Queen Mary* (1936) at the start of a liner voyage from Southampton to New York, 30 July 1964. (Author)

(*Left*) The shell in the early days of construction, before work was stopped on the hull in December 1931 due to the Depression.

(*Bottom left*) Partly plated hull seen after work resumed in April 1934. Every shell and deck plate overlaps adjacent plates by up to one foot depending on the number of rivets required in the overlap.

(*Above*) Grand main hall and shops reflecting the art deco mood of the period.

(*Below*) Traditional main lounge.

King George V wryly commented on the years of the Depression in his address:

> For three years her uncompleted hull has lain in silence on the stocks. We know full well what misery a silent dockyard may spread among a seaport and with what courage that misery is endured. During those years when work upon her was suspended we grieved for what that suspension meant to thousands of our people …

Of the many other wonderful ships built on the Clyde, John Brown also had the millionaire's steam yacht *Nahlin* on the stocks alongside the slip where the Canadian Pacific Line's *Empress of Britain* was rising in 1930. *Nahlin* was yard number 533, while yard number 534 was, of course, *Queen Mary*. Ordered by Lady Henrietta Yule, husband of David Yule, who had made his millions as a merchant in India, the yacht was the last steam yacht to be built in the UK. *Nahlin* was designed by G L Watson & Company of Glasgow, a company founded by its namesake George Lennox Watson, who was renowned for racing yacht design, including four America's Cup contenders, in the late

Empress of Britain (1931) was built alongside the luxury yacht *Nahlin*, Yard Number 533, at John Brown's yard at Clydebank.

nineteenth century. The yacht cost £250,000 and offered a gymnasium and a dance floor but required a crew of fifty to keep her on the move! She was also renowned for having as a figurehead an American Indian Chief with a full feathered headpiece.

In the immediate post-war period John Brown built the *Arnhem* and *Amsterdam* for the railway packet route between Harwich and Hook of Holland. Not particularly striking ships in themselves, they become more significant when it is realised that their hull design was modified for the Royal Yacht *Britannia* completed in 1954 at the same yard; her four sets of turbines were almost identical to those installed earlier aboard *Amsterdam*, giving both ships a service speed of 21 knots. The last big John Brown passenger ship was the *Centaur* built for Blue Funnel in 1963. She was essentially a passenger and livestock carrier on the Fremantle to Singapore route, sheep to Singapore and cattle from north Australian ports to Fremantle. She could accommodate two hundred passengers. The last big passenger ships built at Clydebank were the ocean liners *Queen Elizabeth 2* and *Kungsholm* which, although completed for the Swedish American Line by Upper Clyde Shipbuilders, was contracted for by John Brown (Clydebank) Limited. *Kungsholm* was the last two-funnelled liner to be built, losing her forward dummy on sale to P&O as the cruise ship *Sea Princess* in 1979.

A full list of Clyde-built merchant vessels is given at www.clydebuilt.com: it is an intriguing list which contains many well-known names. The last of

Kungsholm (1966), last of the graceful two-funnelled Clyde-built liners, lost her forward dummy when she became P&O's *Sea Princess* in 1979. (Author)

the big passenger ferries to be built on the Clyde was North Sea Ferries' 31,750 tons gross *Norsea*, which was delivered by Govan Shipbuilders in May 1987 and since renamed *Pride of York*. The Ferguson yard has subsequently delivered several small coastal roll-on roll-off passenger and vehicle ferries for Caledonian MacBrayne.

The contract for the *Norsea* was placed in February 1985 and the vessel was launched by Her Majesty the Queen Mother in September 1986. This was the first passenger ship built at Govan for twenty years, and required an influx of new skills. There were a number of constraints on the design: a two-compartment damaged standard with the damaged draught not exceeding 6.08m, a total deadweight of 6,300 tons plus size constraints at ferry terminals, particularly at Hull. The power margin was designed for the largest diameter propellers possible, bearing in mind that much of the design route to Belgium is over shallow water. The ship provided for over 1,250 passengers in 1,124 berths, divided between 446 cabins and an additional 152 reclining seats plus 2,250 lane metres of vehicle stowage on three decks.

Walter Weyndling (see references) sums up the attitude to shipbuilding in the 1950s, and wrote fondly of his time at the Alexander Stephen yard:

In the 1950s Stephen embarked upon a period of modernisation. They were among the first to make a sizable investment in electric mono-tower travelling cranes and in welding technology. As their order book diminished Stephen engaged a management consultant and acquired a 'productivity office' filled with bright young men and women plotting curves and sticking wee flags in them. Another brave step of that period was Stephen's absorption of the Simon-Lobnitz shipyard and the production of three self-propelled suction dredgers for the Soviet Union, which are still operating in Russia. In the late 1950s Stephen shared with Harland & Wolff an order for six medium sized [all welded] BP tankers.

Weyndling concludes:

Stephen's repair department was looking after some of the ships of the Brocklebank wing of the Cunard Group. They were mostly in the Indian trade and carried Indian crews. These ships, when in Stephen's yard, were especially popular with the surveyors as their Goanese cooks were renowned for their curry lunches.

In more recent years a great deal has been written about the decline of the Scottish shipbuilding industry, much of it with considerable emotion, and some authors even pointing fingers towards a multi-party array of politicians. But no single group of people can be blamed for the inevitability of the decline. Shipbuilding enjoyed a boom in the very early 1920s – John Brown delivered the battlecruiser HMS *Hood* in 1920, one of seven large fighting ships it had built over the previous twenty years, and at the same time many merchant shipowners were rebuilding their fleets both to replace war losses and to modernise. One of the key decisions of the shipbuilder was whether to retool and go for the lucrative Admiralty contracts or whether to stay in the traditional comfort zone of building merchant ships to the speciality chosen by each specific yard.

In the early 1920s the attraction of Admiralty work was compelling, as Colin Castle described in his book on Clyde shipbuilders and shipowners:

> In the post-war period of 1919–1920 shipyard expansion continued on the Clyde. Fairfield's Board authorised the spending of £70,000 on the development of its West Yard and a further £30,000 on the engineering and boiler works. £27,500 was expended on the formation of Berth Number 6 to the east of the yard. Farther down river at Linthouse, Stephen's extended their engine works to such an extent that they were capable of producing output in excess of the yard's capacity to produce hulls. By December 1919 the shipyard found itself short of capital and unable to finance expansion plans estimated to cost £100,000. Beardmore too built four new berths at Dalmuir in anticipation of further Admiralty contracts.

At Belfast, Harland & Wolff was grateful for such attention by the Clyde to the Admiralty. Belfast continued to reap the benefits of orders that the Clyde was unable to accommodate. But the boom did not last, as Admiralty orders dried up in anticipation of long and lasting peace while the world slowly slipped towards recession.

The saviour of many yards was investment by shipowners in the immediate period of post-war euphoria. They not only provided desperately needed capital, but also a guarantee of orders at a more or less predictable rate. The shipowners were anticipating a boom, and their collective and misdirected investments demonstrated a complete lack of understanding of the post-war global economy. When the Royal Mail group bought Harland & Wolff in 1919, it also acquired Harland's subsidiaries on the Clyde, the London and Glasgow Shipbuilding and Engineering Company – later the Harland & Wolff, Govan Shipyard and Caird & Company of Greenock. Lord Pirrie, Harland & Wolff's Chairman, along with Sir Owen Philipps concluded the purchase of the Pointhouse yard of A & J Inglis and the Meadowside yard of D & W Henderson. Dr Dennis Rebbek, a senior executive with Harland & Wolff, much later commented that this move provided a fall-back position for the company should Home Rule in Ulster have deteriorated into civil war, a situation likely averted by the Great War. Indeed these purchases gave them shipyards, engine works, boiler works, a dry dock (Henderson) and outfitting, repair and heavy lift capacity in the River Kelvin (Inglis and Henderson).

Meanwhile, Lord Inchcape's mighty P&O group acquired Alexander Stephen & Sons in 1920. Christopher Furness's Northumberland Ship-building Company acquired major interest in both Fairfield and in the Blythswood Shipbuilding Company. As time went on Owen Philipps, later Lord Kylsant, took his Royal Mail group of companies almost to financial ruin, before he and the Royal Mail group fell from honour as the recession bit. Following the ignominious downfall of Lord Kylsant, Lord Inchape had to submit P&O to external audit at the command of government, the fear being that the UK was on the brink of losing a large and essential part of its Merchant Navy, should both these brands and their associates end in liquidation.

The economic chaos in the late 1920s and early 1930s drove the shipbuilders slowly out of business. Some yards on the Clyde chose to lay off their workforce in the hope of an upturn in demand for new shipping. Those that survived did so by canny marketing of niche areas – Denny continued with fast cross-channel ships and large and fast cargo liners, while John Brown stayed with the big-ship market. But the downside was an almost universal lack of reinvestment in any of the yards, all of which continued to use slipways designed for yesterday's ships, and most still using tools that had been in use since before the Great War.

The long anticipated recovery kicked in during the second half of the 1930s, with merchant ship orders picking up significantly from 1935 onwards with rearmament soon also accelerating. The war years that followed were good for the shipbuilders, and as peace again returned they enjoyed a late 1940s post-war boom, little realising that their industry was now inevitably destined to fail. The Clyde yards, like those in England and Northern Ireland, were hampered by lack of investment and increasingly sullied by restrictive practices and demarcation disputes caused by poor management–labour relations and strong reactionary unions, notably in the boilermakers' sector. Meanwhile, brand new shipyards were rising from the ashes in Germany, ironically funded by the Allied Nations, and America was busy single-handedly rebuilding the war-torn Japanese yards. Neutral Sweden was also well placed, as that country's undamaged shipyards were immediately able to accept orders once war had ended.

The situation on the Clyde worsened in the early 1960s as air travel slowly invaded the passenger liner market, at first on the Atlantic and later also on the longer hauls to the Antipodes and Asia. Cargo liners soon began to enjoy economies of scale, with bigger and faster ships needed to be built on larger slipways which only John Brown and Fairfield already had. Big bulk carriers and tankers could be built much cheaper overseas, and by 1966 government intervention into the shipbuilding industry was all that could save it. The Geddes Report recommended the creation of Upper Clyde Shipbuilders, a grouping of John Brown, Fairfield (Glasgow) Ltd, Alexander Stephen, Charles Connell and 51 per cent of Yarrow Shipbuilders, the remaining 49 per cent being retained by Yarrow & Company.

Lithgow and Scott's Shipbuilding & Engineering were similarly coerced into a Lower Clyde group called Scott Lithgow. In an attempt to improve profitability and cut out wasteful competition, Lithgow closed two of its loss-making engine works, David Rowan & Company and Rankin and Blackmore,

The Scott Lithgow crane with the stern half of *Cartsdyke Glen* (registered at Glasgow) ready for launch in September 1976. The forepart was launched nearly a year later and the two parts welded together as *World Score* and completed in 1978 for Dolman Shipping of Liberia.

but retained their interest in the still profitable John G Kincaid. Scott Lithgow built its largest vessels, the super-tanker *Nordic Clansman*-class, in 1974. First the after half of the *Nordic Clansman* was launched, and while this was being fitted out, the forward half was built and launched, and the two matched up afloat, and not in dry dock, to make a ship 1,100ft in length and 66ft broad. The *Nordic Clansman* had a deadweight of 268,235 tons and cargo tanks with a total volume of 322,337 cubic metres. She was one of an order of four ships designed in the wake of the closure of the Suez Canal, when economy of scale had become critical. However, there were to be no more super-tanker orders, despite Scott-Lithgow having earlier received a grant towards a new goliath crane; joining two parts of a ship afloat could never compete in cost with ships wholly constructed in a dedicated building dock.

Almost inevitably Upper Clyde Shipbuilders failed. Faced with the prospect of massive unemployment and possible civil unrest, the then Conservative government made a massive U-turn, after having described shipbuilding as a 'lame-duck industry', and sold the profitable Yarrow Shipbuilders back to the Yarrow Group and created the publicly supported Govan Shipbuilders and Scotstoun Marine (formerly Connell) in 1972. The latter two yards were successful for a time at building bulk cargo carriers to a standard design. After the ill-starred attempt at nationalisation of the shipbuilding industry and the vicissitudes thereafter, both the Govan and Yarrow yards continue to this day as warship builders under the ownership of BAE Systems. The John Brown's former yard was sold off privately to American oil rig interests and continued fairly successfully in that market for a number of years under several owners.

Nationalisation of the whole industry in 1977, by the then Labour government, led to the next Conservative government privatising what it could offload and progressively closing what it could not. Today shipbuilding is still carried on at Port Glasgow by Ferguson, and BAE Systems Surface Ships – but the industry is no more than a very pale shadow of its former self.

On the east coast, Hall Russell, at Aberdeen, completed its last ship, passenger and cargo liner *St Helena* for the British government in 1990, and finally closed the yard gates once and for all in 1992. The ship was delivered 60 per cent or £13 million over budget, as Hall Russell were unable to complete the contract. *St Helena* is currently operated by Andrew Weir Shipping, running between St Helena in the South Atlantic and Cape Town, with twice yearly calls to the UK. She is the last UK-registered vessel to qualify for the prefix RMS, or Royal Mail Ship. Henry Robb's yard at Leith amalgamated with the Caledon Shipbuilding & Engineering Company of Dundee in 1968, when the merged companies also bought equipment from the Burntisland Shipbuilding

Yard number 721, *Loch Shira* (2007) at Ferguson Shipbuilders' yard in Port Glasgow on launch day, 8 December 2006. (Donald Meek)

Sealink Isle of Wight ferry *St Helen* (1983), along with her sister *St Catherine* were the last ships built by Henry Robb at Leith. (Author)

Company which went into receivership that same year. Caledon survived in business until 1981, and two years later the last ships were completed at Leith, the Sealink Isle of Wight ferries *St Catherine* and *St Helen*, the latter still in service at Portsmouth.

Scottish shipbuilders and engineers did not just design and construct, however, they also trained up the next generation. Training to be a seagoing engineer in the 1880s started with an apprenticeship with one of the shipbuilders and engine manufacturers. Arthur James wrote in *Sea Breezes*, January 1980:

> The indenture of Apprenticeship makes fascinating reading. Every line in the beautifully lithographed document, with its copper plate writing, is suggestive of an attitude to work and a manner of living that seems not merely one century away from today's standards but several. Hall, Russell & Company undertook to give … training in 'the art and craft of engineers … as carried on at their works at Aberdeen'. The term of the apprenticeship was six years 'full and complete', and the wage paid was 4 shillings per month in the first year, rising by a shilling a year to nine shillings in the sixth.
>
> In consideration of such training and remuneration the apprentice 'binds and obliges himself,' to behave, not only while at work during the 60 hours of the working week but also outside working hours, when he would still be in the surveillance of his masters as the agreement required him to 'reside within one half mile of their works'.

The apprentice also agreed to a host of other rules – not to marry, and to 'avoid gambling, night walking, drunkenness and all other vice and immorality … and to demean himself as a dutiful apprentice'. But at the end of his six years the apprentice left Aberdeen as a competent, but uncertificated engineer officer to get sufficient sea time to allow him to sit for his first certificate of competency. Thereafter it was chief engineer's 'ticket' and onwards up the promotion ladder.

But righteous and strict though the shipbuilder was upon his apprentice, mistakes did occur and while some were glossed over, others were blatantly concealed and never admitted. One of the nicest stories is that of the North British Steam Packet Company's Clyde-based paddle steamer *Talisman*. She was built by A & J Inglis and handed over to her owners in 1896. She was measured by the Board of Trade who calculated her gross registered tonnage to be 394 tons, almost exactly the same as her near sister *Kenilworth* which was delivered from the same yard two years later. But the entry in *Lloyd's*

The Clyde steamer *Talisman* (1896) spent her entire career with an incorrectly recorded tonnage.

Register somehow transposed the number to 294 tons gross. As harbour dues and other charges were based on tonnage, a possible vow of silence crept across the mouth of the owner. Exposure of the truth was anticipated when the 333-ton *Kenilworth* was correctly registered in 1898, but somehow the mistake was still not revealed, the original registered tonnages of the two ships, right or wrong, still carved as they should be on the vessels' main beams for all to see. When both ships had their fore saloons widened after the Great War, only the additional capacity was added to the recorded gross tonnage, so that *Talisman*'s new tonnage became 293 and *Kenilworth*'s 390! The secret was even maintained long after both steamers were withdrawn for breaking up in the 1930s. Even Christian Duckworth and Graham Langmuir, among many other authors, perpetuated the obviously incorrect tonnages in three editions of their seminal book *Clyde River and Other Steamers*, first published in 1937.

8

Innovators, Investors and Entrepreneurs

CAREFULLY MANAGED RISK-TAKING ALLOWED Scotland's innovators, investors and entrepreneurs to lead and dominate the global merchant marine for much of the nineteenth and twentieth centuries. There were risk-takers on the Thames and Mersey as well, but the combination of natural resources available to the Scots put them at a distinct advantage. 'Clyde-built' was the recognised standard 'Kitemark' of its day. Scottish shipowners also set high standards by which the ships were manned and maintained, schedules were adhered to, and safety and reliability were paramount. In addition to an outstanding skills base, the 'Scottish navy' was also blessed with merchants who looked kindly on its services. In due course, merchants' banks were established that were willing to support and invest in the industry, encouraged by a team of innovative thinkers and the support of entrepreneurial businessmen. Without the input of these three sectors – merchants and their banks, innovators and their ideas, and businessmen ready to take risks – the engineering and seagoing skills that drew from both Lowland industry and Highland seamanship could never have become as successful as they did.

Innovation is not always recorded in history, while the innovators themselves may so often be displaced in time by the implementer. But these 'ideas people' are so important that their efforts should be recorded alongside those who are praised for utilising the innovator's work. So who were they and what did they do? They were the inventors, the people who asked, 'What if ...?', and the people who suggested to the company manager that 'if we could sail our ships to India, calling also at South Africa on the way, we could double our market'.

Robert Napier (1791–1876) is one of the greatest of all the engineering innovators. He has been widely acknowledged as the father of Clyde shipbuilding and marine engineering, serving his apprenticeship as a blacksmith and wright with his father in Dumbarton. After completing his apprenticeship he joined Robert Stevenson, the lighthouse engineer, for further experience before setting up in business as an engineer and blacksmith in Glasgow in 1815. He quickly made a name for the construction of reliable and often innovative engines, which were much sought after by the expanding industries in Glasgow and elsewhere. In 1818 he married his cousin, Isabella, who was the sister of David Napier, and soon after he took over the latter's works at Camlachie in the east of the city.

Assisted by his works manager, David Elder, father of John Elder, he secured his first marine engine contract in 1824 for a small steamer called *Leven*, which was so well-constructed and successful that it gave him entry into the world of marine engine building. This engine is still on display outside the former Denny Ship Model Testing Tank in Dumbarton. With his success came a need for larger premises and in 1828 he acquired the Vulcan Foundry just off the Broomielaw in the middle of Glasgow Harbour, and the Lancefield Foundry of his cousin David Napier when he moved to London.

It was during these years that Samuel Cunard was directed to Napier for advice on a suitable ship design and more importantly for introductions to interested financial backers. Cunard's visit to Glasgow and introduction to Napier was successful and he went back to London with backers and a marine engine builder who could be trusted to provide the type of ships that Napier had insisted were necessary for the North American mail contract.

Following upon his pivotal role in the founding of the Cunard company, Napier, like many other marine engine builders after him, decided that it would be in his best commercial interests if he built his own hulls rather than subcontract them to other shipbuilders. To achieve this he acquired ground in 1840 in Govan, on the south bank of the Clyde, where he laid out a modern iron shipbuilding yard with all the latest facilities. With subsequent expansion by acquisition of more ground, the yard operated until sold to William Beardmore & Company at the close of the nineteenth century.

Napier's reputation was of such high standing that he was entrusted from the 1840s with orders from the Admiralty as well as contracts for what were to become known as passenger liners – ships that were technically advanced and were finished to the highest standard of passenger accommodation.

Samuel Hall of Aberdeen proposed the concept of the surface condenser, but it was Napier who first built one, and installed it in the transatlantic paddle steamer *British Queen*. Napier, unlike other engineers, also gave every assistance to teaching and giving experience to his apprentices whilst also providing seagoing experience to aspiring young trainees. This allowed them access to a marine engineering appointment in the Royal Navy in the early days of steam.

Another of the great Scottish maritime engineering innovators was John Elder (1824–1869). MacLehose wrote in his *Memoirs and Portraits of 100 Glasgow Men*:

Pioneer passenger ship *British Queen* (1839) was the test-bed for the first surface condenser.

Perhaps no greater loss ever befell the leading industry of the Clyde than the premature death of Mr John Elder, in 1869. He was a foremost leader in the science of marine architecture and in the art of steamship construction. He was at the head of an enormous engineering establishment employing several thousand skilled workmen; and was, up to the close of his busy life, engaged in such extensions as would have made it unrivalled, for magnitude and completeness. The ships built by him were to be found in all harbours and upon every sea. They were famous everywhere for beauty of form, excellence of arrangements, and efficiency of performance.

John's father David Elder was manager of Robert Napier's engineering works at Camlachie, and was himself responsible for numerous adaptations to the early steam engines and the bracing necessary in the hull to support the weight of the machinery. John served his apprenticeship under his father, and then moved to pattern-making in England until his return to Napier's in 1848. At the age of twenty-eight, he joined Randolph Elliott & Company, as a partner in a successful millwright's business. John Elder was able to bring with him the skills of designing and building engines, and in due course designing and building the ships in which to place the engines. In 1868 the company was renamed John Elder, following the retirement of his partners. Various innovative adjustments to the steam engine were made by John Elder, but his greatest achievement was the development of the compound engine, first successfully trialled in the small paddle steamers *Inca* and *Valparaiso*, built in 1856 for the Pacific Steam Navigation Company. Elder took out various patents on his new engine, which was set to revolutionise steam navigation with its higher pressures, improved thermal efficiency and greater developed horsepower from the same quantity of steam, all made possible by improved boiler design capable of generating greater volumes of steam at higher pressures. His untimely death at the age of forty-five was a great loss, and occurred shortly after he had been unanimously elected as President of the Institution of Engineers and Shipbuilders in Scotland.

Innovation was also the byword of John Ure (1820–1883). Ure started work at Robert Napier's yard at Lancefield when he was fifteen. MacLehose wrote:

… then under the able management of David Elder, whose eminent son John subsequently married Mr Ure's only sister, the liberal-minded and highly-esteemed Mrs Elder, who has, in the most munificent manner, founded and endowed the Elder Chair of Naval Architecture in the University of Glasgow, added an endowment of £5,000 to the Chair of Engineering there, bestowed on the inhabitants of Govan the Elder Park in memory of her husband, so early removed from the scene of his triumphs, and of his worthy father, and has gifted to the citizens of Glasgow the Queen Margaret College for Ladies.

Ure next turned to land surveying, and joined the firm of William Kyle, Glasgow, and later served as chief assistant to Andrew Thomson, another well-known Glasgow civil engineer. After various spells of study at Glasgow University, he entered the service of J M Rendel of London, and was engaged on work on the rivers Tyne and Lea, on railways in Lancashire and Cheshire, at the East and West India Docks, London, the Devonport Dockyard Steam Basin, the Guernsey Harbour Works, and the docks at Garston, Grimsby, and Birkenhead. In 1852 he was appointed resident engineer of the Clyde Navigation and Harbour of Glasgow and one of his first tasks was to commission Mr Kyle to undertake a survey of the river. Ure was then able to develop several comprehensive schemes of harbour and river improvement, at an estimated cost of nearly £1 million. Some seventy-five yards of quay were built in anticipation of greatly increased trade, but more importantly Ure initiated work on widening and straightening the river, and developing

Glasgow Harbour in 1876 after John Ure had completed his engineering works and the deepening of the Clyde channel. (*Illustrated London News*)

the new channel opposite Port Glasgow. He went on to undertake similar work for the Tyne Improvement Commissioners, and in failing health died at the age of sixty-two.

But so many Scottish innovators were at work in the nineteenth century that it is not possible to cite them all. Nor did innovation end at the turn of that century, when the Merchant Navy still reaped the benefit of a host of far-sighted men. Among the incidental involvements with innovation, but nevertheless worthy of record, and more an Italian innovation than a Scottish one, was the first applied commercial wireless messages sent from ship to shore in July 1898. The ship was the Clyde Shipping Company's iron-hulled paddle tug *Flying Huntress*. Guglielmo Marconi was asked by the Dublin *Daily Express* to help report the Kingstown Regatta using a wireless link from an offshore vantage to connect with the onshore telegraph link to Dublin. The embryonic Marconi Telegraph Company speedily established a base station in the harbourmaster's office at Kingstown (now known as Dun Laoghaire) and looked round for a steamer that could be chartered to act as a floating platform to carry both the wireless transmitter equipment and observers of the regatta. The Clyde Shipping Company's tug stationed at Dublin at that time was *Flying Huntress*, and she was duly taken aside and fitted with the necessary batteries and wireless telegraphy equipment, ready to report the winners in time for the evening edition of the *Daily Express*. An innovative Italian first with a Scottish flavour!

A great Swedish innovator was Alfred Nobel, and he set up his British explosives plant on the dune spit at Ardeer to exploit the manufacture of his new invention, dynamite. Founded in 1870, the Ardeer Nobel's Explosives Company became part of the newly grouped ICI industries in 1926, the site now abandoned after it was sold in 2002, and badly damaged by fire in 2007. Until then its safety record was second to none, and so was that of the fleet of small cargo ships which exported the explosives for onward transhipment overseas and to quarries and other users around the UK. The first ship was a small sailing cutter, *Jeannie*, which was loaded on the beach at low tide. The first steamer was *Maggie*, bought second-hand in 1874. By the turn of the century the benefit of a deep water quayside was realised; the Garnock Wharf was completed in 1905. This allowed bigger ships to be loaded so that parcels of up to 300 tons of dynamite and detonators could be dispatched. The first purpose-built explosives carrier, *Lady Tennant*, joined the fleet in time for the opening.

Transhipment for export generally took place to larger ships in sheltered anchorages. This largely ceased after the Second World War when the ICI coasters voyaged directly to the Caribbean, South American, Africa, and many European destinations. The remarkable thing about the fleet was its safety record. Indeed, several of the small explosive carriers enjoyed exceptionally

The attractive lines of the explosives carrier *Lady Dorothy* (1916) belie her trade – seen leaving Birkenhead at the end of her career. The brand new ferry *Royal Iris* (1951) is lying at Seacombe Landing Stage and one of the two Cunard Line intermediate liners *Media* (1947) or *Parthia* (1948) is in mid-river.

long careers, notably *Lady G Cochrane*, built in 1910 and retired only in 1952, and *Lady Dorothy*, commissioned in 1916 and scrapped in 1957. Such was their safety record that the shipping office did a good trade in advisory work, helping shipping companies around the world in how best to handle explosive cargoes, knowledge that was widely sought after in two world wars. The last ship in the fleet was *Lady Helen*, but she was sold in 1984, following the decline in the use of blasting explosives, so ending a Scottish shipping interest that had survived over a hundred years.

One of the really far-sighted Scots innovators was John Paton, whose fleet of motor coasters all began with the prefix *Innis-* (Gaelic for 'island'). In 1911 he left shipowners Paton & Hendry to found the Coasting Motor Shipping Company. John Paton set about developing a fleet of motor coasters, the first *Innisagra* being commissioned in 1912, when the ubiquitous steamer was not only perceived to be efficient, but also integral to all the coasting fleets the world over. Seventeen motor ships were built in all; the first eight were small ships of just 140 gross tons and a length of 67ft, and were all built at Kirkintilloch and launched broadside into the Forth & Clyde Canal. The other nine were larger, and ranged up to 400 gross tons and these were built at yards on the Clyde and at Leith. Part of the experiment was to test different 'hot bulb' engines that had been developed by manufacturers such as Bolinder, Skandia, Beardmore and Tuxham. The vessels were engaged largely in the coaling trade around Scotland and Northern Ireland, settling on the beach at a suitable state of the tide to be discharged, of which the distillery run was described by H W Bristow in an article first published in *Sea Breezes*, November 1950:

> The vessel was beached, and horses and carts came down alongside and took away the quantity required. The distilleries we went to were Oban and Islay. The men engaged to work the coal out would be given whisky – strong doses of it – and it would not be long before silence reigned in the hold while the men slept off the effects. ... we would meet with one or more of the steam puffers so well known in these parts of Scotland. It would be a race with them, and we were evenly matched for speed, our only advantage being that we could forge ahead for a little when the puffer's engineer had to clean his boiler furnaces.

The small motor ships had 80 brake horsepower (bhp) engines. They were not a great success, their engines really being unsuitable for marine use, and were sold in the Great War, most being deployed in Scapa Flow on Admiralty duties. Some were used as munitions carriers working from Irvine to deliver to warships lying at various locations off the west coast of Scotland.

Inniskea was typical of the larger vessels, at 250 gross tons and completed for John Paton at Leith. Four other vessels of similar dimensions, *Innisshannon*, *Innistrahul*, *Innisulva* and *Innisvera* were built by William Chalmers & Company at their shipyard in Rutherglen to the east of Glasgow, some miles above the limit of the Clyde Trust's navigation, and with ten overhead bridges between the shipyard and the sea! Unlike the smaller ships, *Inniskea* and her sisters required two engineers to man the 120bhp engines as part of a crew of eight. The engineers were themselves the main drawback to the motor fleet, because suitably trained and certificated engineers were not available, and a number of the ships remained tied up for want of an engineer. The throttle comprised a gas tap on the fuel line from the twin 500-gallon tanks, although starting the engine required some nifty work with a steel bar and brute force, while the propeller was disengaged by a crude and grinding clutch arrangement. The clutch was either in or out: there was no in-between position!

The early hot bulb internal combustion engines were very susceptible to scaling, should the drip feed water be at all brackish. Once the scaling reached a certain degree, the two cylinders would start to run irregularly and heat up. Stress could quickly develop and connecting rods break. Sadly, both *Innisagra* and *Inniskea* were wrecked after only a few months' service while their engines were disabled. Bristow again:

> We arrived in the Forth on a Sunday morning. I had a middle aged marine engineer from Glasgow who was learning to drive the engine. A big-end bearing had heated up and we anchored beneath the shadow of the Forth Bridge to take off the bearing, scrape the molten metal, and refit. Meanwhile the captain had the hatches taken off ready for discharging. We had not finished our job when the weather changed and a strong south westerly gale sprang up. It was a case of slipping the anchor cable and 'running before it'. We started the engine up on one cylinder, which was all we could do, and the gale drove the ship to the other side of the Forth. Then seas broke over us … the vessel took a list and the Captain tried to beach her on a patch of sand between two piles of rocks. He could not make it, and with a sickening crash we struck the rocks, just about at high tide.

Despite these early setbacks John Paton pursued his dream of developing a fleet of motor coasters. As engine designs quickly became more suitable for the maritime environment and trained engineers became more plentiful, his larger class of motor ships at last became more profitable. However, those that survived the Great War and had not been purchased by the Admiralty were sold, and the company was disbanded in 1920. One of the little ships, *Innisbeg*, made it to Sierra Leone, later to be converted into a barge, while *Innisdhu* found itself part of the New Medway Steam Packet Company's fleet, better known for its Thames excursion steamers, in 1937. The 75ft-long *Innishowen* was the longest survivor in gainful employment, under a number of different owners until scrapped in 1947.

As with innovators, there have also been numerous far-sighted investors. Samuel Cunard was one of many to benefit from the collective vision of the Glasgow merchants keen to invest their own resources into shipowning, which many saw as complementary to their own merchant businesses. Others, such as Charles Cayzer, looked to the shipbuilder to sponsor his shipowning aspirations, but again it was on the understanding that good times were ahead. In the early days of the steamship, however, the capital outlay on a new ship was divided into sixty-four parts so that investors could buy an agreed share. Total unit costs were such that families or even individuals could afford to fund the purchase of a vessel without the need for much outside financial support. As unit costs rose, in keeping with the engineering sophistication of the steamship, so the 64th principle was abandoned. Corporate funding, supported by mortgages provided by the burgeoning finance industry, took its place.

When the Western Isles Steam Packet Company was incorporated in 1873, some four thousand shares were issued to raise capital of £20,000. This company was intended to trade in direct competition with established companies such as David Hutcheson (later David MacBrayne). The key subscribers were all Glasgow businessmen, principally wine merchants and grocers, bent on extending their own catchments into the Western Isles. Local Hebridean subscribers made up the majority shareholding, but after only two years trading the company folded. From its ashes was formed John McCallum & Company, and David MacBrayne Limited later became a major shareholder in the company when McCallum merged with Martin Orme & Company in 1929, in response to government pressure for streamlining of Hebridean shipping interests.

Investment by a shipping company in a rival enterprise was quite common in the nineteenth century. The cross-fertilisation of available funds in the Burns and MacIver days of steam navigation on the Clyde and Irish Sea coastal routes was quite remarkable. So too was that of the big banking institutions who would underwrite Cunard, while at the same time providing loans to White Star, Allan Line and the other competitors on the transatlantic trades.

But investors were not only interested in shipowning but also took a keen interest in the profits that could be made in shipbuilding. Shipbuilding was a less secure investment, as new orders were unpredictable and when times were hard, orders were few and far between. Many shipbuilders would bid at cost, or less than cost, to secure an order that was likely to lead to repeat orders from a particular shipowner, a risky business if the gamble should not pay off. The major investors only came along when they perceived good times ahead and profits for the taking. A significant investment was the steel-mill owners who were keen to secure a regular market for rolled steel plate. Two such were John Brown & Company of Sheffield, which paid £923,255 for J & G Thomson's long established, loss-making Clydebank yard in 1899, and William Beardmore, the Glasgow armaments manufacturer, who acquired the Robert Napier & Sons' interests. The Thomson shipyard was an early example of a 'greenfield' site, as they had been required to relocate from their Govan site to an unnamed location down-river, due to their existing Clydebank shipyard being required by the Clyde Navigation Trustees for harbour expansion. Besides building a shipyard, the Thomsons had to build tenements to house their workers, as well as providing accommodation for schooling and religious observance. However, the town rapidly grew and when it became a police burgh, a referendum was held to decide whether it should be called Clydebank (after the shipyard) or Kilbowie (where the huge Singer Sewing Machine plant was located). The vote was in favour of Clydebank, and so the name of a Govan shipyard ultimately named a town! The shipyard under the ownership of John Brown & Company went from strength to strength until the decline of the industry in the 1960s.

Another example was the interest of the coasting firm Clyde Shipping Company in the Dundee shipbuilders W B Thompson & Company, as told by Messrs Harvey and Telford in their history of the Clyde Shipping Company:

> George Jardine Kidston [Clyde company chairman] having many financial involvements outside the company had become closely involved with the Dundee shipbuilding firm of W B Thompson & Company. … it is believed that he had given a cash injection during a critical period. Through this connection the Clyde Shipping Company opened a long relationship with Thompson's by placing the first of many orders for ships during 1886. Their relationship continued with Thompson's successors Caledon Shipbuilding Company, so that by 1950, a total of one tug, 32 coasters and two tramp steamers had been built for company account.

A large part of the investment process was managed by accountants on behalf of shipowners and shipbuilders alike. Of these, one of the Glasgow-based accounting firms was held in great esteem for its honesty and integrity, and its services were highly sought after. This was Thomas McLintock &

Company, which dated from 1877, and it was this company that was brought in by the Bank of England to unravel the mess that Lord Kylsant had created with the collapse of the Royal Mail Group of companies in 1931. John Morison was put in charge of bringing Royal Mail back to some form of economic viability: this was no easy task, as first he needed to settle claims being brought in the American courts from relatives of the dead following the loss of Lamport & Holt's liner *Vestris* off New York in 1928, Lamport & Holt being a Royal Mail Group company. Morison's subsequent success in selling off parts of the group in order to finance the remaining business is well known, and the goodwill generated was a welcome boost to the Scottish financial sector during the early 1930s.

Among Morison's innovative solutions was the merger of the Roal Mail group's Glasgow-managed J & P Hutchison steamship company with James Moss & Company of Liverpool. The latter purchased the entire shareholding of Hutchison in 1917, but had kept the companies separate, even though their respective trades to southern European ports overlapped. The sale of the merged Moss Hutchison Line was a superior offering to the sale of the two

Procris (1924) was typical of the steamers in the fleet of Glasgow based J & P Hutchison trading to the Mediterranean.

companies as separate entities, and in 1934 was rapidly purchased by General Steam Navigation Company of London, then a part of the P&O Group.

While the many innovators and financiers were themselves entrepreneurs, there is also another breed of men associated with the Merchant Marine who were solely entrepreneurs. These were the men who launched a new business, willing to accept the risk-taking that was involved; many of them, though not all, were hugely successful. The successful entrepreneurs were able to weigh up risk-taking against investment and potential profit when viewing a commercial proposal. Many of the more successful names in the shipping industry fall into this category, not least people like Samuel Cunard and his contemporaries such as John Burns.

One of the first displays of entrepreneurship was by Archibald Glen Kidston who owned an iron business in Glasgow, which had a couple of sailing ships to support its trade. Archibald had three sons, George Jardine the youngest, John Pearson, and Richard the eldest. Their father was keen that they set up in business, but was reluctant to set them up in his iron factoring works as he saw little immediate prospect for growth. But he was undoubtedly a man of wisdom and foresight, because he recognised the future of the steamship, and in particular the potential of the steam tug. It was this far-sightedness that led him to purchase the embryonic Clyde Shipping Company in 1848 as an investment for his sons to develop. The opportunity arose when the existing partnership of the Clyde Shipping Company, formed in 1815, broke up under the chairmanship of Sir James Lumsden, when the assets of the company needed to be realised. Kidston senior bought three wooden-hulled paddle tugs and one iron-hulled tug, three river luggage boats and eight lighters, plus the goodwill of a viable company.

Kidston financed the purchase of the Clyde Shipping Company with fellow investors William Ferrier, his cousin, and two Glasgow merchants. Under the subsequent directorship of George Kidston, the investment developed into the world's longest surviving steamship company trading specifically from the Clyde to Irish and English coastal ports and providing much of the towage and tendering capacity on the Clyde and in Ireland. The wealth of the family following Archibald's entrepreneurial investment allowed his great grandson, Glen Kidston, to become a celebrated aviator and racing driver; he lost his life in an air crash in 1931. The Kidston family remained involved with the company which survived until 2002, while one of its later chairmen was London-based banker Archie Kidston, who died in 1977 at the age of fifty.

Perhaps the ultimate entrepreneurial followers were the brides and grooms that cemented relationships between various companies. There are many examples, so close-knit were the shipbuilding and shipowning families in Scotland, including the tie between Paddy Henderson & Company and the Ben Line described in chapter 4. Another 'partnership' was the marriage of John Inglis, son of founder Anthony Inglis, who with his brother John created A & J Inglis, the shipbuilders, and who married Agnes Denny in 1867. This formal link between two shipbuilding families served both companies equally well for many years.

But in the true sense of the word 'entrepreneur', it is men such as Charles Connel, who left the comfort zone of Alexander Stephen & Son to set up his own shipbuilding yard at Scotstoun, that stand out. Charles Connel & Company was hugely successful, and passed out of family ownership when Upper Clyde Shipbuilders was created in 1967. David Tod and John MacGregor did broadly the same thing when they left David Napier in 1836 to set up on their own in Glasgow and later at Meadowside. But perhaps the most flamboyant display of entrepreneurism in the Scottish shipbuilding fraternity was Messrs Hugh McMillan and Donald Bremner, respectively of Fairfield and John Brown, who could smell the money to be made after the Great War and set up on their own as the Blythswood Shipbuilding Company. The new company quickly developed a liaison with the Furness Withy group of companies, and went from strength to strength in building the oil tankers that were in great demand from 1919 onwards.

There were notable entrepreneurs on the shipowning side of the industry as well. Many of these saw an opportunity and grasped it, aware that their actions could lead to the big time, but equally aware that disaster was a possible outcome. Indeed, the old adage 'the right place at the right time' certainly holds true for many. Bob Campbell, having been forced to sell his Clyde steamer business to Captain Buchanan in 1884, rebuilt his business, only to be faced by a new threat from the Caledonian Railway. The Caledonian Railway had tried and failed to interest independent steamer companies to operate from their new railhead at Gourock, and decided to institute their own steamship services by founding the Caledonian Steam Packet Company – a name which lives on to the present day in Caledonian-MacBrayne. In the midst of this development Bob Campbell died and left his sons Peter and Alec in charge. On 1 January 1889 *Meg Merrilies* and *Madge Wildfire* were sold to the Caledonian Steam Packet Company, along with the Campbell goodwill of the Glasgow and Holy Loch routes. This sale gave the Campbells the capital required to develop their Bristol Channel business, but as part of the deal it was agreed that Captain Peter Campbell would remain on the Clyde in command of one of his former ships for two years, to help promote confidence in the new railway-owned company.

Campbell's *Madge Wildfire* (1886) was one of the Clyde steamers sold to the newly formed Caledonian Steam Packet Company in 1889. (From a painting by John Nicholson)

Campbell's other steamer, *Waverley*, had been losing money on the Glasgow to Ayr excursion trade, and a charter was agreed for her with a group at Bristol for the 1887 season. The problems were immense, not least because Alec Campbell had to devise a timetable that allowed the steamer to berth at Bristol Channel piers when the tide permitted (the tidal range is up to forty feet here, immense compared to the moderate range in the Clyde). *Waverley* was a success and Alec returned the following year to operate the steamer under his own name. It was not until the end of 1891 that Peter was able to join his brother at Bristol to help set a firm course for the new company of P & A Campbell. Expansion to the south coast followed later, where competition was intense. The brothers never forgot their Scottish roots, and gave their paddle steamers beautifully contrived Scottish/South Wales names such as *Glen Usk* and *Glen Gower*. But the early years at Bristol were hard, and the company only prospered because of the charismatic energy that Alec brought to everything he did. Here indeed was a man with true entrepreneurial skills, and a clear vision of what was needed to succeed.

One of P & A Campbell's south-coast steamers *Bonnie Doon* (1876) which started life on the Clyde, was not the most reliable of vessels, and was known by the English excursionists at Brighton and Eastbourne as 'Bonnie Breakdoon'!

A similar visionary worked on the Forth. This was Captain John Galloway, who had the vision of a towage and excursion business. Galloway was able to obtain financial support from Edinburgh merchant Donald MacGregor, and together in 1854 they bought the tug *Carrs*. It was not long before a fleet of passenger-carrying tugs was built up, serving Aberdour, Inchcolm, and occasionally also Kirkaldy and Inverkeithing. The partners' first proper excursion boat was *Lord Aberdour*, which was purpose-built ready for the 1866 season. In 1869 the company focussed on the new Portobello Pier, with local excursions to Prestonpans and Inveresk, but sadly its founder John Galloway died just as the summer season started. Galloway's vision had, nevertheless, become a success.

Various metamorphoses followed until in 1886 the Galloway Saloon Steam Packet was formed with Matthew Pearson Galloway, son of Captain John Galloway, one of the majority shareholders. Thereafter the company was kept afloat largely by Matthew Galloway's efforts, until in 1898 financial difficulties required that the two best steamers, *Tantallon Castle* and *Stirling Castle*, be sold. That same year the North British Railway attained a 62 per cent majority shareholding in the company in an attempt to better integrate its services with the rail network. North British soon realised that the Galloway company was outreaching itself with orders for new steamers and paying no dividend on its investment. While Galloway was able to defer enquiries from the NBR accountancy office about the viability of the excursion steamers, the Galloway company experienced modest prosperity and expansion until the Great War. So much so that the North British Railway Company ordered two identical paddle steamers in 1914 from A & J Inglis of Glasgow; the *Fair Maid* for service on the Clyde and *Duchess of Buccleuch* for the Forth. Both ships were updated versions of the company's 1899 *Waverley*, but *Fair Maid* was lost in active service in the Great War, while *Duchess of Buccleuch* survived. Before completion, both ships were requisitioned by the Admiralty for service as minesweepers. As the other members of the Galloway fleet had been sold to the Admiralty during the war, it was not considered financially viable to run a single ship service; the *Duchess* was not refitted and was scrapped soon after the end of the First World War, thus closing the business of the Galloway Saloon Steam Packet Company.

Two of the classic entrepreneurial developments overseas were the successful Irrawaddy Flotilla in Burma and the equally unsuccessful attempt

The Galloway Saloon Steam Packet Company's flagship *Tantallon Castle* (1887). (Oil painting by author)

to transfer the Irrawaddy success to the River Plate. Rudyard Kipling's soldier, retired to London, looks back fondly on his service years in Burma, and reflects on the Irrawaddy Flotilla (*Mandalay*, first published in the *Scots Observer*, 21 June 1890):

By the old Moulmein Pagoda, lookin' lazy at the sea,
There's a Burma girl a-settin', and I know she thinks o' me;
For the wind is in the palm-trees, and the temple-bells they say:
'Come you back, you British soldier; come you back to Mandalay!'
Come you back to Mandalay,
Where the old Flotilla lay:
Can't you 'ear their paddles chunkin' from Rangoon to Mandalay?
On the road to Mandalay,
Where the flyin'-fishes play,
An' the dawn comes up like thunder outer China 'crost the Bay!

… and those paddle steamers flew the house flag of P Henderson & Company of Glasgow (see chapter 4).

The foundations of the Irrawaddy Flotilla Company were laid in 1852 when the Governor General of India, Lord Dalhousie, ordered four steamers, *Lord William Bentinck*, *Damoodah*, *Nerbudda* and *Juma*, to be sent out from England, and four flats. They ran between Rangoon (now Yangon) and Thayet three hundred miles up the Irrawaddy River (now Ayeyarwaddy River). Twelve years later, in 1864, the Secretary of State for India decided to privatise the service. Todd, Findlay & Company of Rangoon, run by its namesake Scotsmen, James Todd and Thomas Findlay, and already managers of the Burma Steam Tug Company, bought the vessels and goodwill for £16,200. The contract stipulated that there must be two sailings a week between Rangoon and Thayet Myo, connecting with the mail ship from Calcutta. Finding costs higher than anticipated, Todd and Findlay transferred the contract to the newly formed Irrawaddy Flotilla & Burmese Steam Navigation Company of Glasgow in order to recapitalise the business. A partner was found in P Henderson & Company, running steamers between Glasgow and Liverpool via Suez to Rangoon. Thomas Findlay was appointed chairman and Messrs John Galloway and John Galbraith from the Henderson Board were made managing director and secretary.

The company was restructured in 1875 as the Irrawaddy Flotilla Company, and in 1876 William Denny, having been invited by the company to inspect conditions first-hand in Burma, delivered the first of his many shallow-draught steamers, the *Taiping*. Denny had designed earlier steamers which had been built by Duncan at Port Glasgow. But the tie between the Irrawaddy Flotilla and the Denny family enabled Denny to become world-renowned for shallow-draught river vessels for export the world over. The Irrawaddy company went from strength to strength, and by 1930 it was carrying nine million passengers a year. With the invasion of the Japanese in 1942, following the bombing of Rangoon on Christmas Day 1941, almost five hundred units of the entire fleet of 267 steamers and 383 flats was scuttled in the upper reaches of the Irrawaddy and Chindwin rivers. The British then hastily escaped over the Assam hills to India. About a hundred vessels were put back into service in 1946, and following independence being granted to Burma, the Irrawaddy company was nationalised in 1948, before going into voluntary liquidation in 1950.

The obvious commercial success of such entrepreneurial enterprise in Burma led the Henderson management to believe that they could transfer their experience directly to the River Plate in South America. Denny had delivered steamers to two companies working on the Plate but neither had been paid for and part-ownership remained with Peter Denny. La Platense Flotilla Company of Glasgow was registered in 1886 under Peter Denny's chairmanship; the vice chairman was none other than John Galloway from the Henderson Board, and the secretary was his colleague Matthew McKerrow. The risk-taking was immense, and assumed that the political and commercial constraints on the River Plate paralleled those on the Irrawaddy.

Nagama (1898) was just one of many William Denny products built for the Irrawaddy Flotilla Company. Note cargo flats to port and starboard. Hulked in 1921 she later became a houseboat at Nyourghia.

Scuttling the Irrawaddy Flotilla Company fleet in April 1942. (Drawing by J Burnie, first published in Laird 1961, *Paddy Henderson*)

William Denny and John Galloway sailed for Buenos Aires in June 1886 to consolidate their affairs. They purchased one local company and tried to purchase another potential competitor. John Galloway returned home shortly afterwards, and it was in despair that William Denny took his own life in Buenos Aires in March 1887. Sadly, the Henderson and Denny-owned company was to suffer at the Argentine Revolution and failed in July 1889, following the collapse of the Argentine economy. The entrepreneurial spirit of both William Denny & Brothers, the shipbuilder, and P Henderson & Company, the shipowner, was forever dented. It is a sad postscript that the close relationship enjoyed by the Denny and Inglis families never recovered from William Denny's suicide, as John Inglis had developed close commercial ties with Nicolas Mihanovich, who was a major Argentinian shipowner and a competitor of Denny's La Platense company, and who finally bought the failed Denny company for the proverbial song.

But perhaps the greatest innovators and entrepreneurs of all are the people themselves, as shown, for example, by those faced with the Clearances in the early nineteenth century. The notorious land clearances gave the displaced crofters two options. The majority opted for the arduous passage aboard the emigrant ship in the hope of a new beginning, while a few opted for alternative employment (see chapter 3). Many of the new factory jobs created in the

Industrial Revolution were regarded as semi-skilled or at worst unskilled, and the Highlander's aptitude for such work was sorely taxed. An alternative industry was fishing, and the east-coast boatbuilders, innovative as always, were able to produce a simple lugger for the landlubber to try his hand on the high seas and cast his nets. These small half-decked boats were limited by the area of sail they could carry, which, in turn, was limited by how much sail one farmer and a boy could hoist and set. The boats were vulnerable to being overwhelmed in a big sea because of their size and open construction, and the casualties were enormous. But the risks the men regularly and willingly took were considered acceptable in order to keep their families housed and fed. The sails were of canvas made heavier with homespun preparations such as catechu and linseed oil which protected against water and rot.

A remarkable series of new hull designs emerged during the latter part of the nineteenth century, incorporating a deep keel and a handsome streamlined, double-ended hull. Known as 'Scaffies', 'Fifies' and 'Zulus', these attractive looking wooden-hulled boats provided greater efficiency in the water, and allowed the farmer-fishermen, now fully fledged, to travel further offshore seeking their catch with increased safety. Nevertheless, these by now decked boats, with up to a mile of nets overboard, were vulnerable to any change in the sea conditions, and casualties still occurred on a regular basis. The new boats were still limited in size by the ability of the crew to raise larger sails. This problem was finally overcome when a small steam capstan, 'the iron man', was installed on deck, so that a larger sail could be hoisted by just one man keeping a rope taut around the revolving capstan. The capstan was also invaluable for hauling in even longer and heavier nets. Larger sail meant larger hulls, allowing the steam-assisted Fifies and Zulus to sail down as far as the Dover Strait in search of the 'silver darlings'. Having fitted steam capstans, the next logical step was to fit a larger boiler and a main propulsion engine which, in turn, ushered in the era of the steam drifter and side trawler. The fisher-girls travelled with the boats, taking up residence in Grimsby, Yarmouth, Lowestoft and finally Margate as the season progressed southwards, gutting, cleaning and barrelling the fish ready for the quayside market. The stories of mayhem created by these hordes of roving fun-loving girls are legion, and although their job was unforgiving, by all accounts they certainly lived life to the full.

But it was the arrival of the steam drifter which revolutionised the harvesting of fish to create the burgeoning fishing industry. Fish was a cheap and nutritious food that a hungry nation could afford when the steam drifters and trawlers first went to sea in large numbers in the late Victorian era. Indeed, the global image of the British soon became that of a working man clutching his fish supper wrapped up in yesterday's newspaper. In the 1960s the inshore boats became more dependent on technology, with all kinds of electronic gadgets to guide them to the catch. The basic shape of the wooden hull remained the same, double-ended, although some had transom sterns to provide more working deck space, beamy with a high flared bow and high bulwarks. Scottish builders tended to use larch planking on oak frames with steel deck beams (all-steel hulls are now preferred), and a typical inshore seine trawler is typically about 80ft in overall length and perhaps 22ft beam. The new fishing industry blossomed, and continued to thrive until fish stocks, both in home waters and in the cold waters to the north, were threatened – in the meantime the Scottish fishing industry had a clear one hundred highly profitable years. The remnant of this once great industry is now represented by a considerably smaller fleet.

Matthew Pearson Galloway of Leith (1843–1913)

Mathew Galloway was the son of John and Margaret. Captain John Galloway had formed a partnership with Donald MacGregor of Leith in 1854 to run the paddle steamer *Carrs* as both tug and seasonal excursion steamer on the Forth. The excursion business focused on the Leith to Aberdour passage, fighting off competition until John died in 1869. His share of the business went to his son Matthew, but not until 1876, just before the last of the ships had been sold by Donald MacGregor to John Kidd. Matthew Galloway's passion for the steamers was such that he managed the Kidd fleet through his own ship chandler and shipbuilding supplies business which was also registered at Leith.

Galloway maintained a two-ship excursion service offering cruises up river to Alloa and down the Forth round the Bass Rock, as well as a weekly cruise to Dundee. Economics were such that only one ship, *Lord Elgin*, was in service for the summer of 1879. But when John Kidd died in the spring, *Lord Elgin* was sold to English operators and remained in service in the Solent area until 1953 – she was eventually broken up two years later at the remarkable age of seventy-nine.

In 1879 Galloway hosted a consortium to form the Forth River Steam Shipping Company to maintain the excursion service between Leith and Aberdour. Trading was initially poor due to intense competition and Galloway realised he needed to offer modern steamers to attract patronage.

At this time in his career Galloway was described as 'Ironmonger' of 24 Shore, Leith, in the *Edinburgh Gazette*; in his own right he was purveyor of iron and steel fittings to the shipbuilding and repairing industry, notably to J Cran & Company and John Menzies, Shipbuilders. The excursion steamer *Lord Morton* was commissioned in 1883, followed by the first *Stirling Castle* in 1884. Life for the *Stirling Castle* did not start well as she struck temporary staging beneath the Alloa Railway Bridge on a trial run up-river, her owners being accused in court of careless navigation by the Caledonian Railway Company.

In 1886 the Forth River Steam Shipping Company was owned by the traditional 1/64th share as follows:

Matthew Galloway	12	Andrew Wallace	12
John Wallace	12	Annie Kidd	10
David Kidd	5	Anthony Watson	5
Robert Croall	4	Thomas Aitken	4

Under this ownership Galloway, aided largely by Aitken, reformed the company as the Galloway Saloon Steam Packet Company, with shares issued appropriately to the respective proprietors. The company received the new *Edinburgh Castle* later that year, complete with deck saloons that extended the full width of the ship, and the following year also the *Tantallon Castle*. New calls were introduced, including the ever-popular embarkation point at Portobello, and destinations such as Elie and North Berwick, while the core service was still to Aberdour and Stirling from Leith.

All would have been well for Galloway's new company had not the North British Railway complained that it was interfering with its potential passenger traffic. With no response from Galloway, the North British moved in during 1889 and acquired 62 per cent of the company shares. The board was reformed with a strong North British bias. At first little changed and the 1890s saw the 'Leith yachts' emerge from hibernation each spring to take up their excursion duties as normal. The former railway company steamer *Gareloch* was ceded to the company in 1891 to become the *Wemyss Castle*, a poor sister to the real Galloway steamers, but all that the North British Railway board would allow Galloway to fund.

Company expenditure began to exceed income due to upkeep of piers and other shore-side assets, as well as storm damage to four ships at

Leith in the summer of 1891. Although the company entered the 1898 season, as before it quickly sold its two best ships, the *Tantallon Castle* and *Stirling Castle*, after the May Edinburgh Week. This was necessary to pay for extensive repair and maintenance costs coupled with starvation of resources by the parent North British Railway. But Galloway bounced back with a new *Tantallon Castle* and the smaller *Stirling Castle* ordered from John Scott & Company of Kinghorn. The fitting-out of the two ships was magnificent: the first-class lounges had alcoves behind Greek-style pilasters in walnut and inlaid in gold, the couches were upholstered in Utrecht velvet, and the after windows were in stained glass.

Sadly, the *Tantallon Castle* was critically stern-heavy and handled very poorly, so a replacement was designed. Galloway went for a Parsons direct-drive turbine in the style of the pioneer Clyde turbine steamer *King Edward*, and immediately had a sturdy extension built to Portobello Pier to take the new ship. But the North British Railway objected to the plan, expressing 'extreme dissatisfaction with the company accounts', and the order for the turbine steamer was blocked. Matthew Galloway managed to put off the railway company's demand to inspect his balance sheet until 1901, and in May 1903 the railway company asked for dissolution of the partnership with Galloway. This should have been his downfall as a shipowner.

Despite a policy of attrition from the North British Railway, Galloway and Aitken maintained a five-ship service throughout the summers of much of the 1900s. The fleet included the new *Roslin Castle*, driven by twin screws and powered by two sets of triple expansion engines, but a poor second to Galloway's triple screw turbine steamer he so much yearned for.

Thomas Aitkin died in 1907 and was replaced on the Galloway board by a railway man, Henry Grierson. Grierson's remit was to constrain the Galloway Saloon Steam Packet from competing with the railway shipping and rail services and to make it profitable, but also to return any profit directly to the North British Railway. Both Matthew Galloway and Henry Grierson died in the winter of 1913/14. Matthew's son John took up the reins and tried to revitalise the steamers. The intervention of the Great War put paid to his vision and the company was wound up in 1919.

9

Missionaries, Explorers and Traders

MANY A SCOT WAS born to travel. Even the more remote trading posts around the world generally hosted at least one expatriate Scot, eking out a living as merchant or other service provider. There were a number of reasons behind the need to leave home, not least periodic hardship that peaked in the era of the Clearances in the first half of the nineteenth century. Key to global travel were the missionaries and explorers who opened up new trade routes and, of course, the increasingly tight web cast by the 'Tartan Navy' to carry the goods dispatched by the traders and merchants far and wide. It was a web that quickly passed through the Iberian Peninsula into the Mediterranean and later expanded south and east into Africa and Asia and ultimately to Australasia. At the same time the web moved west and southwest to encompass the Americas.

At the end of the eighteenth century the famous master mariner and explorer James Cook was making history. James Cook was the son of a Scots farm worker who had moved south to Yorkshire. Cook joined the Navy and rose rapidly through the ranks. In 1766 the Royal Society engaged Cook to travel to the Pacific Ocean. Cook was promoted to lieutenant at the age of thirty-nine and was to be commander of the Royal Society expedition. The expedition sailed in 1768, rounded Cape Horn and continued westward across the Pacific to Tahiti to make astronomical observations. Cook then commenced phase two of his voyage aboard *Endeavour* which was to search the South Pacific for signs of Terra Australis. Cook later mapped the complete New Zealand coastline, making only minor errors, and sailed west, reaching the southeastern coast of the Australian continent in April 1770. In so doing, his expedition became the first from Europe to encounter the eastern coastline of Australia.

Cook's second voyage of discovery was aboard *Resolution* to the deep south. Although he did not find the Antarctic coast he did map South Georgia. Cook entered historical legend as 'Columbus of the Pacific' when he stumbled upon Hawaii while searching for the elusive Northwest Passage. Columbus, of course, had 'discovered' America on his mission to India. On 29 March 1778, Cook's flagship, *Resolution*, accompanied by *Discovery*, arrived at Vancouver Island. Sadly, the most famous Scottish sea captain of his generation died in

Hawaii in 1779 after an unexpected return to the island with a broken spar; he was killed as he turned on the beach to protect his men while launching one of the boats to return to the *Resolution*.

A dominant force in the early days of trade was the Honourable East India Company, an autonomous institution with its own military to defend its outposts. Essentially London-based, the East India Company had a preference for Scottish seamen, as it recognised their special skills as navigators (the islander element) and as innovators and traders (the lowland element). The company's mighty wooden walls were, almost without exception, built on the Thames. There was strong resistance to Scottish engineering innovation when the steamship arrived on the scene: the East India Company claimed that the distances involved in sailing round the Cape into the Indian Ocean precluded any idea of deploying steamships. This resistance was one of the larger nails later driven into the East India Company's coffin as various companies, led by Arthur Anderson's Peninsular and Oriental, deployed steamships successfully, using the overland connection across Egypt and, later still of course, developing a through route via the Suez Canal.

Various missionaries had family links with Scottish shipowners and shipbuilders, some receiving direct sponsorship. David Livingstone, for example, was born on 13 March 1813 at Blantyre in Lanarkshire (the town of Blantyre in Malawi was named in his honour). Livingstone was brought up to respect personal piety, poverty, hard work and learning. When he had travelled north of Bechuanaland and the Kalahari Desert, rivers became his natural means of travel. Often shallow and subject to shoaling, a shallow-draught steel hull was preferred, as these could be carried beyond obstructions such as waterfalls. One of the famous builders of such craft was Alfred Yarrow on the Thames (later to move to Scotstoun on the Clyde) but Livingstone stayed faithful to his countrymen and worked closely with Tod & McGregor.

Having published his book on his southern African travels and now with people clamouring to fund his work, Livingstone ordered *Ma Robert* from Laird Brothers at Birkenhead for the Zambezi Expedition in 1858. Her thin steel hull quickly perished and he replaced her with HMS *Pioneer*, as he reports in a letter to Lord Kinnaird dated November 1861, a letter written aboard the boat on the Shire River below Lake Nyasa (now Lake Malawi):

I suppose that the Government will pay for the steamer after we have put it on the Lake – but do not know. It was built by my friends in Glasgow and the builders Tod & Macgregor take nothing [from me] until they see whether anything will be granted. The expenses of this steamer and all her crew are

David Livingstone's *Ma Robert* (1858) on the Zambezi. From a lithograph in *The life and explorations of Dr Livingstone*, published by Adam & Company, London in 1875.

great, £11,000, but next year they will be less. The *Pioneer* is unfortunately too deep. A splendid strong good vessel with this one fault. Were she on the Lake she would be admirable. I do not grumble about her I am most thankful to have her, but with half her draught as was intended in the plan she would have gone up any of the East African rivers.

Sadly, Livingstone's vision of *Pioneer* as a lake steamer did not materialise, as the river shoaled below the lake and access was denied. Livingstone's vision included use of the boat to prevent transport of slaves to East Africa and for use as a mission ship and clinic.

Then there was *Lady Nyassa* which, undeterred, he also ordered from Tod & Macgregor. In 1861, iron-hulled, twin-screw *Lady Nyassa* was completed and dismantled for shipment to Africa in crates, to be reassembled for the

Zambezi Expedition. Being a river steamer, she did not require registration, but is recorded to have been of 123 gross tons. Livingstone later rather recklessly sailed her to India, where she was sold and only then in 1866 was she registered.

River transport on the Shire River and Zambezi commenced in 1879. The African Lakes Corporation, sponsored by the Free Church of Scotland and the Church of Scotland Missions, commissioned the stern wheel steamer *Lake Nyasa* to run fortnightly from below the Murchison Cataracts on the Shire River to the Zambezi delta. Local management comprised two brothers from Glasgow, John and Frederick Moir, and shipping soon spread to planting and trading. At home a key advocate was John Stephen of Alexander Stephen & Son. The fleet was soon developed with stern wheelers on the river and screw steamers on Lake Nyasa running in competition with the British Central Africa Company and the African International Flotilla. Donald Anderson reported in *Paddle Wheels*, spring 1975:

The ALC ordered two stern wheel steamers from Ritchie, Graham & Milne of Glasgow who, apart from already having supplied in 1896 the 100 foot *Queen Victoria* for the service on Lake Nyasa, were shareholders in the ALC. One of the stern wheelers was launched from the Clydeholm Shipyard in Whiteinch on 14 June 1898. Built in seven floatable galvanised steel sections, the steamer as yet unnamed, was 120 feet long, with a 21 feet beam and a moulded depth of 3 feet 3 inches. Fitted with a pair of non-condensing compound engines of 130 indicated horse power built by Messrs Campbell & Calderwood of Paisley, the vessel, after trials, was dismantled and shipped out to the port of Chinde on the Zambezi Delta, where on re-assembly she was christened *Princess*. By 1899 the other steamer, *Empress*, had arrived at Chinde, though she was 14 feet shorter and 3 feet wider in the beam. Both sternwheelers were the showpieces of the ALC river fleet for they incorporated such luxuries as electric lighting.

Livingstone's vision of a mission ship and clinic on Lake Nyasa finally came about in 1901. The 150-ton steamship *Chauncy Maples* was ordered in 1898 by the British Universities' Mission to Central Africa. She was designed by Henry Brunel (the son of the great Isambard Kingdom Brunel) and by Sir John Barry, and was built and bolted together by Alley & MacLellan (also makers of the famous Sentinel steam wagon) on the Clyde, at a cost of £13,500. Her parts were all numbered and catalogued and she was disassembled into 3,481 pieces. They were then galvanised and crated up for shipment. The crates were brought up the Zambezi and Shire rivers by boat and unpacked so that they could be carried on the heads of men and women to the shore of the Lake. Only then was it realised that the part numbers stamped on each plate and each frame had been obliterated when they were galvanised before being packed.

Nevertheless, by 1901, two years after leaving Britain, the *Chauncy Maples* was finally launched on Lake Nyasa. She had three purposes: a missionary school, an emergency refuge from Arab slave traders, and a hospital ship. She was named after a Bishop who had earlier drowned on the lake.

During the Great War *Chauncy Maples* was requisitioned as a troop carrier and gunboat. She otherwise served the Universities' Mission to Central Africa until 1953, when she was sold for use as a fishing boat, and later bought by the Malawi government for use as a passenger and cargo vessel when she was also refitted with a diesel engine. She is currently being renovated and rebuilt by the UK-based Chauncy Maples Malawi Trust with the intention of putting her back into service as a mission school and clinic with a future expected design life of at least thirty years. Remarkably, this Clyde-built ship, with a riveted steel hull, has so far survived over 110 years of service on the lake, and much of this time has been spent on her original role as a missionary school ship.

There were other great explorers from Scotland, many driven as much by enquiry as they were by commercial prospects. Notable among these were

Missionary ship and clinic on Lake Nyasa, Clyde-built *Chauncy Maples* (1898) seen celebrating her fiftieth anniversary on the lake in 1951.

Chauncy Maples on the slip at Monkey Bay under renovation in March 2013. (Jeff Davies)

the various expeditions to the Antarctic. Proudly preserved at Dundee is the locally built Royal Research Ship *Discovery*. She was completed in August 1901 at the Alexander Stephen yard of the Dundee Shipbuilding Company, especially for the National Antarctic Expedition under sponsorship from the Royal Geographical Society and the Royal Society. But she was by no means the first *Discovery*. The first of her earlier namesakes was used by the East India Company to explore the Northwest Passage; the second, a collier, accompanied Captain Cook's fateful voyage of the *Resolution*; the third was an improved version of the collier used by Captain George Vancouver in his voyage of circumnavigation in 1791; and the fourth was the converted Dundee whaler *Bloodhound*. She was commissioned as HMS *Discovery* as consort to Admiral Sir George Nares's expedition towards the North Pole in 1875.

The fifth *Discovery* was built entirely of wood as she was intended to study magnetic fields in Antarctica. It was also believed that a strong wooden hull would better withstand the pressures of the Antarctic ice. She also had to be self-sustaining for a minimum of two years. So, despite available modern technology, a rather unbalanced looking and old-fashioned ship emerged on the slip at Dundee. It has subsequently been admitted that financial constraints also meant cost savings which could not accommodate the price of a steel hull. Although the new *Discovery* was based on traditional whaler design, her naval architect, Mr W E Smith, gave her several distinct features: the bow was given more 'ice-breaking' rake and a cruiser stern was provided instead of the normal transom. Ingeniously, the rudder and the propeller could be lifted free of ice by means of a block and tackle and a well in the main deck. The ship was also longer than a whaler to accommodate personnel, additional bunkers and the main engine.

The timber frame of the hull is massive. It includes a keel made of elm which is 11in wide by 22in deep with 11in closely-spaced English oak frames rising to an 11in mahogany lower deck frame and a 10in oak weather deck. The cladding of the hull is primitive and should really have played no part in a twentieth-century research ship. It comprises an inner skin of 4in thick Riga fir with 6in Canadian elm and pitch pine, and below the water line the hull is sheathed in 4in planks of elm and greenheart. The gap between the outer and inner planking was once packed with rock salt as a preservative. The whole was sheathed in steel plate to just above the water line. Her two-bladed propeller was driven by a triple expansion engine built by Gourlay Brothers, and supplied by steam from two Scotch boilers. Finally she was rigged as a three-masted barque. She was truly a throwback to days long passed! She also had a leak which was a constant source of difficulty to her crew. Ironically, Robert Falcon Scott wrote at the time of her construction:

> The art of building wooden ships is now almost lost to the United Kingdom; probably in twenty or thirty years' time a new *Discovery* will give more trouble and cost more money than a moderate sized battleship. This is natural enough; it is the day of steel, of the puncher and the riveter; the adze and the wood plane are passing away.

Discovery sailed from Spithead, arriving in New Zealand in November. Her departure from Spithead was accompanied by controversy. Professor Jack Gregory, subsequently appointed Professor of Geology at Glasgow, was invited to be the scientific leader of the expedition and hence also leader of the team. The picture was muddied by Sir Clements Markham, President of the Royal Geographical Society, who stated: 'The Navy needs some action to wake it up from the canker of prolonged peace. Polar exploration is more wholesome for it, in a moral as well as sanitary point of view, than any more petty wars with savages', and he specifically asked that the Navy provide Lieutenant Robert Falcon Scott as leader of the expedition. This made Gregory's position unclear. What was clear was that Markham's real intention was not scientific research and exploration, but a determination to get a man to the South Pole before any other nation. Gregory's resignation was published in the journal

Discovery (1901) alongside the Victoria Embankment in London.

Nature, and Scott was able to pursue a voyage of adventure without being held back by the needs of scientific enquiry.

Discovery returned eighteen months later. She was sold to Hudson's Bay Company in 1905 and again later to the British Inter-Departmental Committee of Research and Development for work on behalf of the Falklands Island Administration in 1923. Prior to her departure to the Falklands under Captain Stenhouse, she was extensively refurbished, but the rot and decay that her timbers had suffered required a major rebuild. She was found too slow for her new role and was replaced in 1929 by *Discovery II*, completed by Ferguson Brothers at Port Glasgow. The survey work of the old *Discovery* now over, she returned to the Thames in March 1931 and continued to decay during various static roles: firstly used by the Boy Scouts Association, and latterly as drill ship for the London Division of the RNVR. Minus engine and all yards she was acquired by the Maritime Trust in 1978 and rebuilt in her 1925 configuration for public display, not as originally envisaged at London, but at Dundee.

During the original National Antarctic Expedition, of course, Scott had gone 'furthest south', leaving Ernest Shackleton, a Merchant Navy officer, behind to look after the dogs. Friction between the two men led Shackleton to mount his own expedition in 1907, which prompted Scott to seek funding for a further expedition south in 1910. The ship he chose was the whaler *Terra Nova* which was purchased from Bowring Brothers, Liverpool. This ship had previously escorted *Discovery* out of the ice in 1904, prior to which the two masters had considered abandoning *Discovery*, which was trapped eighteen miles into the ice after wintering where she lay. *Discovery* eventually came free with the aid of explosives and made her way back to the open sea.

Terra Nova was of standard whaler design and had been built by Alexander Stephen at Dundee in 1884. Again funds were short and she was registered as a yacht to avoid Board of Trade regulations for commercial shipping. Scott was obsessed with beating rival Norwegian explorer Roald Amundsen to the South Pole. With a ship now so packed with fuel and equipment that it nearly foundered in the Southern Ocean, Scott did, of course, reach the South Pole, although just over a month after his rival had planted the Norwegian flag at the Pole. Sadly, all five of Scott's party perished on the journey back to the ship. *Terra Nova* returned to the UK and was sold back to Bowring Brothers to resume work as a whaler. While still working at the age of sixty, this sturdy timber vessel foundered in September 1943 off the west coast of Greenland. No lives were lost.

Ironically, the Scottish National Antarctic Expedition of 1902 bought a Norwegian whaler, *Hekla*, for conversion for the journey south. Refitted by Ailsa Shipbuilding Company at Troon, she bore little resemblance to her former self when she emerged as the research ship *Scotia*. *Scotia* had a new compound engine fitted that gave her a speed of about 8 knots. Under the supervision of Mr William Bruce, a meteorological station was established at Scotia Bay, and later handed over to Argentinian management at a ceremony that saw the St Andrew's Cross lowered in favour of the Argentine flag, the first time the latter had ever flown in the Antarctic.

The division between explorer and trader is a narrow one that is exemplified by Captain Archibald Currie's wanderlust, and his desire to find overnight riches on the Australian gold mines. Born at Saltcoats in 1813, he left school at fourteen to become apprenticed to the Greenock shipowner John McCunn & Company. At the age of twenty-two, and now armed with his master's certificate, he signed on as third mate on the barque *Sir William Molesworth* for a one-way passage to Australia. Realising gold would not jump into his hand, he recognised that his career really lay at sea, although he hankered after shipowning as well.

In time, Currie bought part shares in various wooden sailing ships, and later in Melbourne met importer and merchant James Service, none other than his old schoolteacher from Saltcoats. Between them they built up a fleet of iron-hulled sailing ships, and then developed a steamship fleet by developing the trade between India and Australia. Known as Melbourne's Currie Line, its enigmatic leader was so respected as businessman and trader that he rose to a number of senior roles in banking and in public office. Currie also undertook salvage work and was not averse to buying wrecks from the insurers to reclaim cargoes and valuable fittings. Indeed, one ship he refloated and then added to his own fleet.

By the turn of the century, Archibald Currie had the major share of the Australia/India trade to his name, and in 1907 received a government subsidy from the Victorian government to run also to Singapore. Northbound he carried coal and horses, while southbound it was tea and jute, but his steamers were also equipped to carry passengers. Among his senior staff were the second-generation New Zealanders, brothers Captain Murdo and Captain Colin Macdonald. His undoing was the threatened Navigation Act, delayed only by the Great War and implemented finally in 1921. This forbade any Australian ship from being crewed by other than Australian nationals. Currie knew that without his Indian crews he could not compete with foreign flag tonnage and approached British India to buy him out. Lord Inchcape responded with an offer of £269,000 for the business, assets and goodwill of the Currie Line, and the sale was completed in January 1913.

Currie died in Melbourne aged eighty-four. Six year earlier, in 1908, the *Melbourne Punch* ran a piece on Archibald Currie:

> A little man with a hard Scotch face fringed by a rim of hard Scotch whisker. A pair of keen grey eyes glint from under shaggy grey eyebrows. His walk has the roll of the sea in it. He is redolent of salt ... but there is Presbyterian severity grafted onto it all ... He is in short the personification of all the oatmeal virtues. Seamen touch their hats to him. Lascars salaam violently at his approach. Shipmasters quake when he frowns. He is as well known in Calcutta as in Melbourne. He is Archibald Currie, the little strong masterful Scotchman who has forged a link between India and Australia and built for himself a fleet of big ships ... Whatever Melbourne has done for Archibald Currie he has done well by his adopted city and owes it nothing. He is not the sort of man to owe anybody anything for very long.

There were of course, many other Scots who sailed to a faraway port to set up in business. Merchants, shipping agents, shipowners ... the list is unending, but to list even the key expatriate Scots maritime businessmen would be a long and tedious duty. Many deserve particular notice, as their roles not only helped British industry and wealth creation, but were also fundamental to the economic development of Empire; their companies included Paddy Henderson and its work in Burma, Anchor and City lines in India, Ben Line throughout Asia, Anchor Line and America, Aberdeen Line and Canada, Albion and New Zealand, and so on.

The Scottish visionaries also worked from England. These included Shetlander Arthur Anderson with that archetypal English company P&O, Lanarkshire-born James McQueen and the Royal Mail Line, and James Anderson of Peterhead and his Orient Line, and Donald Currie of Greenock and the Castle Mail Packet Company. In competition with Donald Currie was Aberdonian John Thompson Rennie, whose Aberdeen Clipper Line of Packets ran between Natal and London. Rennie quickly became established in South Africa and although his shipping interests were taken over by Liverpool shipowner T & J Harrison in 1911, Rennie's Ship Agency survives to this day as a major component of the South African Bidvest group of companies.

Those based overseas, the expatriate traders, were quick to learn. Many were regular visitors to coasts in India, Australia and Africa as seamen, and were able to recognise a need for a specific service, perhaps, for example, a trading link exporting tea and importing horses between India and Australia, perhaps a service such as import and export, merchant, chandler or port agency. The Scots tended to have a canny knack for identifying need which was coupled with a yearning to progress. Obtaining a master's certificate and rising to the command of a ship was not enough for many who also dreamt of becoming the shipowner or director of a shore-based company. Opportunity overseas was the prime way of achieving this goal.

Perhaps the most significant overseas partnership was that of William Mackinnon and Robert Mackenzie, who established the India–Burma trade, and then pursued the trade to and from Asia as successors to the failing East India Company. Their vision, of course, spawned the British India Steam Navigation Company, which became critical to the economic development of South Asia. Others such as Andrew McIlwraith and Malcolm MacEacharn at Melbourne, and William Jardine and James Matheson in Canton, were critical to development in their respective regions (see chapter 4).

Life overseas was not all plain sailing, as William Denny found to his cost when he was driven to take his own life in Buenos Aires in 1887. The benefits to be reaped overseas were nevertheless tremendous. Intertwined within the vision and objective of all the explorers, missionaries and overseas business entrepreneurs was a mixture of adventure, religious fervour and opportunism. The outcome, despite the stated agenda of explorer or missionary, was the promotion of commerce and trade with Britain which was hosted primarily by Scottish companies and carried out in Scottish-registered ships.

10

The Making of the Sailors and Some of their Stories

TRAINING FOR A SEA career in the nineteenth century appears to have centred on hardship and a punitive existence. To a certain extent this was true, but in the context of life ashore, the hardship was not exceptional. There were three routes to becoming a Merchant Navy officer: working a way up through the ranks with training support, specialist pre-seagoing schools and training ships, and more recently through cadetship or apprenticeship and onshore training.

The Navigation School at Leith first opened in September 1855 and was managed by the Town Council under the direction of the Board of Trade Department of Science and Art. The school was closed in 1859 but quickly reopened with the promise of a Government Training Ship, which in the event never materialised. James Bolam was appointed to the school in 1861 where he later rose to become headmaster, a post he fulfilled until he retired at the age of eighty-six. He had begun his teaching career at the Trinity Navigation School in Newcastle. He quickly identified himself with technical education when he was transferred to the Government Navigation School at Leith and lectured in engineering subjects and mathematics.

The Government Navigation School provided instruction in navigation leading to deck officer examinations and certificates. Around 1864 a compulsory examination for engineers was introduced and by 1868 evening classes in marine engineering and naval architecture were started. The school occupied various addresses and in 1903 moved into new premises in Commercial Street, built by public subscription, with contributions from James Currie and other leading Edinburgh-based shipowners. The school was then renamed Leith Nautical College. In 1913 a new course on wireless telegraphy was introduced to the curriculum.

The character of the school is alluded to in the preface of Thomas Walton's book *Know Your Own Ship: a simple explanation of the stability trim, construction, tonnage and freeboard of ships, together with a fully worked out set of the usual ship calculations (from drawings)* (thankfully it just says *Know Your Own Ship* on the spine), first published in 1896 and which ran to at least eighteen revised editions. Walton thanks his boss, James Bolam, the headmaster, for 'the kindly sympathy and interest which he has manifested in the preparation of the book'. More significantly, the following concern is described by Walton at the start of his preface:

> As regards the subject of stability, it has been said that it is useless to provide a captain with curves of stability, for he does not understand them, and if he did, they are of little use, all he requires being a statement of certain conditions of loading, beyond which he must not go, or his vessel will be unsafe. This is all very good in its own way, but why does the captain not understand curves of stability, or, more broadly speaking, the subject of stability? Is not the answer this, that very little indeed has been done to provide the means of his obtaining such important information?

The College prospered under the aegis of the Scottish Education Department, administered by a board of governors. Disciplines included naval architecture, design of marine motors and ship electricity. Marine engineering was introduced in 1920 and the college was recognised by the Board of Trade as a Marine Engineering School. A new Radio Department was opened in 1927. In 1941 special courses were established for the Royal Naval Patrol Service for fishermen. Three years later the first deck courses in Scotland were inaugurated and conducted on board the Training Ship *Dolphin* under the guidance of the Merchant Navy Training Board. *Dolphin* dated from 1882 and was towed from Portsmouth to Leith, ending up waterlogged on the beach at Fisherrow. There she lay for nearly a year before being repaired and berthed at the now infilled West Old Dock, Leith, in 1928. Shetlander Captain Adam Tait was her first commander. In 1977 the old ship was burnt on the beach to recover her metal fittings and copper cladding.

Catering courses were introduced, and radar observer courses came in shortly afterwards, then the only radar instruction available in Scotland. The College continued to expand and by 1974 taught 2,000 full- and part-time students including seagoing personnel. A new site was planned for the college in Milton Road East and this was opened in July 1978.

The Scottish Education Department and Convention of Scottish Local Authorities published a review of nautical education in Scotland, and concluded that nautical training be concentrated at one site in Glasgow. Although Leith Nautical College was well patronised and well equipped, a downturn in demand was foreseen with the decline in the British shipping industry that was then taking place, and Leith Nautical College was closed in 1987.

The Glasgow School of Navigation was only established in 1910 in what was then the Royal Technical College (now part of Strathclyde University), with the sole objective of providing seamen with the technical knowledge necessary to advance their career prospects. Models and apparatus were provided to demonstrate the principles of seamanship, navigation and nautical astronomy. The school's qualifications were recognised by the Board of Trade. After the incorporation of Strathclyde University, the School of Navigation evolved into the Glasgow College of Nautical Studies as a further education college of nautical and maritime studies, including marine and offshore training courses, situated on the banks of the River Clyde. It merged with Central College and Glasgow Metropolitan College in 2010 to form City of Glasgow College in association with the University of Strathclyde. The college currently offers a range of courses including deck officer trainee programmes, advanced tanker courses, and many at HNC and HND level, within a wide range of courses available on a full-time, part-time, evening and Saturday basis.

The James Watt College at Greenock also ceded its nautical training to Glasgow in January 1969. There was a long tradition of teaching at Greenock, which for many years took place in the James Watt Memorial Building constructed at the birthplace site of Watt himself. The engineering classes occupied the ground floor and navigation was upstairs with access to the flat roof for compass and sextant work. The cost of the new building was donated by philanthropist Dr Andrew Carnegie, but John Rankin, of the firm of Rankin & Blackmore, Sir Donald Currie and others also helped raise funds.

A key impetus to the growth of the school was the introduction of arrangements for day release from work for apprentices. The Royal Naval Dockyards had given their apprentices a half-day release from work from 1944, which by 1950 became a full-day release, and the Royal Naval Torpedo Factory in Greenock followed suit shortly thereafter with its apprentices. The local shipyards, engineering establishments and commercial firms quickly adopted the scheme as all saw the economic benefits of the formal training supplemented, as before, with on-the-job training. By the mid 1960s there were 800 day-release and 100 full-time students. Instruction included radio, radar, navigation as well as City and Guilds courses on welding, steel fabrication, fitting, machinery, carpentry and joinery, electrical installation, automobile engineering, and retail distribution. The prospectus also showed courses leading to the Ordinary National Certificate in Mechanical or Electrical Engineering, and to the Higher National Certificate in Naval Architecture. For much of the 1950s the head of the navigation department was the formidable Captain George Davidson and the cadet class instructor was Captain Ian Pearson, a fondly remembered but capable teacher who was responsible for instilling into his cadets the basic rules of seamanship and navigation.

There were, of course, other dedicated training centres in Scotland including the Aberdeen Wireless College and the Dundee Nautical College. Although training opportunities continue at Glasgow, the numbers involved remain few by comparison to the heady days of the 1950s and 1960s. Nevertheless, British officers are much sought after in difficult roles such as anchor handling and dive support ships, and this is a reflection of the formal training that is available in the UK, not least that provided at Glasgow.

The modern approach to officer training has been through cadet seagoing experience coupled with onshore training. By the mid twentieth century onboard cadet training comprised two parts: cheap labour by the cadet and, if he was lucky, training in navigation and other skills from the officers the cadet worked with. The lot of the cadet fell to a large extent on the attitude of the chief officer and the master. John Moffat described his experience aboard *Clan MacNeil* in 1948, as part of his own four-year cadetship, in an article first published in *Sea Breezes*, October 1988:

Captain Carter, the master, was very keen that we should receive good instruction in navigation and when we were on watch we were expected to take sights of the moon, sun and stars. This was really excellent as our calculations were always handed to the master and any errors were pointed out to us, in the nicest possible way. The four noon positions obtained by the second and third officers and we two cadets, were handed to the master, and then the position was plotted on the chart. In this way we were made to feel active members of the bridge team and this gave us the confidence we needed.

And of the Suez Canal:

Our main duties consisted of writing up the bridge notebook and noting the time of passing signal stations and anything else that should be entered in the log. The [canal] pilot conversed verbally with the signal stations as there was no VHF at that time. Canal speed was sometimes 4 or 5 knots and it was not difficult for the pilot to talk to the watch keeper in the station as we passed. We also made tea for the officer-of-the watch and the pilot and the tinned salmon sandwiches were a special treat in Clan Line ships transiting the Suez Canal. They were really for the pilot but we got our fair share.

Mention needs also to be made of the training vessels *Cumberland* and *Empress* which were stationed on the Clyde off Helensburgh and *Mars* off Dundee. The *Cumberland* was built in 1842 and served in the Crimean War with a crew of up to 620 men. In 1869 she retired to the Clyde to become the Clyde Industrial Training Ship Association's vessel 'providing for the education and training of boys who, through poverty, parental neglect, or any other cause were destitute, homeless, or in danger from association with vice or crime', ie one of the many industrial school ships rather than a reformatory ship. Originally, boys were trained for entry into both the Royal Navy and the Merchant Service but once the Royal Navy decided to accept only 'boys of good character', training focused on the needs of the Merchant Navy. Only about half the boys left the ship for a career at sea. Those that did go to sea were undeterred by the bold statistic that in 1861 some four thousand sailors lost their lives, in other words 1 in 56 of the seamen aboard British flagged ships were killed in that one year. This loss compared to the 1 in 350 British miners lost in 1861 suggests that the mining industry was perceived then as a safer haven!

Training ship *Empress* (1859) off Helensburgh, formerly HMS *Revenge*, from a painting by Mary Hunter, 1906.

Cumberland was destroyed by fire in 1889 and was replaced by *Empress*, built in 1859 as HMS *Revenge*. Her previous roles included Flagship of the Channel Fleet and Second Flagship of the Mediterranean Fleet in the 1860s, and Flagship at Queenstown in 1873. She served off Helensburgh as a training vessel until 1923.

Mars was stationed off Dundee from 1869 and was also an industrial training ship. Phil Carradice wrote in *Sea Breezes*, September 1992:

> ... conditions aboard the ships were Spartan, often brutal. A typical day began at 6am, usually with prayers and a frugal breakfast. Exercises and manual work followed. Education was, in general, limited to reading, writing and number work, although in some ships there was an extra emphasis on religious education and on music [the ship's band]. Lunch was taken about midday, tea at 4.30 and lights out occurred at 8pm ... Punishments for wrongdoing were quick and brutal. Corporal punishment was regularly used, but so too was a rewards system where boys who performed well could gain extra marks to earn more leave and other privileges.

The funding for the two schools came entirely from private subscriptions while the ships themselves were loaned by the Admiralty. The operating costs

HMS *Caledonia* (1810) was used as a training ship between 1891 and 1906 for the Royal Navy moored off Queensferry in the Forth.

for the ships in 1889 were £6,390 and £7,078 for the *Cumberland* and *Mars* respectively. In addition the Navy had various training ships in Scotland including HMS *Caledonia* which was stationed in the Forth between 1891 and 1906. The most spectacular naval training ship was another HMS *Caledonia*, this time stationed at the new naval dockyard at Rosyth. She was built as *Bismark* in 1914 for the Hamburg America Line and as part of the war reparations procedure became the White Star Line's *Majestic* in 1922. Increasingly uneconomical, she was commissioned in April 1937 as a gunnery training school ship alongside at Rosyth, following removal of lifeboats and topmasts. At the outbreak of war her cadets were sent ashore to make her accommodation available for naval personnel. At the same time she was moved off her shore berth into the Forth. Barely a fortnight later, while lying unwanted at anchor, she caught fire and later sank, only being recovered for scrap later in the war.

Merchant Navy deck and engineering staff, unless they were on a company contract, were recruited until the 1970s at the Shipping Office, the Mercantile Marine Office. In Glasgow this used to be opposite the offices of the Seaman's Union in James Watt Street, between Argyle Street and the Broomielaw, with the Board of Trade surveyors upstairs and the Sailor's Home next door. This was where the men came to sign on for a voyage and where they looked forward to returning to sign off. The office comprised three rooms: the engagement room, a normally quiet and sombre room, the discharge room, which was known for its rows and arguments and occasional fights, and the accounts office. Bob Rennie was in charge of the discharge room in the Second World War and occasionally would take his books and his staff to a particular ship if trouble was anticipated. He had a knack of calming a situation, as Dorothy Laird (author of *Paddy Henderson*) recounts in an article first published in *Sea Breezes*, March 1992:

> On one occasion I was sent with him to a ship signing-off and signing-on in Rothesay Dock. She was one of 'Ropner's navy', a tramp from the North East Coast which had had an awful voyage. Everyone wanted to complain so while I signed-on those members of the crew willing to sail in her again (always the easier task) Mr Rennie tackled the furious majority.
>
> 'Aye, aye,' he said, 'I can see you have a lot of complaints and we will take them in order. Now you will agree that those with no quarrel should go through first?' He looked at his watch. 'In an hour and ten minutes there is a train to Newcastle and I have ordered a taxi (he had, too) to take anyone to the station who wants to go. Now if we can get going …' Mysteriously the line of complaints almost disappeared.

But if the lot of the ordinary seaman was poor, the engineer thought his was even worse. The steamship engineer was dedicated to his engines and listened for changes in sound and smell as indicators of overheating bearings or excessive wear on some moving part of the machinery in his charge. Rudyard Kipling sets the scene with the opening of his classic ballad *MacAndrew's Hymn*:

Lord, Thou hast made this world below the shadow of a dream,
An', taught by time, I tak' it so – exceptin' always Steam.
From coupler-flange to spindle-guide I see Thy Hand, O God –
Predestination in the stride o' yon connectin'-rod.
John Calvin might ha' forged the same – enorrmous, certain, slow –
Ay, wrought it in the furnace-flame – my "Institutio."
I cannot get my sleep to-night; old bones are hard to please;
I'll stand the middle watch up here – alone wi' God an' these
My engines, after ninety days o' rase an' rack an' strain
Through all the seas of all Thy world, slam-bangin' home again.
Slam-bang too much – they knock a wee – the crosshead-gibs are loose,
But thirty thousand mile o' sea has gied them fair excuse ...

The rhythm of the stokehold was set by the second engineer who was responsible for the day-to-day management of the engine room. The working tempo of the stokehold was set by the desired speed and the consequent steam demand. A typical firing cycle would comprise having the 'bunker rats' bring the coal to the bunker doors where the trimmers would barrow, basket or shovel it to the boiler front. When he was ready, the fireman would open the furnace door and heave the required number of shovelfuls into the furnace; ensuring a full spread of coal over the bed of the fire. Just prior to the next feed of the fire, the fireman would open the furnace door and use his pricker and slice to open up the fire and break up the clinker which would be pulled off the top, and from the ashpit below, along with the ashes, using the slice. When this operation was complete, the firing cycle was repeated until the end of the watch when the last task by the off-going watch was to hoist the ashes up on deck and dump them over the ship's side, that is, unless the ship was fitted with a steam ash ejector.

The true coal-burner fireman could always be recognised in the stokehold from his sweat rag round his neck with one end in his mouth and loose-fitting boots with no laces; easy to kick off if a piece of red-hot coal, ash or clinker should find its way in. The firing cycle was any time between six and twelve minutes and was even controlled by the automatic sounding of a gong in the crack steamships on the Atlantic – as described again by Rudyard Kipling:

A' home again – the Rio run: it's no child's play to go
Steamin' to bell for fourteen days o' snow an' floe an' blow.

No wonder scuffles and fights broke out between the firemen, whose main qualification was a resistance to extreme heat and dirt.

At about the time *Titanic* was lost, a second engineer disappeared without all trace aboard one of the other big North Atlantic liners. Any experienced second would not intervene with the stokehold arguments and fights which were organised on a gang to gang basis. But this one did and the gruesome story that emerged many years later was that the firemen stabbed him to death and then pushed his body into the furnace to destroy the evidence. The official record was 'missing during his watch in the stokehold'!

The engineer's lot in a steamship is aptly described in *MacFadyen's Grievance*, which was written by Scots poet Sydney Brand in the style of *MacAndrew's Hymn*, in which the third engineer bemoans his lot and hankers for the Clyde, or at least promotion to chief. But the classic lines from the original ballad by Kipling sum up the engineer's lot:

Then, at the last, we'll get to port an' hoist their baggage clear –
The passengers, wi' gloves an' canes – an' this is what I'll hear:
'Well, thank ye for a pleasant voyage. The tender's comin' now.'
While I go testin' follower-bolts an' watch the skipper bow.
They've words for everyone but me – shake hands wi' half the crew,
Except the dour Scots engineer, the man they never knew.
An' yet I like the wark for all we've dam' few pickin's here –
No pension, an' the most we'll earn's four hunder pound a year.
Better myself abroad? Maybe. I'd sooner starve than sail
Wi' such as call a snifter-rod ... French for nightingale.
Commeesion on my stores? Some do; but I cannot afford
To lie like stewards wi' patty-pans. I'm older than the Board.
A bonus on the coal I save? Ou ay, the Scots are close,
But when I grudge the strength Ye gave I'll grudge their food to those.

There are so many Scottish deckies' stories that it is hard to choose which to relate. That by Deck Apprentice Scott aboard Clan Line's venerable *Clan Murray* in 1944, docked at Mauritius, shows how quite by accident the lowly can come to the attention of the master to earn praise. Hearing that there was to be a government-sponsored shindig at a posh hotel in the capital, a short train ride away from the port, Scott decided that this was for him. He could not persuade any of his shipmates to join him, others preferring to sample the local bars than travel up-country for the chance of a dance with a pretty girl. Dressed up to the nines in full starched white rig and blue doeskin trousers, Scott duly arrived at the hotel and as he walked into the ballroom was aware that the room fell briefly silent. Thereafter he was invited to join this party and that, would you dance with my daughter …? And not one drink did he have to pay for.

But his popularity was short-lived. The uncanny resemblance of Scott, in full apprentice dress uniform, to the son of the governor of Mauritius was uncanny, and Scott was in no mood to let on. But he missed the last train back to port and had to ask the local police station to put him up for the night; it seems the police constable saw no resemblance to anyone other than a sailor who had lost his way! But the twist to the tale was that the skipper had seen Scott leaving the ship the night before and was so impressed by the way he had turned himself out for the night and taken the initiative to attend the ball in the capital that Apprentice Scott went up in estimation considerably.

Sandy Ferguson in his book *From Burma to Barra* tells the following story:

During my time with Denholms I served mainly on the ore carriers … On one trip to Port Elizabeth, South Africa, when I was second mate on the *Sir Andrew Duncan*, we arrived off the port to be told there was a queue for the iron berth, and that we would be anchored off for about ten days …

After a few days at anchor we were bored to distraction, and a few of us decided to do a spot of shark fishing … We got a length of rope, a meat hook and a big lump of meat and proceeded to the poop deck, where we commenced fishing. It must be said that we really did not expect to catch a shark and had not even considered the consequences of a successful capture.

Shortly afterwards the rope tightened, and the sea boiled in confusion under the stern. We all pulled on the rope, and after a great struggle, the head of a very large Hammer Headed shark appeared over the rail. Stupidly we gave one final heave and this mighty beast was suddenly among us on the poop deck. Everyone scattered and three of us found ourselves shaking on the top of a nearby samson post. The hook came free at that point and the poor shark began thrashing loose on the poop. I don't know how long it was before it worked itself across the deck, far enough away from us to allow a hurried escape but it seemed like hours. We ran for our lives and then roped off the poop deck, warning all crew members to keep clear. The poor creature took a long time to succumb, and we left it well alone until we were sure it was really dead before getting it over the rail into the water, where no doubt it was eaten by its mates. I never fished for sharks again.

Sandy Ferguson's story about a Henderson Line skipper is equally endearing:

That trip on the *Prome* was with a renowned 'Paddy's Captain', known throughout the fleet as 'The Pig', and believe me he was well named. We sailed from Birkenhead for Port Said on a Monday, and on the following Monday morning the Captain was accosted by an elderly lady passenger: 'Captain,' she said, 'you failed in your duty as master of this ship. You did not hold a church service yesterday which was the Sabbath Day.' The Captain looked at her with disdain and commented 'Madam, my duty is to get your earthly being to Rangoon, how your soul gets to Heaven is no concern of mine.'

The Scots built them, the Scots sailed them afar as export, and the Scots stayed with them as expatriates. In 1879 Denny completed the *Rotomahana* for the Union Steamship Company of New Zealand. This little ship had a

Passenger cargo liner *Prome* (1937) accommodated seventy-six passengers in traditional hardwood panelled luxury and was a product of William Denny's yard at Dumbarton. (John Clarkson)

Letter to the author dated 10 August 1962 confirming the impending withdrawal of *Prome* and subsequent demolition at Bruges.

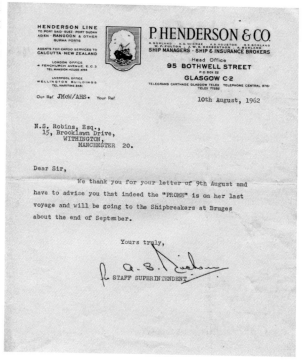

clipper stem with a Maori princess figurehead. Her sheer was such that 'she sat on the water like a duckling' and her hull was one of the first to be built entirely of mild steel plates. This fast steamer is often linked in appearance with David MacBrayne's *Claymore*, delivered not by Denny but by J & G Thomson the following year. *Claymore* was far smaller as she was destined for the shorter runs along Scotland's west coast and across the Minch, rather than the long and usually stormy hauls between Wellington and Sydney.

Rotomahana carried only 700 tons of cargo along with her passengers and she was always maintained in top order as the company flier. Her trials speed amounted to just over 15 knots, but on her delivery voyage Captain Underwood drove her at 17 knots around the Cape of Good Hope, before pointing her bows towards Port Chalmers. Her consort, the steamer *Te Anau*, was of similar design although with a straight stem. Adorned with green hulls and a gold band, both ships were attractive, but it was the *Rotomahana* that really caught the imagination.

In 1884 the Adelaide Steamship Company took delivery from Denny of the crack steamer *Adelaide*. At last a ship was on the seas that could strip the

attention away from the *Rotomahana* and the *Te Anau*. Will Lawson takes up
the tale in his book *Pacific Steamers*:

> The *Adelaide's* extra turn of speed was impressed by degrees upon the engine
> room crews of the older ships, but there was one stubborn Scot who refused
> to believe that the *Adelaide* was any faster than his ship until he had tested
> it in actual fact. This was Jock M'Queen, of the Union boat *Te Anau*, sister to
> the *Rotomahana* in all but speed and the clipper bow. Like a poor relation,
> she always had a little reflected glory from the glamour that gathered around
> the *Rotomahana*. So one evening, when the *Te Anau* had left Hobart and laid
> a course for Melbourne, there was excitement on board when the *Adelaide's*
> smoke was seen astern.
>
> Old Jock called his second and said 'Do ye see yon steamer? Well, if she
> passes us the night, there'll be men on this ship seeking jobs the morn.' The
> second laughed, 'Ye want a fiddle bow and another thousand horsepower gin ye
> talk o' lickin' the *Adelaide*. Ye're no the *Rotomahana*. But we'll gie her a hurr'l!'
> In about three hours the *Adelaide* went past, doing 14 knots and making a
> pretty picture. And Jock shook his fist at her for her audacity in passing the
> *Rotomahana's* sister.

Another story in Will Lawson's book, which underlines the large number
of Scottish engineers then working in Australasian waters, tells of the New
Zealand to Australia steamer *Mararoa*, built by Denny in 1885. She initially
did a few trips to San Francisco, and while there her chief engineer, Mr
MacAllister, visited an American steamer and was impressed by the brass
eagles fixed on spreaders on the tail rods of the triple expansion engine. As it
happened, when he and his fellow engineers were entertained by the Marine
Engineers' Society of San Francisco, MacAllister was presented with three
eagles; these were duly bolted onto *Mararoa's* three tail rods.

> The brass eagles flew on the *Mararoa's* tail rods for many years ... The *Monowai*,
> the *Mararoa's* successor on the San Francisco service, had three tail rods too,
> and her engine room staff began to feel that they should also have three spread
> eagles to adorn their polished rods.

Whenever the ships met they raced and the smaller *Mararoa* usually held
her own. On one occasion they were berthed on either side of the Margaret
Street jetty in Sydney, and later that evening the engineers from both ships
met in a local bar:

'We'll give you five hours' start and lead you in past Tiri,' the youthful fourth of the *Mararoa* boasted. 'We push her along with steam,' was the scornful reply, 'we don't have any wings'. 'Yes, but you'd like 'em,' jeered the youngster. 'Yes, and by Jingo we'll have 'em too, one of these days!' the other retorted.

Mr MacAllister's successor was Mr MacMurrich and he was sitting away from the crews talking to a friend. MacMurrich could not hear the whole discussion, but it was the laugh at the end of it that worried him. On returning to his ship he went below with his spanner and unbolted the eagles and stowed them safely at the back of his chest drawer in his cabin. There was the big low-pressure eagle, the middle-sized one and the small high-pressure one.

The sound he was waiting for came at last – stealthy steps of stockinged feet on the creaking gangway that was not far from his cabin porthole. Then came cat-like movements down the alleyway leading to the engine room companion. As soon as he was sure that the marauder had passed into the engine room the old man slipped swiftly along the alleyway and up to the deck, where he could look down through the skylight. There he saw the burly second engineer of the *Monowai* … The language that rose in muttered tones when the intruder found that all the eagles were gone made it necessary for the amused Scot to withdraw to a quiet place by the rail, lest his chucklings would be heard.

In the morning the eagles were missing and one of the greasers raised the alarm. Mr MacMurrich sent a messenger across the quay demanding that the second engineer aboard *Monowai* return the eagles to their rightful place. Apparently the stink went through the entire ship and everybody came under suspicion from the master down. MacMurrich later slipped down to his engine room and refitted the three eagles – interrupted by one of the greasers whose silence was bought in perpetuity with promises of free beer when next ashore!

And in case we forget that 'the old boys' had emotions too, Captain J Robertson, master of Donald Currie's *Carnarvon Castle*, recorded the following as reported in Marischal Murray's definitive history of Union-Castle:

The stately *Carnarvon Castle* was the smartest and best equipped sailing ship that ever flew the colours of the British Mercantile Marine. It was with anything but a light heart that I furled my canvas to boil the kettles of the Castle Mail …

I was sent by Mr Currie as a passenger for a coastwise trip in a primitive kind of steamer, called *Iceland*, to learn 'steam' …

Iceland belonged to brother James Currie and the Leith, Hull & Hamburg Steam Packet Company, although she was actually deployed on the Liverpool & Hamburg Steam Ship Company route from Liverpool through the English Channel and into the North Sea. Big brother Donald Currie, in partnership with the third brother David, wanted to deploy steamships on the South African mail run, having inaugurated steam on the India service with the delivery of *Dover Castle* by Barclay Curle & Company in January 1872. Donald Currie tried the *Iceland* and then the *Gothland* on the South African route to test the suitability of the steamship, albeit far smaller steamships than would shortly be built for the run, and to train sailing ship crews in the ways of the steamship. Although *Iceland* came back from her charter, her training duties complete, *Gothland* was later purchased by 'Big Brother' and retained on the South African coastal trade. The emotive cry for help from Captain Robertson, as he furled his canvas ready to boil his kettles, is fully understood!

MaFadyen's Grievance

By Sydney Brand (first published in *Sea Breezes*, December 1949)

By just a stroke o' rotten luck, I left Govan yard
An' signed aboard the *Bertha Pyle* instead o' yon Cunard;
The *Bertha* needed engineers an' I was fou' wi' booze,
An' once upon the 'articels' ye canna pick or choose.
So here I sweat in Samarang when I wud just as soon
Be sailin' up the Clyde an' castin' eyes at fair Dunoon.
There's Maggie up in Renfrew an' she doesna write a word
Because I tauld her I was 'Chief', whereas I'm only 'Third'.
But now resigned tae boiler doors an' comin' up for tea,
I'm no consultin' engineer wi' hundreds for a fee.
The thing that irks ma verra life is – Fraser signed as 'Chief'
(A snorin' in a deck-chair – doesna even dae 'relief').
Not that I mind the 'Chief' at all, for him and me were pals
Afore we got our tickets an' we used tae chase the gals.

Oh, life aboard the *Bertha Pyle* is nane tae craw aboot;
If onything is wrang below it's me they mostly shoot.
Now human tongues are silent, but condenser tubes they leak,
An' a stoppage after breakfast – Fraser's almost boun' tae speak.
A clangin' on the telegraph that hasna rung a note
Since four weeks come tomorrow, when we left the pilot-boat,
But, just for sake of orderness, auld Fraser's tauld the 'Skip'
That 'mileage or nae mileage, he wud have tae stop his ship'.
An' what wi' waste an' spanners, block-an'-chain an' oily flares,
The donkeyman produces all, then stands aide an' swears
(I seem tae like auld 'Donkey'. He's a kind o' unco guid;
The sort ye wadna feel ashamed tae touch for half-a-quid).
On Sunday morns I envy such as line the fo'c'sle bench;
Compared wi' engine messrooms there's nae difference in the stench;
The fat auld 'Chiefy' sittin' at the breakfast-table head,
Dividin' egg-an'-bacon an' distributin' the bread;
An' nae one dares tae speak a word an' nane 'Guid mornin' say
For fear o' bein' telt 'That's mine own business onyway'.
The 'Junior' reaches for the salt, but waits until he sees
The 'Chief' and 'Second' an' mysel' have started on the cheese.
An' all the messroom silent, save the rattle o' a plate
Or squeakin' o' the rudder-chains that work an' whine an' grate –
Exep' the Cook is finished an', beneath a paughty chin,
Is scoopin' awfu' noises frae a dirty violin;
It minds me o' a mongrel-pup shut oot for half the night,
Indulgin' in its howlin' for tae put the matter right.
An' I can howl frae Albert Dock tae Argetina's shores
For a special kind o' packin' that I wanted in ma stores;
Long indent sheets for this an' that, an' loads o' scented soap
For stewards who can go ashore while I stay here an' hope;
Way off the Horn the stern-gland takes a fit to go amiss,
Then Fraser says 'We'll get you stuff the voyage after this';
So I puts it in ma inven'try, but when we reach the Tyne
The 'Chief' has drawn a pencil through the special noted line.
My kingdom for auld Bowlin' or a Yoker ferry noo;
We're 'Finisterre for orders', an' its just twa years today
I maundered doon tae Ibrox Park tae see the Rangers play;

But 'Finisterre for orders' doesna strike sae near the Clyde,
It'll likely be the Channel or a port the other side;
Well, Rotterdam or Antwerp or Dunkirk? It all depends:
I need some time in port tae do ma top-an'-bottom ends.
Nae use tae make excuses for an hour ashore the noo,
For Fraser's boun' tae tumble on some rotten jab tae do.
It serves me richt – I shud ha' stayed in Linthouse frae the first,
Here beneath a scorchin' sun I hae a Glasga thirst.
An' brither Bob's a buyer for a firm that deals in jute,
The only trip he ever does is doon the Kyles o' Bute.
An' Maggie wants a photograph 'in uniform of white'
(She oucht tae hae a picture of me doon below at nicht,
A-statin' up the dynamo a quarter after ten,
Instead o' gaun on top tae find the ellecktrish-i-yen;
Black oil across ma shoulder an' a sweat rag in ma teath
Is different, bonnie Maggie, frae a Sunday off in Leith).
There's Meiklejohn, the 'Second', wi' his anchor soundly cast,
He swears by all the stars that every trip shall be his last;
So I stay on a-hopin' that promotion's due tae me;
'That shore-job letter wisna there' – an' back he comes to sea.
Shore-job me boots an' gitter – he expects an easy chair
In sewage-pumpin' station on the skirts o' Aberdare;
He hasna got the courage, he wud miss the gruntin' growl
O' guide-links in a steamship when the weather's getting' foul.
He tried it once an' said that keepin' clean was verra grand,
But longed to feel the swing o' dirty spanners in his hand.
Yes, I stay on an' I stay here an' hope on for the best,
That some wee hot mosquito will alight on Fraser's chest
An' ravin' mad malaria cause the skipper to decide
Tae leave him in a hospital, in case he might hae died.
I'm thinkin' that's the only way tae supplement the rings
Aroon me double-breester cuffs – unless guid fortune brings
Far better than a mon shud die, I much prefer that way.
An' if be so that Fate is kind an' Maggie keeps her word
When I get 'Chief' – well, maybe I'll be wishin' I was 'Third'!

11

Disasters and Lessons Learned

THE SCOTTISH PEOPLE ARE rightly proud of their many achievements. But, proud or not, they have suffered their share of disaster over the centuries. The battle of Flodden Field would certainly be listed as one of the earliest while the collapse of the first Tay Bridge is probably remembered with the most emotion. But there were also a number of maritime disasters, some still remembered, like the sinking of Donaldson Line's *Athenia* in the ninth hour of the Second World War, and the loss of the ferry *Princess Victoria* as she left Loch Ryan on the morning sailing to Larne at the end of January 1953. But there were other disasters that befell the Scottish mariner, some of which are now glazed over into history and are largely forgotten. Of these, the most appalling loss was that at the launch of *Daphne*, from Alexander Stephen & Sons yard at Linthouse, on Tuesday, 3 July 1883.

The specifications for the ship had been drawn up by the marine superintendent of the Glasgow, Dublin & Londonderry Steam Packet Company for service between Glasgow and Derry. Alexander Stephen & Sons

Princess Victoria (1946) seen during trials on the Clyde with the half-deck hinged stern-gate clearly visible. (University of Glasgow)

The *Daphne* (1883) tragedy from a contemporary engraving.

were responsible for the detailed design and tests on the stability of the hull. As the yard did not have a fitting-out quay it was proposed to launch the ship with her engine in place, but with the boiler room left open to the sky so that the boilers could be installed from a quayside crane up river. The plan was to have her ready for the Glasgow Fair holiday so time was all important for the completion of the new steamer. It was for this reason that *Daphne* was launched with nearly two hundred artisans on board, all working hard to complete the fitting out by the deadline.

Just before noon the ship was launched quietly into the Clyde and, as planned, the drag chains restrained her onward progress across the channel. The starboard chain worked well but the port chain slipped so that the hull yawed across the river channel. Only a small crowd had assembled to watch what, to all intents and purposes, was a routine event on the upper Clyde, but of those present, many had relatives and friends aboard *Daphne*. Within a few seconds of coming to rest, the ship heeled to port, juddered and steadied slightly before she heeled over again onto her side and capsized, trapping many of the workmen below deck. The roll was exacerbated by loose gear which slid to port and the open deck above the boiler room, which flooded in an instant. Rescuers were on hand almost immediately, but there was little to be done other than pulling bodies out of the water; only about seventy survivors were recovered, while the death toll was later counted to be as many as 124. Many of the apprentices aboard that day were no more than boys.

The ship was righted a few days later and taken to Salterscroft Graving Dock at Govan where it was subjected to exhaustive tests. Alexander Stephen's naval architects were commended for the assistance they gave the subsequent inquiry; the cause was found to be a lack of initial stability, combined with the weight of loose gear and personnel which slid to port, stopping the vessel from righting herself. The lesson learned that day was that only those necessary to look after the safety and mooring of a newly launched vessel shall be allowed on board during the launch.

The hull was completed as *Rose* for Alex Laird & Company. However, misfortune stayed with her and she was reported aground off Millport inbound from Derry in March 1884. Refloated, Laird sold her to a Prestwick firm, John Bell & Company, but she was stranded in the eastern Mediterranean only three years later and Bell also decided to part with the vessel. Registered in Greece for the rest of her career, the one-time *Daphne* was eventually sunk by a torpedo during the Great War, taking with her the memory of her awful launching.

Of the many disastrous events, great and small, the loss of the Allan Line's magnificent *Bavarian* off Montreal was perhaps one of the more embarrassing, though fortunately without loss of life. A product of William Denny & Bros at Dumbarton, *Bavarian* was the largest liner on the Canadian services when she was delivered in 1899. Sadly, on 3 November 1905 this modern vessel stranded in fog on the Wye Rock off Montreal, later breaking her back. All personnel were safely brought ashore, as was much of the cargo aboard ship, but her loss made a deep mark on Clydeside at the time.

Probably the most notorious Scottish maritime incident, the *Iolaire* disaster, happened during the Great War. When the English naval personnel returned to their respective bases after the Christmas festivities in 1918, large numbers of Scots servicemen prepared to take leave in readiness for Hogmanay. Those destined for Lewis were dispatched by train to Kyle of Lochalsh, there to catch the regular MacBrayne mail boat, *Sheila*, across the Minch. Anticipating that *Sheila* would not be able to accommodate all the men, the officer in charge at Stornoway despatched the duty patrol boat, HMS *Iolaire*, to stand by at Kyle of Lochalsh and to act as relief to *Sheila* as appropriate.

Allan Line's *Bavarian* (1896) was wrecked in the St Lawrence in 1906.

Iolaire (Gaelic for 'eagle') was a former luxury steam yacht built in 1896 by Ramage & Ferguson at Leith as *Doris*. She had various owners and names and was renamed *Rione* in 1897, *Iolaire* in 1899 when she was bought by Sir Donald Currie, and *Amalthaea* in 1907. At the time of her loss she was registered under the ownership of the executors of the late Sir Charles Assheton-Smith. *Amalthaea* was requisitioned in 1915, and modified for patrol work. She was renamed *Iolaire* before taking up duties at Stornoway in November 1918, adopting the name of the local shore base. There she replaced another *Iolaire*, which had previously given its name to the local shore base, and which in peacetime was the late Donald Currie's new yacht. This *Iolaire* had been built by William Beardmore in 1902, and doubled as the Union-Castle Line's training ship, a role she reverted to after the Great War. In World War II she served as HMS *Persephone*. The existence of two *Iolaires*, both linked with Donald Currie, has been the source of much confusion.

Iolaire was commanded by Richard Mason, RNR, and arrived at Kyle at 4pm on New Year's Eve. *Sheila* was already nearly full to capacity with civilians returning home for Hogmanay when the naval harbourmaster learned that two chartered trains carrying the servicemen were due in the early evening. Mason was consulted and he agreed to carry three hundred men bound for Stornoway, despite carrying life-saving equipment for just 180 and, therefore, placing himself and his ship in contravention of the post-*Titanic* statutory passenger-carrying regulations.

Aboard the first train were 190 men destined for Lewis, sixty of whom were the last to be allowed to board *Sheila*. The second train arrived at 7pm, with an additional 130 men destined for Lewis. Those for Harris and Skye were left on the quayside to await further transport. At 9.30pm *Iolaire* set sail for Stornoway, some thirty minutes ahead of *Sheila*. The young men on their way home were in high spirits ready for homecoming and Hogmanay. The crossing was undertaken in clear visibility with a fresh southerly wind, although shortly after midnight the wind increased and visibility was considerably reduced when it started to drizzle. At about 1am, and now on the approach towards the harbour, Mason left the bridge in charge of the first officer, Lieutenant Cotter. Eyewitness accounts from a local fishing boat stated later that *Iolaire* failed to turn to clear the rocks at Holm, Lieutenant Cotter appearing to overestimate his distance from land on an approach both he and his senior officer had made many times before.

Iolaire ran onto the rocks at Holm shortly before 2am. Heavy waves pushed the yacht onto her starboard side just twenty-five yards from dry land. About fifty men panicked and tried to swim ashore – none made it alive through the swirling seas that tore through jagged rocks in a scene that was almost totally devoid of light. Some did get ashore by jumping from the bows of the wreck onto a rocky ledge that ran towards the shore, but again many were swept away to their deaths. A distress rocket was fired which fortunately was immediately reported to the officer of the watch at Battery Point. But it was a while before help could be on its way. Many of those that did survive owed their lives to the courage and determination of John Macleod from Ness who was returning on home leave. Macleod managed to scramble and swim his way to the shore with a heaving line around his waist and four men followed him along the line. Together they were able to heave a rope ashore and so rescue a further thirty-five men.

Neither coastguard nor lifeboat was dispatched in time to help, as shortly after 3am the yacht had a broken back and offered little refuge for any remaining passengers and crew. One man did stay perched up the foremast where he was rescued by boat seven hours later. As news of the disaster spread, the devastated townsfolk slowly set off along the road to Holm to offer what they could. By dawn the scene was mayhem, with the two halves of the stricken ship largely submerged between the Beasts of Holm. The exact number lost that night, and lost almost at their very own front doors, was never established, but it is believed that 205 men died out of a passenger and crew compliment of 284.

At the subsequent naval inquiry it was concluded behind closed doors and in strictest confidence, that without any evidence being presented to the contrary, 'No opinion can be given as to whether blame is attributable to anyone in the matter'. However, a public inquiry was convened shortly afterwards which concluded that:

1. The officers in charge of *Iolaire* had not exercised appropriate caution on the approach to Stornoway.
2. The vessel was allowed to sail without adequate life-saving equipment.
3. That no lookout had been posted.
4. That once the vessel had struck, the officers did not take command of the situation.
5. That there was delay in deploying shore-based emergency services.

A memorial was erected in 1958 at Holm and a stone pillar marks the site of the wreck, which could be seen to starboard on the approaches to Stornoway Harbour for several decades. What lessons were learned that night? While the families of Lewis were convinced that the Navy was somehow culpable in their grief, the benefits of hindsight were clear to all those that followed in the course of *Iolaire*. Every one of the five points highlighted in the public inquiry was in due course encapsulated in what we know today as SOLAS, the International Convention of Safety for Life at Sea. But for the people of Lewis, these were hard-learned lessons indeed.

During the twentieth century Scottish passenger liner operators led an enviable existence as far as their passengers' safety was concerned. There were

Responsibility for the appalling sinking of *Athenia* (1923) at the start of World War Two was initially denied by Germany.

no peacetime losses after the Great War. Even before, when Anchor Line's *Armenia* was wrecked in June 1901 near St John in New Brunswick, there was no loss of life; six months later Allan Line lost *Grecian* approaching Halifax, Nova Scotia, without loss of life; and when *Bavarian* stranded on the Wye Rock off Montreal Harbour in 1906, there was no loss of life. Not surprisingly news of the loss of *Athenia* in the evening of the first day of World War Two provoked anger, indignation and outrage, not only in Scotland but throughout the Allied cause. The background to the loss is worth recounting, as so often it has been told incorrectly because of errors in the original press reports. As it happens, the Scottish Schoolboys' Expedition to Canada, summer 1939, enjoyed the last peacetime sailings of *Letitia* and *Athenia*. The following note was recorded during 2010 by Iain Hope, well-known maritime historian, based on information supplied by his brother Colin:

With regard to Colin's presence in the Scottish Schoolboys' Expedition to Canada in 1939 he explains that the party comprised a total of 80 boys, plus the teaching staff responsible as leaders of the Expedition …

The outward voyage by the expedition was as ordinary passengers on board the regular sailing of *Letitia* on her transatlantic service to Canada in the summer months of 1939. Colin was one of four boys in a modest but quite comfortable 4-berth cabin. The only downsides about this cabin were the noise and vibration when the propellers lifted out of the water in heavy seas. … *Letitia* made the passage from Glasgow to Belfast Lough, where they were met by the tender bringing out passengers from the City of Belfast … From Belfast *Letitia* was scheduled to sail direct to Quebec. But off Belle Isle heading to the mouth of the St Laurence she had to heave-to for almost 12 hours due to fog … Her master and crew would have been only too well aware of the terrible disaster and loss of life (1,014 drowned) in the St Laurence in similar fog conditions with *Empress of Ireland* in spring 1914.

For the homeward voyage … *Athenia* sailed for Quebec where she embarked her final passengers from Canada including the Independent Schools group plus their leaders. While en route homewards across the Atlantic the international tensions with Germany grew worse and at one point *Athenia* was diverted towards Cork in the publically neutral Republic of Ireland. But quickly the international tension seemed to ease and *Athenia* diverted back to her earlier course to Belfast Lough and then on to Glasgow. Unlike several other British liners she was not blacked out at night.

My next memory of *Athenia* was a week later being shown the outraged newspaper headline of the torpedoing of *Athenia* with heavy loss of life, particularly of women and children, off the coast of Northern Ireland within hours of war being declared and without any warning. The liner had been en route from Glasgow back to Canada, having made her usual 1939 call at Belfast Lough (In the newspaper it was wrongly reported at the time that she had made a call at Liverpool en route.)

Athenia sailed from Belfast Lough with 1,418 passengers and crew, including a large contingent of American women and children bent on returning home before war erupted in Europe. Germany had attacked Poland the day *Athenia* sailed from Princes Dock at Glasgow at 11.15am on Saturday, 2 September, twenty-four hours before war was declared on Germany on 3 September. The ship pulled off the berth to the strains of *Will ye no come back again*, while some of the dockers taunted the passengers standing at the ships rails with shouts of 'Cowards, cowards!' That night, off the coast of Ireland, there was a dance, but few took part and the conversation was all about impending war. The following morning, Sunday, an announcement proclaimed that the ship would be sailing under blackout as war had been declared on Germany. The ship settled into a shocked silence as the day progressed.

Two torpedoes ripped into the hull of *Athenia* shortly before 8pm ship's time, although only one of them exploded; the position was 250 miles west of Inishtrahull. The ship sank slowly, remaining afloat for about eleven and a half hours, time enough for rescuers to get to the scene, but 112 lives had been lost in the explosion and the subsequent evacuation, including children and their mothers. Fifty lives were lost when one of the *Athenia's* lifeboats was crushed under the propeller of the tanker *Knute Nelson* while attempting rescue. This same ship later landed 450 survivors in Ireland.

Why had so many lives been lost in a calm sea on a ship that stayed on an even keel until she sank by the stern? The ship was overcrowded; so many Canadian and American passengers had brought return sailings forward that Donaldson staff had arranged two hundred additional temporary berths, many in the ship's gymnasium. The torpedo had created a massive explosion at the after end of the ship, where many passengers were berthed, and had trapped diners in the tourist restaurant. Cabin doors were blown off, those on the lower passenger decks were stunned and shaken, and quickly found sea water rising in the alleyways. The speed of the ingress was such that mothers and children were parted, some children never to be seen again. The third reason was that there was panic. The ship had been tense all day since the morning's announcement of war, and passengers found it hard to find their muster stations, many surprisingly not having attended the muster rehearsal when the ship was off the Lower Clyde. Panic was such that one lifeboat was wrongly released from its falls and the entire complement of the boat tipped into the sea – women, children and supervising crew members.

Survivors were landed at Greenock and transferred to the Beresford Hotel in Glasgow. Crowds awaited their arrival and had to be held back by mounted police as feelings ran high at the thought of the wanton sinking of a passenger ship by a Nazi submarine. Passage west was slowly arranged for those survivors still in need of travel and many were taken by special train to Liverpool and given berths aboard *Duchess of York* three weeks later. There were many children who refused to climb the gangway at Liverpool, even with bribes of teddies and sweets once aboard ship, and crew members spent several hours carrying frightened children and their belongings to their cabins.

Germany feared that the death of American civilians might bring that country directly into the war and so it denied all responsibility for the sinking. The truth that *U-30* had unleashed the torpedoes on the liner only came out in 1946 during the war trials. But the lesson was learned by the Allies that Germany was going to treat the London Naval Treaty of 1930, which secured the safety of civilian passengers at sea, with contempt, and it was clear that Germany was not going to fight holding the rule book in one hand and the sword in the other. Ironically Oberleutnant Fritz-Julius Lemp, in command of *U-30*, and who was decorated for his deed on return to Germany, paid dearly a few months later when a British corvette forced his boat to the surface. In his hurry to get off his sinking submarine, Oberleutnant Lemp failed to destroy the boat's secret papers and these were soon recovered by a British search party before the boat finally sank. The papers included the encryption codes used by the German navy and these were passed to Bletchley Park where they were used to decode German military instructions right up to the end of the war.

A similar outrage was the loss of Ellerman's City Line's *City of Benares*. Despite being based at London, her pedigree was entirely of George Smith & Sons City Line. On Friday, 13 September 1940 she sailed under the command of Captain Landles Nicoll from Liverpool for Quebec and Montreal, a voyage operated for the Cunard White Star Line. The omens could not have been worse as it was also well-known aboard ship that the final design of the ship was known as 'the thirteenth plan' at her builders Barclay Curle & Company. She joined the nineteen-ship convoy OB213 at the head of the central column as commodore ship. There were ninety evacuee children on the passenger list being relocated by the Children's Overseas Reception Board which was

'The Children's Ship' *City of Benares* (1936) was built by Barclay, Curle & Company for Ellerman's City Line.

responsible for taking British children away from the war zone. At night the whole convoy was in blackout and making just 8½ knots.

Late in the evening of 17 September, *U-48* fired two torpedoes at *City of Benares*, which missed. Shortly after midnight the U-boat found its mark and hit *City of Benares* near the stern, a target that had been clearly silhouetted for the submarine by moonlight. *City of Benares* was 250 miles west-southwest of Rockall and started to sink rapidly by the stern, evacuation still incomplete when the stricken vessel sank forty minutes after being hit. Because of the rules regarding breaking out of columns when under attack, other ships in the convoy could not assist. The escorts meanwhile were too busy also to attend and it was a long time before help arrived.

HMS *Hurricane* was able to pick up 105 survivors and later land them at Greenock. One lifeboat was overlooked and was host to its cold and miserable cargo, which included eight of the children, for a further eight days before it was sighted by an escort support aircraft which directed HMS *Anthony* to assist. Twelve-year-old Derek Capel and the other boys in lifeboat 12 were weak, thirsty, starving and frostbitten when rescued, but Derek recalled the wonderful welcome they received in Glasgow:

We came into Gourock, then on to Greenock and they put us to bed and we didn't think any more of it. But the next day they picked us up to take us to Glasgow and there were crowds of people. We thought 'what do they want?' Then we realised that we were headline news.

Derek lost his brother Alan in the sinking. What he did not know until a reunion forty-two years later was that Alan and two other boys had been picked up by HMS *Hurricane* but all three died shortly afterwards of exposure.

All the child survivors' stories are heart rending. Mrs Bech was travelling with her three children, Barbara, Sonia and Derek. Sonia recorded the first moments of the sinking:

I remember a thud and being woken up by my sister Barbara and automatically getting into my duffle coat and putting on socks and sandals and of course carrying my life jacket. There was a sinister atmosphere along the corridors up to the Muster Station in the lounge and I remember an odd smell in the air. The next few minutes are still very vivid in my memory and are like a long bad dream. How I reached the tiny raft beneath I will never understand. When I got onto the raft I remember thinking we were laying very close to the ship's side and I thought we would be sucked under when she actually sank. By some fantastic good luck a strong man was in the water at that minute and he pulled the raft out of danger. I believe his name was Mr Davis: he certainly saved our lives.

Derek Bech, then aged nine, recalled:

Some of the children were killed in the explosion, some were trapped in their cabins, and the rest died when the lifeboats were launched incorrectly and children were just tipped into the sea. All I can remember were the screams and cries for help. It was one of the worst disasters at sea concerning children, and it should always be remembered.

Sonia and Derek and their mother were together in a small life raft. Unbeknown to them, big sister Barbara was safely aboard a lifeboat in relative comfort. Sonia recalled falling out of the raft in the rough seas and being hauled back aboard by one of the seamen. She described a sense of peace when she was underwater but was brought back to life shivering and intensely cold. Eventually, Mrs Bech muttered to her daughter:

'Sonia, let us take off our life belts and go to sleep in the water,' but I insisted that we waited and it was shortly afterwards that our lives were saved a second time. An already overcrowded lifeboat from *Marina*, which had also been sunk, was skilfully brought alongside our raft and we were hauled unceremoniously aboard and plied with rum and Nestlé's Milk.

Dr Peter Collinson, medical officer aboard HMS *Hurricane*, remembers the state of the survivors :

All survivors were suffering from severe exposure, and varying degrees of shock, being physically and emotionally exhausted. Some were dehydrated and most were suffering from bruised and sprained bodies, limbs, and suspected fractures. Several had severe swollen legs due to prolonged exposure to sea water, the so called 'Immersion Feet'. Three little boys could not be revived in spite of the valiant efforts of the Petty Officers' Mess at artificial resuscitation. They were later given a full Naval Burial by the Captain.

Out of the 406 people on board *City of Benares*, 260 were lost, including Captain Nicoll, Convoy Commodore Mackinnon, 124 crew members and 134 passengers. Seventy-seven of the ninety child evacuees died in the sinking. The question was raised in the press on both sides of the Atlantic whether it had been sensible to carry so many child evacuees in a blacked-out ship carrying the convoy commodore. Had Britain declared the passenger list and put the *City of Benares* unescorted with civilian lights ablaze onto the Atlantic crossing, theory had it that the Germans would not have risked attack for fear of an America reprisal.

On a lighter note the loss of the Harrison Line steamer *Politician*, in Eriskay Sound in February 1941, was very much a tragedy to her owners but anything but a tragedy to the good folk of Eriskay. *Politician* had sailed from her home port of Liverpool to join a transatlantic convoy. She was carrying a cargo of luxury goods, including hundreds of cases of whisky, destined for the US as part payment of American military hardware. Bad weather forced her off course and she was wrecked off Eriskay, a location that later became the setting for the film *Whisky Galore*. The stern section of the ship was still visible on the rocks until recently, and the locals will tell you that there is still the odd case of Black Label stashed safely away should there be need for a ceilidh.

Although the immediate post-war years were indeed grey and austere, shipowners queued up to order replacements for their war losses. Materials

Royal Mail Line's brand new *Magdalena* (1949) needlessly lost on 25 April 1949 on the inward leg of her maiden voyage to Rio de Janeiro.

were in short supply and a strict licensing system came into play. Yet again on Clydeside there were pent-up feelings of anger and indignation; the brand new Belfast-built passenger liner *Magdelana* sailed on her maiden voyage in March 1949 on the Royal Mail Line's London to Buenos Aires service to be wrecked on her homeward journey off Rio de Janeiro. The feelings of hopelessness and of waste were exactly not what was needed in a maritime industry that was still trying to pick itself up to service the increasing demands of post-war commerce and industry. Although no lives were lost, the incident did little for morale either in London, or indeed, in Scottish shipping circles.

A few years later, in 1953, the whole nation was caught up with yet another disaster, this time very much both a Scottish and an Irish one. Tuning into the wireless in the afternoon of Saturday, 31 January 1953 the listener not only heard the football commentary, although many matches were cancelled due to awful weather conditions, but also periodic bulletins on the plight of the ferry *Princess Victoria*. These ended in the report on the BBC Home Service which began:

A car ferry has sunk in the Irish Sea in one of the worst gales in living memory. The *Princess Victoria*, a British Railways car ferry, bound for Larne in Northern Ireland, had left Stranraer on the south-west coast of Scotland …

Tragedy struck soon after the vessel had cleared Loch Ryan when Captain James Ferguson sent a message, by Morse code, to alert coastguards that the ferry was not under control and needed a tug. That was just before 9am. The southeasterly gale had exposed the half 'tween-deck height horizontally-hinged stern door to the elements and it was stove in almost as soon as the ferry left the shelter of the Loch, allowing water to flood onto the vehicle deck. Just short of 1pm Captain Ferguson radioed to say that his engine room was flooded and that he was about to issue the command to abandon ship. By now the ferry was listing so badly that it was almost impossible to launch the lifeboats. One was smashed against the ship's side, while another, containing eight women and a child, was swamped by huge waves. The ship drifted west of its last reported position and it was only after a final Morse code message was broadcast by the ferry to the effect that the Down coast was visible, that rescuers were finally able to locate the ship. RAF planes arrived at about half past three and dropped rubber dinghies, but the weather remained atrocious and ships and lifeboats attending the scene could at first do little to help as the tragedy unfolded. Some 139 passengers and crew lost their lives that afternoon out of the 177 who had left Stranraer that same morning.

The *Princess Victoria* was a Denny-built vessel, virtually a replica of an earlier ship of the same name, lost in minelaying activities in the North Sea in May 1940. As with all disasters, lessons were there to be learned. At the subsequent inquiry it was found that the design of the stern door was inadequate and complete watertight enclosure of the vehicle deck was desirable. It is noteworthy that until then the half-height door had been applied on all railway-owned roll-on roll-off ferries including the new *Lord Warden* based at Dover. Indeed the design stemmed from the train ferries in operation at both Dover and Harwich. More significantly the inquiry reported that the scuppers on the vehicle deck were too small to discharge the mass of water that cascaded along the deck, and that the water caused the ship to list violently as it flowed down the incline of the deck to port. It was to be many years before cambered vehicle decks and longitudinal subdivisions by hydraulic barriers were introduced.

The *Princess Victoria* tragedy prevented the railways from considering further roll-on roll-off vessels until *Maid of Kent* and *Caledonian Princess* were completed for the Dover and Stranraer stations in 1959 and 1961 respectively.

Vehicle deck aboard *Princess Victoria* – small by today's standards but a large area for free water to accumulate. (University of Glasgow)

Eventual successor to *Princess Victoria* at Stranraer was *Caledonian Princess* (1961) here showing off her full-height watertight stern door. (Author)

Caledonian Princess was also noteworthy as being the very last cross-channel steamer ever built by Denny of Dumbarton.

The most recent 'Scottish' maritime disaster occurred on the far side of the world at the entrance to Wellington Harbour, North Island, New Zealand on 10 April 1968. *Wahine*, owned by Union Steamship Company of New Zealand, struck Barrett Reef and later foundered near Steeple Rock towards the end of her normal passage from Lyttleton in South Island. There were 610 passengers and 123 crew aboard the ferry – fifty-three of these lives were lost.

Wahine was built by Fairfield Shipbuilding & Engineering and was launched into the Clyde in July 1965, following protracted delays as the builders went into receivership that October. *Wahine* (Maori for 'woman') finally left the Clyde in June 1966. Numerous faults were found on the delivery voyage to Wellington via the Panama Canal, notably in steam lines and valves, and in the boilers themselves. Given the delayed delivery of the ship, there was some bitterness on the part of her owners towards the Clyde shipbuilders, much of it perhaps unwarranted. *Wahine* was designed as a vehicle and passenger ferry and was finally ready to take up service in the Cook Strait on 1 August. Her machinery was innovative, being turbo-electric with twin steam turbine generator sets supplying electric power to twin propulsion motors connected to the propeller shafts. Her service speed was 21 knots.

On the morning of 10 April 1968, the weather near Wellington deteriorated into a severe cyclone. Wind speeds reached over 170 miles an hour and caused extensive structural damage ashore. *Wahine*, meanwhile, was heading into the storm at the end of her overnight voyage from Lyttleton, having had no warning of severe weather. Just before 6am, in wind speeds in excess of eighty miles an hour, Captain Gordon Robertson, a second-generation New Zealander of Scottish descent, decided to enter harbour rather than risk his ship and passengers to the heavy seas that were building. His decision coincided with a significant worsening of the storm, during which the radar mast was blown away leaving the ship near-blind on its approach to harbour. Captain Robertson fought to keep his ship on course, but the wind and waves forced the vessel to turn from the channel. In a bold attempt to complete the turn through 180 degrees, Captain Robertson tried to put back out to sea. With partial loss of control of the engines the turn became a losing battle and the new ferry was soon driven onto the southern end of Barrett Reef, less than a mile from shore. *Wahine* drifted helplessly along the reef ripping a large open gash along her hull. Passengers were instructed to put on lifejackets and report to their assembly points.

Only at 11am did a harbour tug managed to put out to help. Attempts to get a line aboard the stricken ferry failed, and shortly after 1pm tide and weather swung the *Wahine* broadside to the wind, and the ship commenced a slow unending roll to starboard. Only three of the ship's lifeboats reached the shore. As the remainder of personnel aboard the ferry were forced into the water, the weather abated sufficiently for small ships and tugs to come to their rescue. Shortly before half past two *Wahine* rolled onto her side. Scotland, with its sense of ownership of the ship, mourned alongside New Zealand for the loss of fifty-one passengers and crew who were so close to their destination.

The subsequent court of inquiry cited errors of judgement but stressed that the conditions had been extreme. The inquiry did state that the order to abandon ship was given at precisely the right critical moment, ie neither too early nor too late for the optimum survival of passengers and crew. Yet again lessons were learned, this time highlighting the importance of passage planning and voyage risk assessment, especially during the critical stages of entering and leaving harbour, particularly if adverse weather conditions prevail.

In more recent years disasters have tended more towards mishaps, although the loss of the Irish Sea cattle carrier *Hereford Express*, when she was wrecked off the southeast coast of Kintyre in October 1970, was very much a tragedy. Inbound to Glasgow from Derry, the Dutch-registered ship had a full cargo of cattle when she went aground. About a hundred adult cattle and a number of calves were drowned. Badly holed, the ship refloated and was taken in tow by the container ship *Hope Isle*. In the rough conditions the tow parted and again the cattle carrier went aground, this time on Boiler Reef off Sanda Island. By now the RSPCA inspector had arrived on the scene and as many cattle as possible were encouraged to swim to shore; those that could not or would not were shot. Newspaper reports questioned the use of such a small vessel (700 gross tons) carrying 250 head of cattle, and highlighted a transatlantic voyage carried out the previous year by sister ship *Shorthorn Express* between Canada and the Clyde as cruel. In this case the ship was carrying breeding stock. Bearing in mind that live imports from Canada had been stopped before the Second World War in favour of refrigerated meat imports, the viability of live cattle shipments, even across the Irish Sea, remained in question, despite it having been a staple part of the Burns & Laird Lines business for many years.

There were two celebrated mishaps in recent times, neither of which should ever have been allowed to occur. In March 1973 the MacBrayne ferry *Loch Seaforth* was returning on her routine sailing from Lochboisdale and Castlebay via Gott Bay, Tiree, to Oban. Captain Donald Gunn had on board both company chairman and executive director, returning from a business trip to the islands. It was a rough night with a Force 8 southwesterly wind. Approaching Tiree, *Loch Seaforth* hit the Cleit Rock in Gunna Sound and immediately issued a Mayday call just after 5.15am. The second officer was on the bridge and in an attempt to raise the piermaster at Tiree on the VHF, he had turned off the radar which was making a noise. It was too late when he sighted surf breaking on his starboard bow and called to the quartermaster for port helm. The master dashed to the bridge and tried to get the ship to go astern, but the ship was pinned by rock. The rising tide did lift her clear and *Loch Seaforth* drifted in the wind to the northwest. At the same time the engine room was flooding while the chief engineer struggled to cope with a generator fire.

There were eleven passengers and twenty-eight crew aboard that night. All were safely evacuated in the ship's boats, passengers and some crew in the first boat, which was towed by the second motor lifeboat. The master and the two MacBrayne VIPs followed in the third boat. Press coverage obviously picked up on the 'owners' being aboard the abandoned vessel and likened the incident to the sinking of the *Titanic* with Bruce Ismay aboard, although neither the MacBrayne chairman nor his executive director were held to blame as was the case with Ismay! As for the *Loch Seaforth*, she was taken in tow by the salvage tug *Cruiser*. The draught of *Cruiser* was too deep to attempt to beach the ferry which was put alongside Gott Pier where, in due course, she sank in 18ft of water. The hulk blocked the pier to ferry traffic for several months until it could be raised and towed away for dismantling.

The other mishap, highlighted at the time by the media, was the master of the preserved paddle steamer *Waverley* allowing his ship to strand on the Gantock Rocks on approaching Dunoon Pier on 15 July 1977 with 650 passengers on board. Although nobody was hurt, the master swung the ship towards the Gantocks then had to go astern to miss a buoy, so allowing the tide to bring the steamer's stern on to the rocks. The incident was a serious blow to all those who had contributed to the ship's upkeep and the many who spent their winter months working on the ship to get her ready for the new season. This was a seriously embarrassing accident that could have so easily become a disaster; happily, all personnel were brought ashore without incident within forty-five minutes, using Western Ferries' car ferry *Sound of Shuna* as a tender. *Waverley* was banner headlines in the national press the next day, but for all the wrong reasons. That being so, it was only by the narrowest margin that *Waverley* was not lost when she later scraped the edge of the Boiler Reef on an excursion from Campbeltown to circumnavigate the Island of Sanda.

While none of the disasters and accidents could have been readily averted given the knowledge of the day, all could now be averted with hindsight. Knowledge and experience, gained through both technical development and operational experience, has advanced understanding and increased the safety threshold of day-to-day work practices. We should be thankful that we live in a safer world today than our forebears did and that the lives of so many lost in these maritime disasters, through no fault of their own, have not been wholly wasted. However, despite the foregoing, accidents will always take place as a result of errors and carelessness by members of the human race and vigilance must always be the watchword. The needless loss of *Costa Concordia* is a timely reminder to all!

The Clyde Anchorages Emergency Port

The geographical location of the Clyde provided huge benefits in World War II because of its distance from the enemy. In September 1940, following the establishment of the Cloch-Dunoon anti-submarine boom, the Clyde Anchorages Emergency Port was established at the Tail o' the Bank with support from London dockers moved north to a new base at Greenock. The new facility was organised by Robert Letch from the Port of London Authority and the dockers were from the Royal Docks in London which had been closed at an early stage of the war because of bomb damage. The new port facility allowed very large liners to be turned round off Greenock that would otherwise have had to visit the Mersey as ports in southern England were no longer viable, and Liverpool was at severe risk of bombing. The facility was hugely successful and facilitated large troop movements to be made away from the attention of the enemy. The port was also the main arrival point for US troops entering Europe.

The Free French Naval Forces was also based at the Clyde Anchorages Emergency Port. Just before the Free French Naval Forces was formed and while the emergency port was still being created, the Vauquelin-class destroyer *Maillé Brézé* exploded off Greenock with heavy loss of life on 30 April 1940. There were few other major incidents, and many happier ones such as the disembarkation of Winston Churchill from HMS *Renown*, via the MacBrayne steamer

King George V acting as ship's tender, at the end of Churchill's historic visit to Canada in 1943.

Apart from significant naval activity on the Clyde, Loch Ewe also became a busy naval centre used for assembling North Atlantic convoys well away from the eyes of the enemy. Methil, in Fife, was also a focus of activity and was the centre from which North Sea convoys were organised; all convoys from Methil had a large contingent of colliers destined for the Thames.

MacBrayne's *King George V* (1926), in happier times at Fort William. (Linda Gowans)

12

The Atlantic Crossing

NOWHERE WAS THE COMPETITION more intense than on the North Atlantic. It was perceived as a prestigious trade and various Glasgow-based companies were attracted away from serving South America or Asia to join the North Atlantic routes (see chapter 4). Here they focused on the emigrant exodus to North America with guaranteed return cargoes of live cattle and grain. It was a cut-throat business with Glasgow companies competing with their neighbours, and all busy fighting off the 'English' which included Cunard, White Star and Canadian Pacific Steamships. Canadian Pacific was an English company rather than Canadian, as its origins stemmed from the Liverpool-based North Atlantic services of Elder Dempster Line, which the Canadian Pacific Railway bought in 1903.

The key Scottish players were the Allan Line, Anchor Line and Donaldson Line, the Anchor Line heavily involved also in trade with India. However, the first transatlantic steamer company to be registered in Glasgow was the British & North American Royal Mail Steam Packet Company, forerunner of the Cunard Steamship Company (see chapter 2). A contract with the British government established the company, with Samuel Cunard working alongside David MacIver and George Burns to raise the initial capital outlay for the four original paddle steamers. The launch of the first ship, *Britannia*, was described in the *Glasgow Herald*:

> She is to be propelled by two engines, each of 220 horse power and when put to sea will be succeeded by three other ships ... to carry the mails and passengers between Liverpool and North America, a scheme, it will be remembered which was originated by the Hon S Cunard, of Halifax, Nova Scotia, who with a small party of influential gentlemen in Glasgow, is associated with this undertaking.
>
> The vessel's hull and machinery are constructed under the direction and superintendence of Robert Napier, of the Vulcan Foundry, Glasgow, and as we mention this gentleman's name as being connected with such a work, we give a guarantee that when completed nothing better will be found in the United Kingdom.

The Allan Line was founded by the five sons of Alexander Allan. The Allan Line story started in 1819 when Captain Alexander Allan of Saltcoats took shares in the brig *Jean*. Allan built up a fine fleet of wooden sailing ships over the next thirty years, and operated them largely between the Clyde and Canada and also to the River Plate. His five sons James, Hugh, Alexander, Bryce and Andrew all became involved in the business which had offices in Glasgow, Liverpool and Montreal. Given a promise of a Canadian mail subsidy, the brothers took the bold decision to commission four screw passenger and cargo steamers from Denny's yard at Dumbarton. Advertised as the Montreal Ocean Steamship Company, the maiden voyage of the first steamer, *Canadian*, took place in September 1854, instantly making Cunard's paddle steamers on the Atlantic mail services obsolete.

Within five years the Allan fleet had been doubled to eight ships. However, there were some appalling losses. Bad weather in the St Lawrence, coupled with the need to keep steaming despite fog and other hazards, in order to satisfy the terms of the mail contract, saw eight vessels lost in the first ten years of the company's existence, many with significant loss of life. Rebuilding in the 1860s allowed the company to diversify with sailings from Glasgow and Liverpool, with a new service developed also from London. In 1882 Sir Hugh Allan died and the company lost headway against its competitors through indecision. For example, half of the early fleet was registered in Glasgow and half in Montreal, until in 1886 the whole fleet took up Canadian nationality. This only lasted for one year when the entire fleet was re-registered at Glasgow and the company assumed British identity.

The Allan Line was in decline in the early 1890s when many of the older vessels were lengthened and re-engined as an alternative to new tonnage. Its involvement with the River Plate traffic was intermittent, although it remained a member of the River Plate Conference. It suffered a number of accidents (see chapter 11) and near-misses. One of the more bizarre was the incident that befell *Parisian* when she was unexpectedly rammed in clear calm daylight conditions outside Halifax harbour on 25 March 1905. On board was Dr Kirkpatrick, Professor of Divinity at Cambridge, and Master of Selwyn College. He wrote in a letter to England:

Here I am, thank God, under Bishop Worrell's roof, but I have been within a very little of what might have been an awful catastrophe. We made good running and stopped at the mouth of the harbour of Halifax to take up a pilot between 5:30 and 6 o'clock. We had been watching a German steamer, the Hamburg-American liner *Albano*, from Hamburg, coming down from the

Parisian (1881), lying half submerged alongside the pier at Halifax with collision damage that occurred on 25 March 1905. She was later raised and eventually scrapped in 1914.

north, also making for Halifax. I thought she was coming too near us, and to my horror saw her making straight at us, we being practically stationary. What happened I cannot say. Whether she would not steer or what I do not know, but for half a minute it was a bad time to know if we could escape or where or how badly we should be struck. Into us she came, but mercifully only struck us aft of the engines. For a few minutes it was doubtful what damage was done and the order was given to clear the boats, but as the engines were undamaged we took up a pilot and steamed on. Apparently only a stern-most compartment was damaged, but evidently it was leaking considerably, and we soon got pretty well down in the stern. However we got safely to the pier. There was no panic on board though there were a good many anxious faces. But I shudder to think what might have happened if that clumsy German had rammed us in the engine room and our fires had been put out or the ship sunk quickly. The idea of the sudden sinking of a ship with 800 or 900 people on board, at the very mouth of the harbour is too terrible to think of, but it seemed to me that we came very near and for a few minutes I thought it was not impossible that I should be landed a destitute alien in the clothes I stood in, with all my possessions including my lectures at the bottom of the harbour. I am most truly thankful that we were preserved from disaster but we were certainly very near it.

Facing up to the need to modernise, the Allan Line Steamship Company, as it was recast in 1897, placed orders for new and larger vessels of modern design with various yards. The first new ship was *Castilian*, but she did little to improve the company image as she was wrecked on her maiden homebound voyage in the Bay of Fundy. Malcolm Cooper described what happened next in an article which first appeared in *Ships Monthly*, May 2008:

> The arrival of the new ships finally cleared the way for the disposal of the older part of the fleet. A total of twelve veterans went to the breakers between 1896 and 1902, including two that had been built in 1861. Pressure from competitors, however, was unrelenting. The formation of J P Morgan's International Mercantile Marine company in 1902 brought modern White Star liners onto the St Lawrence in a joint service with the Dominion Line, which itself had just reached peak strength. Even more ominously, the Canadian Pacific Railway bought its way into the UK-Canadian passenger liner trade in 1903 with the acquisition of Elder Dempster's North Atlantic business.

This time around the Allan Line responded magnificently by commissioning the first triple screw turbine steamers for the North Atlantic to operate its core Liverpool to Montreal service. Originally ordered as twin screw quadruple expansion engines, the design was changed in favour of turbines at an early

An impressive contemporary painting of the turbine steamer *Victorian* (1904), used for advertising the Allan Line service.

stage, a bold move into such untried technology by the owners. Nevertheless *Victorian* was launched only ten months after keel-laying and was delivered in 1905 by Workman Clark at Belfast and *Virginian* by Alexander Stephen closer to home. Contract speed was 18 knots and this they exceeded comfortably. Canadian Pacific countered by commissioning their first purpose-built liners for the North Atlantic, *Empress of Britain* and *Empress of Ireland*, which were delivered from the Fairfield Shipbuilding & Engineering Company. They were faster than the Allan Line ships at just half a knot short of the '20 knots to Canada' aspiration canvassed by a number of Canadian business people at that time.

The relationship between Canadian Pacific and the Allan family was closer than some would at the time have believed. Sir Hugh Allan, founder member of the Allan Line had been appointed in 1873 as president of the new company created in Canada in 1871, when construction work started on the transcontinental Canadian Pacific Railroad, later to become the famous Canadian Pacific Railway. Initially dogged by inadequate funding, the Canadian government stepped in to pay for what it saw as an essential part of national infrastructure, and it was government that invited Sir Hugh to oversee their investment.

The Allan Line planned to build two 18-knot turbine steamers to compete with the Empresses but realised it could not afford them so it compromised with the order for *Corsican* and *Grampian* which were 15-knot triple expansion engined ships. An article in *Sea Breezes*, October 1961, takes up the subsequent collusion between the Allan family and Canadian Pacific:

> Even then, however, there were signs of compromise in the operation of the Allan and Canadian Pacific fleets, for the two Empresses and *Victorian* and *Virginian* were sharing the mail contract, and it was this tendency to compromise that eventually led up to the amalgamation of the companies in January 1916.

Among rumours that later turned out to be true, the Allan family had secretly sold out to Canadian Pacific in 1909. Clearly very good terms had been agreed for the family, but just why the need for secrecy remains a mystery to this day, and it was only in July 1917 that news of the sale was released. Under Canadian Pacific ownership the Allan line retained its identity; a number of innovative new ships were built. The largest and youngest of the sixteen Allan line ships to enter the Canadian Pacific fleet were the 18,481-ton *Alsatian* and her near sister *Calgarian* built on the Clyde in 1914. They were

The oldest of the sixteen Allan Line ships transferred to Canadian Pacific ownership in 1917 was *Sardinian* (1875).

Only *Alsatian* (1914) was good enough to merit 'Empress' status when she joined the Canadian Pacific fleet as *Empress of France*. Sister *Calgarian* was lost in the Great War.

distinctive as they had the modern spoon-shaped cruiser stern instead of the traditional counter stern. The oldest of the sixteen ships was veteran steamer *Sardinian* which had been commissioned in 1875. Heavy losses during the war persuaded Canadian Pacific to amalgamate the surviving Allan liners into its own post-war fleet; *Alsatian* became *Empress of France* while the remainder adopted the 'also ran' Mar- names of the secondary fleet. Even *Victorian* was only fit to become *Marloch* while sister *Virginian* was sold to the Swedish America Line as *Drottningholm* in 1920.

The River Plate service had become a joint service with Ellermans in 1903 but was operated under the Allan Line brand, due to objections about Ellerman entering the Conference from Lamport & Holt and others. The arrangement did not last long and Ellerman withdrew in 1907, leaving Henry Allan to struggle on alone until he, too, withdrew a few years later.

Another key player in the transatlantic trade, and important also in the trade to India, was the Anchor Line of Glasgow. Nicol and Robert Handyside established themselves in Glasgow as shipbrokers and merchants in 1838. N & R Handyside & Company used chartered ships to trade with the Baltic and Russia; Nicol even became the Russian consul in Glasgow. Thomas Henderson joined the business in 1852. He was one of four brothers from Pittenweem in Fife, all four of them gaining master's certificates and all distant relatives of the Hendersons of P Henderson & Company (see chapter 4). Thomas wanted to develop a steamship line based at Glasgow, operating in the transatlantic trade.

Captain Thomas Henderson was in command of G & J Burns steamer *Orion* when she was wrecked off Portpatrick in June 1850 while cutting in too close to the coast in order to make best time to Glasgow. Contemporary press commentary wrongly reported that the master was a Captain McNeil, and that his body had not been found (*Illustrated London News*, 29 June 1850). Thomas Henderson, however, was later identified as the master and charged with culpable neglect of duty by the owners, no doubt because another of the Burns brothers, Dr Burns, Regius Professor of Surgery at Glasgow University, was one of the many who lost their lives that night. Thomas Henderson was given an eighteen-month gaol sentence; his criminal record, however, was not to prevent him from pursuing his transatlantic vision on his release.

Thomas Henderson became a full partner in 1855 and Handysides & Company was retitled Handysides & Henderson. The Anchor Line of Steam Packets' new transatlantic service, in line with Henderson's long standing vision, with Handysides & Henderson as managing owners, was first advertised in the *Glasgow Herald*, 1 May 1856:

Anchor Line of Steam Packets sailing regularly between Glasgow and New York:

John Bell, 1,800 tons James Alexander Commander and *Tempest*, 1,500 tons, John Henderson Commander.

Fitted up with a view to the comfortable accommodation of all classes of passengers. The splendid Clyde-built iron screw steamer *Tempest*, A1 at Lloyds for 12 years, will shortly be at a loading berth, and is intended to sail with goods and passengers directly from Glasgow to New York early in July.

Handysides & Henderson, 45 Union Street, Glasgow.

The service had to be suspended from 1856 after the *Tempest* was lost, and *John Bell* and *United Kingdom*, which had also joined the New York service, were chartered by the East India Company to take troops to India. In summer an infrequent service was also maintained to Quebec and Montreal. In 1857, John Henderson, Thomas's brother, joined Handysides & Henderson. At the same time Thomas's other brothers, David and William, founded the Finnieston Steamship Works Company to build steam engines. In due course the company evolved into the shipbuilders D & W Henderson.

Handysides had managed the four ships of the Glasgow & Lisbon Steam Packet Company for some years and the trade was taken over by the Anchor Line of Peninsular & Mediterranean Steam Packets in 1863. A Naples–New York route was inaugurated in 1869 after the company identified the potential of the Italian immigrant trade and the lack of suitable Italian tonnage.

A remarkable story of the loss of a captain, first and third officers is told by R S McLellan through the eyes of a passenger in his history of the Anchor Line; *Europa* sailed from Glasgow on 25 February 1871:

By eight o'clock (on 3 March) the situation was terrible. The wind screamed and whistled through the rigging and huge waves struck heavily against the sides of the gallant vessel … The Commander, Captain MacDonald, whenever he could snatch a moment from his duties on deck, used his utmost endeavours to calm his passengers and allay their apprehensions. About 9.30 on that Friday evening he left the cabin where he had been sitting in conversation with the passengers, and in company with a New York gentleman, who wanted to take a look at the storm, went on deck.

One look was enough for the passenger, for he immediately returned to the cabin. He had scarcely seated himself when a tremendous sea struck the bridge under the starboard side, twisting the horizontal iron railing into a perpendicular position and tearing the planking up like paper. This broke the wave, and its crest fell with a crash upon the leeward side of the bridge, snapping the stanchions and grinding that part of the flooring into kindling wood. The almost solid mountain of water then bounded off into the sea again, staving in two boats and breaking the main boom. In its passage it overwhelmed the Captain and the first and third mates and swept them far into the ocean.

The engines were stopped by the second mate, still half dressed, when he reached the bridge. However, he soon had to ring down for slow ahead to keep the ship head to wind. With the second mate in charge, the *Europa* finally arrived at New York ten days later without further mishap.

India became an attractive trade partner once the Suez Canal opened in 1869. Earlier the Mediterranean service had linked with the overland trek to Suez to connect with British India and P&O services onwards to India, but once the canal opened, Anchor was free to move east to complement its business on the Atlantic. Anchor Line's *Dido* made the first British merchant ship journey, southbound through the Suez Canal, on the day following the opening.

In 1872, the Anchor Line and D & W Henderson jointly bought the shipyard of Tod & MacGregor at Meadowside, Partick, to build the hulls into which the engines from D & W Henderson's Finnieston works could be fitted, and

Anchor Line Offices, 7 Bowling Green, New York, in 1872, leaves little to the passer-by's imagination!

Arabia (1884) was one of many Anchor Line ships built by D & W Henderson.

between 1876 and 1911 a total of thirty-two ships were built for the Anchor Line at Meadowside. Typical were the sisters *Persia*, *Arabia* and *Asia*, built in 1883 and 1884, with accommodation for about forty cabin passengers. The last of the Hendersons died in the 1890s and the D & W Henderson shipbuilding and ship repair interests were later sold to Harland & Wolff.

Also in 1872 was formed the Barrow Steam Ship Company, its champion being the Duke of Devonshire, who was keen to develop industrial interests in Furness, and the port of Barrow in particular. Thomas Henderson bought heavily into the initiative and sold the embryo company his two newest ships, *Ethiopia* and *Bolivia*. Devonshire's Barrow Shipbuilding Company was commissioned to build a new crack liner for the Inman Line, but when she was delivered in 1882 *City of Rome*, despite her handsome appearance, was found sadly lacking and Inman would not take delivery after testing her on the North Atlantic. After a considerable upgrading of machinery, ownership inevitably reverted to the Barrow Shipping Company when no other purchaser was forthcoming, and the Anchor Line was looked on to manage the ship like much of the rest of the Barrow fleet. *City of Rome* was a singleton and without a pair maintained a monthly departure on the Liverpool to New York run before she was relegated to the Clyde services in 1891, for which she was really too big. While most other Barrow ships were subsequently bought by Anchor,

Barrow Steam Ship Company's handsome but unwanted liner *City of Rome* (1882) seen in service with the Anchor Line.

Astoria (1885) was built by William Denny for Shaw Savill & Albion and named *Tainui*, and was bought and renamed by Anchor Line in 1899 and resold in 1910.

Elysia (1913), a product of D & W Henderson, carried a hundred cabin-class passengers on the Glasgow to Bombay service. (B & A Feilden)

City of Rome remained registered at Barrow until sold in 1902. The ship's only redeeming feature was her distinctive and handsome Allan Line profile.

Anchor Line operated twenty-two ships with an aggregate gross tonnage of 79,343 at the start of the twentieth century. Its latest acquisition was the venerable steamer *Astoria* which it bought from Shaw Savill & Albion for use on the Bombay and Calcutta services. In the twentieth century the Anchor Line went through various ownerships. Cunard Steamship Company bought the company in 1911 as part of a massive shopping spree which also included what was to become the Port Line, as well as the Brocklebank Line (at the invitation of the Brocklebank family). It was acquisition of the Anchor Line that finally gave Cunard access to the Indian trade, while Port Line and Brocklebank Line completed the global arena for Cunard. Significantly, Cunard also bought Cairn Thompson, which gave it a foothold in the Canadian trade. The Anchor–Brocklebank consortium was set up in 1912 to serve India, the Anchor Line Calcutta Conference rights being transferred to Brocklebank, thus preventing Anchor from sailing to and from Calcutta thereafter. Therefore at the start of the First World War Anchor was left with three core routes: Glasgow to New York operated by the passenger liners *Columbia*, *Caledonia*, *California* and *Cameronia* and joined in 1915 by the nearly-new former Cunarder *Transylvania*; Glasgow to Bombay operated by the *Massilia*, *Scindia*, *Circassia*, *Elysia*, *Olympia* and *Castalia*, most of which had berths for up to sixty cabin-class passengers, 100 aboard *Elysia*, and the Mediterranean to New York route maintained by steerage-class emigrant ships *Perugia*, *Calabria* and *Italia*.

A new company called Anchor-Donaldson was consolidated in 1916 in partnership with Donaldson Line of Glasgow. But by the end of the Great War the three largest and newest ships on the prestigious Glasgow to New York run had been sunk and some of the ships from the India service stood in until better vessels could be found. *Perugia* had also been lost leaving only a two-ship service between Genoa and New York. The big cargo liner *Tarantia* was bought in 1916 to fill the gaps and, once she stood down from government duties after the war, was deployed on Italy to New York services. Post-war rebuilding provided the Clyde-built single-funnel passenger liners *Cameronia*, *Tuscania* and *California*, a new *Transylvania* and *Caledonia*, the latter pair with a dramatic three-funnel profile (two dummies) and all intended for the transatlantic services, while *Tuscania* and *Transylvania* were destined for the Mediterranean–New York emigrant run. However, the five new ships were soon to provide Anchor Line with an embarrassment of over-stocking. Cruising became part of the routine from 1921 onwards when

Tarantia (1911), built by Russell, Port Glasgow, as *Kirkfield* for the Kirkfield Steamship Company, purchased by Anchor Line in 1911 and renamed. (B & A Feilden)

Cameronia made a Mediterranean cruise from New York. Then in 1922 the emigrant trade was greatly reduced by the US authorities necessitating the withdrawal of the Mediterranean service, neither *Tuscania* nor *Transylvania* ever managing to sail from an Italian port on their design route. While *Transylvania* was reconfigured on the stocks for the Glasgow and Liverpool to New York service, *Tuscania* was found employment on a new London to New York run operated by Cunard. She served briefly under Cunard colours during 1926 until in 1929 she was reconfigured as a cabin-class ship and operated occasional trips to Bombay for her owners. In April 1929 she arrived back in the Clyde from Bombay to be quarantined at the west end of Yorkhill Quay with forty cases of smallpox aboard. Two people died.

The Bombay service received its first new ship for eighteen years when *Britannia* was delivered by Alexander Stephen & Sons in 1926. Unlike her sixty-passenger cabin-class consorts, the *Britannia* brought the welcome luxury of 175 first-class berths to the route. In addition, the former German liner *Assyria* was transferred from the Atlantic to provide an additional 300 berths to Bombay. Thereafter the Bombay service was periodically supplemented with sailings by *California* and *Tuscania* from the Atlantic routes.

The Atlantic service enjoyed the regular patronage of the Order of Scottish Clans of America and the Lewis and Skye Societies in America. Anchor Line also brought a good many of the 1,500 attendees to the unveiling of the American-Scots Memorial of those fallen in the Great War in Princess Street Gardens, Edinburgh, in September 1927. Thereafter, patronage on the Atlantic route declined as the recession advanced towards Depression. In 1928 the *Assyria* ran a successful series of cruises from Glasgow while other ships ran booze cruises from the States for those frustrated by Prohibition. From the mid 1920s, one of the New York ships was seasonally deployed on the Bombay route during the winter off-season. As time went on, the luxury of the big passenger liners on the Bombay service became almost the standard and the older ships became less popular with the travelling public. But even the Indian service suffered as political difficulties hindered trade between Britain and India in the early 1930s.

The Anchor-Donaldson Line served Canada until 1935 when Anchor was restructured and Donaldson bought the majority shares in the North Atlantic company. The chairman of the new company was Cunard's Sir Alfred Booth and members of the Donaldson family served on the board. Anchor Line (Henderson Bros) had been forced into liquidation in May 1935 as a result of worldwide trade depression and a surplus of tonnage, and control passed to Runciman (London) with the majority of the shares owned by a consortium formed by Dawnay, Day & Company. The company was incorporated anew as Anchor Line (1935) with Lord Runciman as chairman. Anchor-Donaldson became Anchor-Cunard and calls at Liverpool ceased as these would have competed with Cunard ships, although the outward call at Belfast was retained. Then in 1936, Cunard started a Clyde service which did little to help matters.

The new Anchor company recognised the need for new tonnage on the Bombay service and orders were successively placed for two new passenger liners with the Fairfield Shipbuilding & Engineering Company; they were the attractive, although traditional-looking, motor ships *Circassia*, delivered in

Circassia (1937) boarding passengers bound for India at Prince's Landing Stage Liverpool, 5 October 1963. (Author)

1937 and displacing *Tuscania*, and *Cilicia* in 1938. They could accommodate 300 first-class passengers in modern, light and airy accommodation and had numerous en suite staterooms, very much a novelty other than aboard the crack liners on the North Atlantic. The new motor ships partnered *Britannia*.

As war approached once more, the five-ship New York service plodded on, ever fearful of competition from all directions. Among the war losses was *California*, bombed and sunk by aircraft in July 1943. The survivors were taken to Casablanca where they were looked after, fed and clothed at an American army base. Eventually repatriated to Avonmouth, the crew were put on a train home to Glasgow. One of them, Charles Aitchison, reported in *Sea Breezes*, July 1997, that Scottish humour was still plentiful even under such grim circumstances:

> There was an amusing incident on the way home. We stopped for ten minutes at a station and, just as we had arrived, another train full of GIs drew up at the next platform. Quite a few of our party had visited the USA on many occasions and we had picked up some of their dialects. We shouted across to them in Brooklynese and southern drawls and, together with our US military garb, they were completely taken in. Just as our train was about to depart we lapsed into broad Glasgow patois; the expressions on the GIs' faces are something I shall always remember.

Another of the happier tales is reported in the official Anchor Line history by R S McLellan:

> For four and a half years, from August 1939 to February 1944, the *Cilicia* was in service as an Armed Merchant Cruiser. It was on 25 March 1941, while she was on patrol in the Atlantic, that she picked up the signal sent by *Britannia* reporting that she was being attacked by a surface raider. Surgeon in the *Cilicia* was Dr Thomas Miller whose daughter was surgeon in the *Britannia*. As no further signal was received it was clear that the raider's attack had been successful and Dr Thomas Miller had three anxious days to wait before his mind was at rest. Twenty-four hours after Dr Nancy Miller's lifeboat pulled away from the doomed *Britannia* it was picked up by the Spanish steamer *Bachi*, having made some twenty-eight miles to the south in this time. The sixty-three survivors in the lifeboat were taken aboard and the Spaniard resumed her voyage. The scene now shifts to *Cilicia*. At 6.25am on the 28th she sighted a small steamer and at 7.15 sent away a boarding party to investigate her. It was the *Bachi*, and a signal

came from the boarding officer reporting that she had picked up survivors. By 9.30 they were alongside *Cilicia* and the first to reach the deck was Dr Nancy Miller, to be greeted by an overjoyed father. Two days later the survivors were landed at Freetown.

Post World War II, only *Cameronia* survived out of the newer transatlantic liners. The prospects were such that Anchor Line decided to withdraw altogether from the New York passenger trade in order to concentrate on cargo earnings with three sisters, *Egidia*, *Elysia* and *Eucadia*, equipped for just twelve discerning passengers. *Cameronia* found gainful employment as an Australian emigrant ship, ending her days as the troopship *Empire Clyde*, although she was still managed and crewed by Anchor Line. Only in May 1947 was *Cilicia* released from official duties and ready to resume her Bombay passenger service alongside the elderly *Castalia*, while in the following year she was rejoined by *Circassia* and by a third Fairfield sister, a new *Caledonia*, completed in 1948, not long after the war ended. The three-ship Indian service was well patronised and settled into a long-standing routine.

The company went through various ramifications and was owned by the United Molasses Company from 1953 with Runciman (London) Ltd retained

Seen at Avonmouth on New York duties in the early 1950s, *Elysia* (1945) was one of three sisters that were later transferred to the Indian routes.

as managers. In 1965 Moor Line Ltd of Newcastle upon Tyne (managed by Walter Runciman & Company) acquired Anchor Line, and in 1966 Moor Line purchased the managing company, Walter Runciman & Company. The final passenger voyage to India took place in 1966 after which selected cargo ship sailings from Glasgow via Liverpool to Bombay carried only twelve passengers.

In 1968 Moor Line changed its name to Walter Runciman & Company and transferred the ownership of the entire fleet to Anchor Line Ship Management. Anchor Line finally withdrew from the transatlantic trade in 1969, but became agents for the Atlantic Container Line traffic from Scotland and providing ancillary shore services for containers. The Runciman Group expanded again in 1969 with the acquisition of the Currie Line of Leith and in 1972 acquired George Gibson & Company, shipowners also of Leith. In 1976 Anchor Line had five operating divisions: Anchor Line Eastern Services (Far Eastern commercial activities); Anchor Line Ship Management (bulk carriers and managed vessels); Currie Line (European services, warehousing and road haulage); George Gibson & Company (gas tankers); Runciman Shipping (administration). Services diminished and shipowning ceased in the 1990s.

The Donaldson Line, which bought the Anchor-Donaldson company in 1935, owed its existence to the brothers William and John Donaldson. In 1855 they entered the South American trade using a series of chartered sailing ships. By 1858 they were sufficiently confident in their business to order a wooden barque, *John Taylor*, of just 299 tons gross, from MacMillan's shipyard at Dumbarton. She was followed by two larger barques from the same yard in 1860.

In 1870 the brothers announced their intention to start a steamship service from Glasgow to Montevideo and Buenos Aires. Later that year Barclay Curle delivered the *Astarte* and *Marina*. But after a fourth steamer had joined the fleet in 1874, the brothers realised that profits on the route would always be hindered by the seasonal summer downturn in trade. The company took the bold move of switching its fleet onto the Glasgow to Quebec and Montreal route in direct competition with the Allan Line. But it did this little by little, at first chartering its steamers to J & R Young & Company who were established in the Canadian trade from Glasgow, and only advertising its own services on the route from April 1878. Any idea that the Allan Line entered the South American trade in November 1876 in retaliation is incorrect, as the occasional Donaldson sailings to the St Lawrence were advertised under the sponsorship of Young & Company. In any case, Donaldson still maintained sailings to the River Plate and put its Canadian steamers back on this route during the closed winter freeze in the St Lawrence.

But the focus slowly changed in favour of Canada. A contemporary report states:

There was a lack of outward freight and it was uphill work competing with the Allans, but the rapid increase in the live cattle trade helped them materially and led to success. The ships do not carry many passengers either outwards or homewards, but they are favourite boats with cattle shippers and carry many fine horses from Canada for western breeders.

Indeed the two competing companies met head on, physically on one occasion, as T E Hughes reports in *Sea Breezes*, May 1967:

... on 22 May 1899 the *Cynthia*, inward bound for Montreal, had been in collision in the St Lawrence with the outward bound Allan liner *Polynesian*. According to contemporary reports the ships met head on. The *Cynthia* sank in a matter of minutes with the loss of seven lives; the *Polynesian*, saved by a strengthened fore peak, managed to reach Quebec where she was repaired in the recently opened graving dock. At the subsequent Court of Inquiry the pilot of the *Polynesian* was found to be in fault and damages were awarded to the Donaldson Line as owners of the *Cynthia*.

By 1900 the core Donaldson product had become Glasgow to Quebec and Montreal in summer and to St John, New Brunswick, in winter, along with a year-round service to Baltimore. In 1904 Donaldson took delivery of the four-masted *Athenia* from Vickers Son & Maxim at Barrow-in-Furness. After only a couple of voyages she was sent back to Barrow to be altered for the carriage of emigrants with berths for 450 third-class with just fifty berths upgraded to 'Intermediate' class. She was shortly joined by three more passenger carriers, *Cassandra* and *Letitia* from Scotts Shipbuilding yard at Greenock, and *Saturnia* from Connel & Company. Then in 1913 Donaldson returned to the South American trade by buying the three-ship Allan Line service to South America and its goodwill. In 1919 it formed Donaldson South American Line to amalgamate its own interests with the Glasgow Steamship Company which was managed by John Black & Company of Glasgow.

Anchor-Donaldson thrived post-war. Respectively in 1923 and 1925 the famous sisters *Athenia* and *Letitia* were delivered by Fairfield Shipbuilding & Engineering Company. The *Athenia* was laid down to Cunard order as the seventh in their A-class intermediate liner series, of which four maintained the company's London–Canada route and two its new Liverpool to Montreal service. While still on the stocks the unnamed 'A-class No. 7' was sold to Anchor-Donaldson and laid out internally to their specification. The *Letitia* was a repeat order. Unlike the Cunarders, which had counter sterns, the two Donaldson ships were built with the more modern-looking cruiser stern. Oddly, they were built with furnaces that could burn either coal or oil to provide steam to the turbine units. *Athenia* had bunker capacity for 1,442 tons of coal or 2,103 tons of fuel oil while the *Letitia* had slightly less capacity for 1,289 tons of coal or 1,877 tons of oil.

Athenia and *Letitia* were occasionally painted in Anchor colours, sometimes losing the white Donaldson band on the funnel. From 1923 a joint Cunard & Anchor-Donaldson service commenced with *Athenia* and *Letitia* sailing via Liverpool and the Cunarders sailing via Greenock. Anchor was now over-stocked with tonnage and suffered badly in the Depression. In 1932 it pledged 50 per cent of its holding in Anchor-Donaldson to the Union Bank and when the end of Henderson's Anchor Line came in 1935 the company was split thirty-six parts to the bank and sixty-four parts to Donaldson. Donaldson was financially strong enough to buy what remained, including *Athenia* and *Letitia*, and it registered the new company under the name Donaldson Atlantic Line, which then traded successfully until September 1939.

The tragic and untimely loss of *Athenia* nine hours into World War II is described in chapter 11. Needless to say, the loss left Donaldson without any passenger tonnage after the war, as the *Letitia* was sold to the Ministry of Transport as the troopship *Empire Brent*, and later took up the New Zealand emigrant trade as *Captain Cook*. Named after the explorer, one of her masters was another Captain Cook, the master of the ill-fated *Athenia* when she was sunk at the start of the Second World War. *Captain Cook* remained in service until the late 1950s.

In 1938 the managing company, Donaldson Brothers, changed its name to Donaldson Brothers & Black. After the war, the company resumed cargo services to North America, and in 1948 a passenger service was reinstated to Canada with the converted wartime standard Victory-type ships *Laurentia* and *Lismoria*. T E Hughes reported the arrival in service of the first of this pair in *Sea Breezes*, June 1967:

> The *Medina Victory* had been taken over from the Americans in June 1946, and operated under the ownership of the Ministry of Transport, managed by the Donaldson Line, until September 1947. She was then sent to the shipyard of Barclay, Curle & Company where she was refitted as a cargo carrier with accommodation for twelve passengers, and renamed *Laurentia*. She began her

Laurentia (1945) was built for the US Maritime Commission as the wartime standard ship *Medina Victory*. Converted by Donaldson Line in 1949, she could accommodate fifty-five passengers.

first voyage in Donaldson service on 30 December 1947, when she left for the US and Canadian west coast ports of Los Angeles, San Francisco and Vancouver with a cargo including 25,000 cases of Scotch whisky and 200 motor cars.

The sale of *Letitia*, although still crewed by Donaldson and wearing the company funnel colours, meant that the Donaldson Line now only offered twenty-four berths on the Canadian run. With support from the Scottish Tourist Board both *Laurentia* and *Lismoria* were taken in hand in 1948 and reconfigured to accommodate fifty-five first-class passengers. Ironically, it also meant a return of Donaldson passenger ships to Princes Dock, *Athenia* and *Letitia* generally having used the more easily accessed King George V Dock. The two former Victory ships, *Laurentia* and *Lismoria*, were very successful and for the next eighteen years spent their summers plying from Glasgow to Montreal and Quebec, and their winters to Los Angeles, San Francisco and Vancouver via Panama.

In 1955 *Captain Cook* was chartered back to the Donaldson Line to trial a Glasgow to Montreal and Quebec service, with a call at Liverpool, with cheap economy fares for 950 one-class passengers. The former *Letitia* managed only seven voyages before the experiment was deemed unsuccessful. She left the Clyde for the last time in October, returning to her New Zealand emigrant duties. *Laurentia* and *Lismoria* continued the passenger service but from the late 1950s both Cunard and Canadian Pacific started to call off Greenock on

Canadian Pacific's *Empress of England* (1956) arriving at Prince's Landing Stage, Liverpool, on 19 May 1964 before sailing to Canada via Greenock. (Author)

their co-ordinated summer schedule between Liverpool and Canada. The comparative luxury of the modern Cunarders *Carinthia* and *Sylvania* and the new 'White Empresses', *Empress of England* and *Empress of Britain*, and from 1961 *Empress of Canada* as well, were hardly fair competition for the Donaldson twins. But in 1961 *Sylvania* was transferred to New York duties and the Empresses were increasingly deployed on cruising. *Laurentia* and *Lismoria* were finally withdrawn at the end of the 1966 summer season. The Canadian Pacific service transferred to Southampton in 1970, maintained solely by *Empress of Canada*, and she closed that route just two years later.

Like many other shipping companies post-war, Donaldson had an eye on the burgeoning aviation industry. Its stated aim was to invest in British Overseas Airways Corporation and help develop air transport between UK and Canada. However, in 1946, chairman Norman Donaldson informed his shareholders 'The government have since decided that this development will be under their control, and the steamship lines are now precluded from participating'. A new cargo service commenced into the Great Lakes once the St Lawrence Seaway opened in 1959. The last ship built for the company was another *Letitia*, completed in 1961, and designed for the St Lawrence Seaway and Great Lakes service, complete with twelve passenger berths. But with the advent of containerisation, the company quickly became uncompetitive and was liquidated in the late 1960s. The chairman's report for 1959 summed up the position:

> I cannot foresee at the moment any improvement in the immediate future because of the large amount of laid-up tonnage throughout the world, and the continuing depressing effect which this has on the freight market. The results of the first few voyages in 1959 are very similar to those of last year, but I am glad to say that so far we have not had to cancel any voyages. There is still a grave shortage of homeward cargo, however, and if this continues it will, combined with the present unremunerative freight rates, again adversely affect our results and may further affect dividend distributions.

Although not in the transatlantic trade, but rather simply the Atlantic trade, it is interesting to note that G & J Burns looked out from its coasting business to the deep ocean in 1912. The *Evening Citizen*, a Glasgow-based newspaper, carried the report:

> Though there has been for a long number of years during the season a regular service between Leith and Iceland, there has never been one with this port, and Messrs Burns's new venture, in sending their *Ermine* to Iceland, opens up a new trade.

Ermine, fresh from the builder's yard, Fairfield Shipbuilding & Engineering, ran from Glasgow to Iceland calling at Oban for two summer seasons, 1912 and 1913, but the venture was not profitable, even carrying 'cruise' passengers, and was abandoned. *Ermine* reverted to her design route serving between Glasgow and Dublin; she was lost in the Aegean in 1917.

13

Bens and Clans – Cargo Liners to the Orient

THERE HAS ALWAYS BEEN a close association between the Scottish merchants and their associated shipping links with the Far East and Australia. This may have developed from the Scottish involvement in tea 'clippers' running the first of the season's tea crop back from China to London. But if it did, it also stemmed from the Scottish expatriate involvement with these regions from the early nineteenth century onwards. Whatever the reason, Scottish shipowners had a strong focus on Asia and Australia, whilst their English counterparts, also keen to compete, developed trading links more with the Americas, including the Pacific ports in South America.

Two of Scotland's best remembered shipping liner companies were the Henderson Line, Paddy Henderson & Company, which provided the link between Glasgow via Liverpool to Rangoon, Burma, and the Anchor Line running passenger cargo liners down to Karachi and Bombay (see chapters 4 and 12). Both companies played a strong part in support of Empire and in providing transport for the bastions of Empire, be they large and important commercial centres, or the more remote stations situated along the Burmese highway of the River Irrawaddy, or in the many trading centres up-country in India.

The cargo liners running to the Far East and Australia were equally important and in some circles better known. Those companies with a Scottish link included the famous Ben Line Steamers of Leith and Glasgow's Clan Line, formerly of Liverpool. Perhaps the most successful of the British cargo liner companies in the Far Eastern trades was Ben Line Steamers of Leith. The foundations of this company were laid in 1839 when Alexander and William Thomson bought the tiny barque *Carrara* to carry marble from Leghorn to supply building contractors with material that would help mark the prosperity Scotland then enjoyed. William Thomson & Company soon expanded operations beyond Italy, voyaging with an expanding sailing fleet first to Canada, then to Australia and in 1859 to the Far East. It was this latter trade that the Ben Line then focused on, adopting its new title when it started to name ships after Scottish mountains. Opportunity had allowed the family to move into the Baltic trade in 1865, bringing timber into east-coast UK ports until it sold this part of the company in 1927.

The Suez Canal opened in 1869 and steamships owned by P&O and Alfred Holt (Blue Funnel Line) were able to beat the fast clipper ships with ease by taking the shorter route through the Mediterranean. Some of their faster steamers were a match for the sailing ships, even before the canal opened. Conscious of the opportunity that the canal offered, William Thomson commissioned his first steamship, *Benledi*, in 1871. She was designed specifically to trade to the Far East. She was rigged as a brig and carried a full set of sail and extra deck crew to sail the ship. Three more steamers quickly followed, *Benarty* and *Bengloe*, built by Barclay Curle in 1876, and *Benalder*, built by Alexander Stephen & Sons. *Benarty* sailed on her maiden voyage from Glasgow and London for Japan and China and returned with a cargo of tea. *Bengloe* started life on charter to the Anchor Line taking pilgrims to Jeddah, while *Benalder*'s first voyage took her to China and then to New York, again with a full cargo of tea. Nevertheless, Thomson clearly hankered for the days of sail and built four more sailing ships before he retired, much to the consternation of the younger members of his family.

All of the ships belied the sailing era with classic bowsprits and figureheads to the fore – *Benlomond* of 1890, 2,670 tons gross – was typical of many. It was only after the Great War that the company commissioned straight-stemmed steamers. The family business was a proud and close-knit concern in which

Benlomond (1890) was built by A Stephen & Sons and was typical of the sail-rigged steamers commissioned by Thompson's Ben Line. (B & A Feilden)

high standards were maintained, and an intense practical and technical interest was always given to the finest detail. Sail was carried on all the company ships until 1906, but once it was abandoned fewer deck crew were needed.

The second generation Thomsons, James and a second William, steered the business forward so that by 1900 the Ben Line was firmly entrenched on the Far East routes, with regular voyages also on a number of other services. The next generation took over the business just before the Great War and it was they who had to contend both with war and the difficult trading patterns of the early 1930s. The company coped with the Depression by trading to many parts of the world, wherever cargoes needed uplifting and unloading. The fleet comprised twenty ships at the onset of the Second World War, of which fourteen were lost in the ensuing hostilities. Ben Line was able to buy a number of fast wartime standard turbine steamers after the war, including the turbo-electric heavy lift ships *Benarty* and *Benwyvis* which had been built by the Greenock Dockyard Company as *Empire Wallace* and *Empire Byng*, and the conventional turbine driven heavy lift ship *Benledi* which was built at Barrow as *Empire Admiral*. Each ship had three 120-ton derricks.

The new *Bencruachan*-class of steamers enabled Ben Line to get back quickly to a position of full trading after the war. *Bencruachan* was built by J L Thompson of Sunderland in 1946 and was followed immediately by

Benarty (1945) was one of three wartime standard heavy lift ships acquired by Ben Line after the war.

Benvorlich which was delivered by Connell & Company of Glasgow. The ships proved to be a little under-powered for the Far East trade in later years but could manage a stately 15 knots, match for most cargo liners that Blue Funnel or P&O could muster in the late 1940s. Thereafter, Ben Line Steamers became a progressive component of various Far Eastern conferences in which it was continuously upgrading standards. In 1963 the great-grandson of founder William Thomson became a senior partner.

The company was always on the lookout for suitable second-hand tonnage. Perhaps the oddest were the former escort aircraft carriers USS *Willapa* and USS *Perdita*. They were from a class of nineteen carriers built in 1943 and 1944 from standard C3 cargo ship hulls for the US Navy and converted at Seattle for use by the Royal Navy. Mitchell and Sawyer in *Wartime Standard Ships* described the conversion:

> The flight deck was lengthened, Asdic for tracking submarines was installed, fire-fighting arrangements and air ventilation were increased, torpedo and bomb storage altered to accommodate both British and American types and steam lines were installed for de-icing. Internally, the ships contained hardly any wood, but the 450 feet long by 80 feet wide flight deck, unlike British built carriers, was planked.

The nineteen carriers were sent to Britain as part of the Lend Lease Programme, the USS *Willapa* became the Canadian-crewed carrier HMS

Former aircraft carrier, *Bennevis* (1944), at Southampton, August 1964. (Author)

Puncher and the USS *Perdita* the British-crewed HMS *Trouncer*. They each had a crew of 890 and supported thirty aircraft. In 1946 they were converted to cargo ships and in 1957 acquired by Ben Line and given the names *Bennevis* and *Benrinnes* respectively. Most of the other carriers were returned to the United States after the war and also converted to cargo ships, but another pair, HMS *Reaper* and HMS *Premier*, were converted in 1948 for Blue Star Line as *South Africa Star* and *Rhodesia Star* respectively. The *Bennevis* and *Benrinnes* survived in the fleet until sold for demolition in 1973. In the meantime, the fleet was upgraded with the new 20-knot *Benloyal*-class coming into service from 1959 onwards.

Ben Line pursued a vigorous post-war rebuilding programme of which the *Benmacdhui* and *Benavon* were typical of the 15-knot steam turbine ships then in vogue. The company built up a fleet of thirty-three modern cargo liners by 1970, many built by Charles Connell & Company of Scotstoun, with seven departures each month to the Far East from a variety of British and European ports. Flagship of the fleet was *Benlawyers*, completed by Upper Clyde Shipbuilders, into which Connell had been subsumed, in 1970. She had an operational speed of 21½ knots. The fleet was sustained by numerous shore offices in Europe and overseas, all of which were dedicated to providing customers with a service that was trusted, reliable, rapid and, above all, good value for money.

Benavon (1949) approaching the King George Dock entrance in the Humber in July 1968. (Author)

Ben Line started to collaborate with Ellerman Lines in the early 1970s when five Ellerman ships were given Ben Line livery – effectively sold by Ellerman, although with rights of ownership still retained by Ellerman. In 1965 Ben Line had become a consortium member within ACT – Associated Container Transportation – and this eventually led Ellerman Lines and Ben Line to develop Ben Line Containers. In 1972 and 1973 it introduced three large container ships to the Far East run: *Benalder*, *Benavon* and jointly

Benedin (1956), newly renamed in February 1968, was an example of increased collaboration with Ellerman Lines. Formerly Ellerman's *City of Winnipeg* and later reverting to Ellerman's City Lines as *City of Delhi* in 1970. (Author)

Container ship *Benavon* (1973) was one of the three 58,000 gross ton container ships. (John Clarkson)

owned with Ellerman, *City of Edinburgh*; each was a massive 58,440 tons gross. The new container ships carried 2,687 TEU (twenty feet equivalent units) at an amazing 26 knots. Ben Line Containers was part of 'Trio' Lines jointly maintained with Hapag-Lloyd and the Japanese lines NYK and Mitsui-OSK lines. From then on conventional cargo liner services were pooled with Liverpool's Blue Funnel Line and its associated Glen & Shire Line, under the trading name Ben Ocean, with Ben maintaining commercial management of the combined fleet.

Ben Line, with its entire fleet still registered at Leith, went into bulk chemical transport jointly with an American company, into bulk transport of timber and plywood imports from the Middle East in collaboration with the East Asiatic Company, and also into ship management. In 1976 Ben Line acquired the Newcastle-based Sheaf Steam Shipping Company. By the mid 1970s Ben Line was one of the first shipping companies to invest in the offshore oil development industry when it commissioned the self-propelled jack up rig *Ocean Tide*. In 1976 the *Ben Ocean Lancer* was commissioned with a capability of drilling over 3,000ft of water. But like so much of the British mercantile marine, competition from foreign companies with lower overheads and staff costs made inroads into the fortunes of the Ben Line, which soon became vulnerable to a hostile takeover. The board, still including a number of descendants of the Thomson family, combined its interests with that of the Danish East Asiatic Company in 1991. Reluctantly, it decided to sell its shipping interests altogether the following year. By 1996 its only asset was a single drilling rig, although Ben Line exists to this day as an active shipping agency.

When in 1959 Ben Line Steamers introduced its 20-knot *Benloyal*-class and reduced the passage time between London and Hong Kong to nineteen days and to Shanghai to twenty-one days, the Glen Line response was the 24-knot *Glenlyon*-class. But the closure of the Suez Canal from 1967 to 1970 put extraordinary pressure on the operations of Ben Line, reducing the trade between Europe and China to a minimum. The merger of Ben and Glen Line interests in 1974 under the Ben Ocean Services banner effectively brought the Glen Line back to its Scottish roots.

The Clan Line was born in England but moved north across the border at an early age. The founder of the Clan Line, Charles Cayzer, was born in July 1843 in London to Charles William, a school teacher, and Mary Cayzer. Charles had six sisters, all of whom died from tuberculosis as children. Charles worked first as a master's clerk aboard a sailing vessel destined for Japan and India. At Bombay he left the ship and worked at William Nicol & Company, the agents for the British India Steam Packet Company, where Cayzer soon became familiar with the business of the agency. He married Agnes Elizabeth Trickey from Bristol in May 1868. Five years later they returned home on leave, and it was then that Cayzer formed a vision of a steam packet company running between Liverpool via Suez to Bombay. Charles's next post was with Gray, Dawes & Company in London, associates of British India. He then took his family to Liverpool, where in 1877 he created ship chandlers Rudstad & Cayzer and became a shipowner, acquiring the majority 64th shares in the 27-year-old barque *Jalawar*.

Jalawar made a number of profitable trips to Bombay before Cayzer was able to invest in the larger *North Star*, his resources unable to extend to a steamship. In 1878 Cayzer approached shipbuilder Alexander Stephen of Glasgow to ask if he would be willing to help resource a new shipping company. Alexander Stephen's shipyard was then short of orders and Stephen recognised Cayzer's proposal as a win-win deal. Two iron-hulled screw steamers were laid down in 1878. Each cost £34,000 and Cayzer was to find one-third of the cost of each vessel, while Stephen covered the other two-thirds, which was to be repaid within three years of delivery.

Charles Cayzer took his friend Captain Alexander Irvine into partnership. Irvine, a Scot and former British India master, had first met Cayzer in Bombay where they developed a great respect for each other. Irvine was put in charge of the new Liverpool office and Cayzer, Irvine & Company began trading in March 1878. Irvine did little to promote the new company, however, and he died the following year.

Cayzer Irvine's first ship was launched as *Clan Alpine* in September 1878, followed two months later by *Clan Fraser*. The ships' compound engines sustained a speed of 10 knots although they were also rigged as brigs with a full set of sail. Accommodation was provided for thirty-six first-class passengers on the upper deck. The single fare to Bombay was 25 guineas (£25 25s, or £26.25 in decimal currency) with concessions available for family groups, missionaries, railway employees and servants. The fare included all meals, but any alcohol required during the voyage had to be brought aboard by the passenger.

Two more steamers were ordered from Alexander Stephen and a further two also from Archibald McMillan at Dumbarton. The six-ship fleet then comprised the original *Clan Alpine* and *Clan Fraser*, plus *Clan Ranald*, *Clan Gordon*, *Clan Stuart* and *Clan Lamont*. A new monthly service commenced. A significant expense in running the service was the canal dues for passage through Suez, almost as much as the combined cost of the bunkers and crew wages for each voyage. The service was extended to include Colombo, Madras, and Calcutta in 1881. Calls also commenced at South African ports on some voyages after *Clan Lamont* had experimentally called at Cape Town in September 1881 to test the market. In due course ships also started to call at Lourenço Marques (Maputo), Beira and Mauritius. The company appointed the best cargo agents it could find; these were Turnbull & Martin at Glasgow, Gellatly, Hankey & Sewell at both Liverpool and Manchester, J & R Grant at London and Tellefsen, Wills at Cardiff. Overseas agents were Aitken, Spence & Company at Colombo, Gordon, Woodroffe & Company at Madras, Findlay, Muir at Bombay and James Searight & Company at Cape Town.

Further expansion was inhibited by lack of cash. With the help of Alexander Stephen and others the Clan Line Association was formed in 1881 by a group of merchants in Glasgow. It quickly raised £720,000 which could be used both to pay off Alexander Stephen and to assure a supply of new ships. Cayzer, Irvine & Company, the Clan Line, had always aspired to be Scottish even from its base at Liverpool, and it now moved its allegiance to Glasgow. From then on it also provided a regular service from west-coast UK ports to South Africa and was a founder member of the South African Conference in 1883. Both Ellerman and the family-run Thomas & James Harrison Company of Liverpool looked on with envy as reported by James Taylor in his history of Ellermans:

> Discussions with Clan Line ensued and an agreement resulted which was designed to provide sufficient regular sailings to keep away any opposition and at the same time be adequate to accommodate the growing trade which was moving to South Africa and Mauritius. It started with a fourteen day service to be provided by Clan, Ellerman and Harrison lines, with Clan taking the lion's share of the arrangement. As an entrance fee, it was agreed that the newcomers would pay Clan 5 shillings per ton on all freight exceeding 25 shillings per ton, for a period of three years ... At this time, trade from the west coast of the United Kingdom was outwards only, the ships thereafter shifting elsewhere for homeward employment.

In June 1890 Clan Line Steamers was formed at a meeting of subscribers to the new company. Charles Cayzer held the majority of shares in the thirteen ships that the new company owned. The company issued 5,000 shares at a value of £50 each and raised mortgage debentures to allow six new steamers to be ordered, three from Alexander Stephen and three from William Doxford of Sunderland. In the meantime some of the existing fleet were upgraded: *Clans*

Clan Macarthur (1883) was one of the original Clan Line fleet lengthened in the 1890s.

Macarthur, Macintosh, Macpherson and *Matheson* were re-engined with triple expansion machinery and crew and passenger accommodation upgraded. In 1893, when the six new ships were in service, the company was able to start a new service between New York and South Africa. In 1894 the Persian Gulf was accessed by buying into the Persian Gulf Steamship Company.

In 1895 the Clan Line gained access to the new port of Manchester. This came about because of the failure of the Manchester, Bombay & General Navigation Company registered in Manchester by Christopher Furness in 1894. Furness planned to carry finished cotton goods to India and bring raw cotton and other goods inbound. But Furness had overlooked the strength of the Conference system. He was bought off the route by the Conference members for £11,000 and as a consequence, two of those members, Glasgow's Clan Line and Anchor Line, became established at Manchester right from the very early days of the port. The first sailings on the lucrative Manchester cotton route took place in January 1895: Anchor Line's *Hispania* on the 5th, Clan Line's *Clan Fraser* on the 15th, both to Bombay, and the *Clan Drummond* on the 16th to Calcutta. The new Indian service attracted a premium bulk tariff of 20s per ton, 3s 6d more than the existing service to Liverpool, but a significant saving on the combined Liverpool rate plus forwarding by rail to Manchester.

Clan Matheson was used as a cruise ship when it carried Charles Cayzer and his guests to the opening of the Kiel Canal. Sir Donald Currie took *Tantallon*

Castle to Kiel for the same purpose with Mr Gladstone as one of his guests. Charles was knighted in 1897 and was present at the Diamond Jubilee Naval Review aboard *Clan Macpherson*.

A service to southern India began in 1896 at the invitation of the Chartering Coalition, formed by coffee growers in 1886 to ensure a regular service for coffee exports. Several Clan Line ships were requisitioned as transports during the Boer War and this served to consolidate the Cape trade for the company. Clan Line ships did not initially have return cargo rights in Africa and went light to Mauritius and India to return via the Suez Canal with full loads comprising sugar, hides, tea, cotton and grain.

The first of five big 'turret' steamers was delivered in 1897 after a trial period using Angier Brothers' *Imperialist* and *Bullionist*. The turret-deck ships were built to take advantage of the Suez Canal dues, which were based entirely on the area of the main deck. They had very narrow main decks stepped down onto the hull to form low harbour decks. Consequently there was a loss of stability when the ship rolled due to the lack of buoyancy on the stepped-down hull. In addition, whenever the harbour deck got submerged the ship was severely inhibited from self-righting. They did roll heavily, sometimes not altogether in sequence with a beam sea, but careful loading with dense and

Clan Macdonald (1897) was the first of the turret ships and was built by William Doxford and launched into the Tyne.

heavy goods stowed low in the holds ensured that the ship's centre of gravity was kept reasonably low. *Clan Macdonald* was the first of thirty Clan Line turret ships, the last of which was *Clan Buchanan*, completed in 1907. They were all built at William Doxford's yard in Sunderland, except *Clan Cumming* and *Clan Ferguson*, which were built under licence by Vickers Sons and Maxim at Barrow. A total of 180 turret decks were built, all but four by Doxford.

Two of the Clan Line turret-deck fleet did indeed capsize. *Clan Ranald*, under the command of Captain Arthur Gladstone, had 6,500 tons of Australian grain aboard, a further 70 tons of bunker coal on the turret deck, and 50 tons more on the 'tween deck. She developed a slight list at her anchorage before leaving Adelaide on 31 January 1909, was soon hove to and anchored, but nothing could stop her eventually rolling right over with significant loss of life. The outcome of the inquiry was an instruction that the bottom tanks should be flooded if bulk cargo was loaded above the turret deck. In July 1919 *Clan Gordon*, another product of Doxford and, like *Clan Ranald*, completed in 1900, was also lost when her master decided to ignore the earlier loading and ballasting instruction. The ship was on passage from New York via Panama to China. Two days into the voyage the master tested his ship's stability by steering hard a-port and then hard a-starboard without undue heeling. This result prompted him to pump out the ballast in the two forward bottom tanks to raise the bows and give the propeller better submergence with the idea of increasing the ship's speed. Within hours *Clan Gordon* developed a noticeable list to starboard and when the ship was put to port for sun bearings in the late afternoon she heeled right over never to recover. *Clan Gordon* capsized in a slow roll that allowed the entire crew to walk over the side and on to the upturned bottom of the vessel to await rescue. At the Board of Trade inquiry the master took full blame for the loss.

In 1910 a consortium of Clan, Ellerman and Harrison lines muscled in on the German-dominated trade from the Continent to East Africa and the British India company's services from United Kingdom east-coast ports to East Africa. The consortium became members of the East African Conference in 1913. A rift between Ellerman and Clan developed in the Great War regarding the Indian services, but this was amicably resolved by letting Ellerman's Hall Line have 7/24ths of the homeward trade from the Malabar coast and allowing Ellerman up to twelve sailings a year to Madras. Clan then raised an objection about the Hall Line loading at Glasgow, and so continued the never-ending tiff.

Charles Cayzer died at the age of seventy-three at his home near Aberfoyle in September 1916. His third son, August Cayzer, became Chairman. Clan

Line owned sixty ships at the outset of the Great War, but only thirty-two of these survived the hostilities. All the losses were due to enemy action save *Clan Macnaughton*, which foundered in the North Atlantic in 1915 while serving as an Armed Merchant Cruiser.

In 1918 the company acquired Scottish Shire Line from Sir James Caird. Scottish Shire was in the chilled meat trade from Australia and New Zealand. Clan Line also bought the Houston Line, also in the chilled and refrigerated meat trade, but to South America and South and East Africa. These acquisitions were a useful way of replacing lost tonnage and getting the company back into full civilian trading mode. They also gave Clan Line access to new Conferences; Robert Houston had for years denied Charles Cayzer full access to the South African Conference, yet for the right price was willing to be bought out. Clan Line now had return loading rights from South Africa and access to the important South American meat trade. Clan Line also bought the Greenock Dockyard Company which became its main supplier of new ships.

The entire fleet was kept occupied during the difficult trading period of the later 1920s and early 1930s. However, August Cayzer led a restructuring of the company in 1926 and again in 1932. Only four new vessels were ordered between 1924 and 1936, and two of them *Clan Macdonald* and *Clan Macdougall*, built in 1928 and 1929 respectively, were motor ships, the first in the fleet. They were equipped with Burmeister and Wain double acting four-stroke air injection engines. They were also the first company ships to have a long foredeck with a single 120-ton derrick for heavy lifts.

In 1938 Clan and Anchor lines signed a new agreement with the Manchester Chamber of Commerce and the Bradford Chamber whereby all the Lancashire cotton imports to Manchester would be by Conference members' ships. This meant additional business for Anchor and Clan lines in the Bombay Conference.

Clan Line lost twenty-seven ships in the Second World War; *Clan Chisholm* was the first loss, torpedoed in the North Atlantic on 17 October 1939. Clan Line ships were present at almost all the more hazardous arenas of the war: Dunkirk, Aegean, East Africa, Malta convoys, Singapore and Java. Many men were lost; 541 men died including 507 Lascars, while 111 men were taken prisoner. Significantly the president of the Chamber of Shipping and subsequently chairman of Clan Line, Herbert Cayzer, who had adopted the title Lord Rotherwick in 1937, helped to promote the arming of merchant ships. In 1943 chairman Sir August Cayzer, also a director of the Suez Canal Company, died. His successor as chairman of Clan Line was Lord Rotherwick.

There are many Clan Line war stories but that of the loss of *Clan Fraser* and *Clan Cumming* are tragic. *Clan Cumming*, under the command of Captain J D Matthews, had limped into Piraeus after receiving a torpedo in No. 1 hold on 12 January 1941. Following dry docking, she moored three ship lengths from the newly arrived *Clan Fraser* which was unloading a cargo of ammunition and TNT. On the night of 6 April *Clan Fraser* was bombed and set alight. Captain Matthews, OBE, recalled the incident in an article in *Sea Breezes*, January 1948:

> I watched her burning from the lower bridge until 2am, and by then she was red hot fore and aft. I then retired into my cabin and lay down half dressed. I was nearly asleep when the whole world seemed to burst asunder. The *Clan Cumming* heeled over till she seemed to be on her beam ends and then rolled heavily for some time. All the woodwork in the room crashed down and then came the rain of molten metal which had to be seen to be believed – the *Clan Fraser*, which still had some explosives on board, had blown up. Among other things, we had one of her plates, 23 feet by 3 feet by 5/8 inch wrapped round our main-top and about half of her windlass had crashed through our No. 4 hatch and set fire to timber in our 'tween decks. Later a section of her structure weighing 12½ tons was found nearly three quarters of a mile away, and about 30 feet of her 40 ton derrick was found in a nearby park.

Clan Cumming was one of the few survivors of the fourteen deep-sea ships in port that night. Captain Matthews finally sailed from Piraeus on 14 April, only for his ship to hit a floating mine. As *Clan Cumming* settled rapidly by the stern, the ship's company took to the boats, to be rescued by a Greek destroyer some five hours later.

After the war, the losses were made good by purchase of twenty-six former government ships and a programme of new building, much of it innovative. The Greenock Dockyard company delivered a new *Clan Cumming* and *Clan Maclaren* in 1946, and a further quartet up until 1949, but with austerity measures still in place, neither vessel had hot water on tap, even in the officers' cabins, and a steward had to fetch water from the galley. But conditions on some of the older ships were primitive indeed, as John Moffat described in an article first published in *Sea Breezes*, October 1988:

> After passing Gibraltar we changed into tropical gear as it was very warm in the Mediterranean. Bathing facilities in the *Clan MacNeil* fell somewhat short of modern standards. We only had running salt water in the bathrooms and to

have a bath we obtained a bucket of hot water from the 'hotwell' in the engine room. This was emptied into a small galvanised bath which fitted into a hole in a specially constructed wooden board which rested in the large bath.

The next move was to go to the pump in the working alleyway and pump up two or three buckets of cold to tepid fresh water which was then poured into the small bath so that we could have a stand-up wash. It was a bit primitive but we kept ourselves clean and managed to wash our clothes afterwards.

The Scottish Tanker Company was created in 1951 by Cayzer, Irvine & Company in recognition of the growing oil tanker market and managed by Huntly Cook & Company. The ships carried the Clan Line funnel of black with two broad red bands, save that the narrow black band between the red bands was painted pale blue. The first new ships were *Scottish Lion* and *Scottish Eagle*. In 1956 Scottish Tankers became part of British and Commonwealth Shipping, still under the control of Cayzer, Irvine & Company. In 1962, after the termination of the Norwegian whaling industry, two whaling ships from the Hector Whaling Company were transferred into the Scottish Tanker Company (now Thompson Steam Shipping Company) fleet following the acquisition of Hector Whaling the previous year.

The routine company operations rarely made the news. Indeed, few noticed the merger of Clan Line and Union-Castle Line to form British &

Scottish Lion (1952), along with sister *Scottish Eagle*, were the first tankers in the newly formed Scottish Tankers fleet.

Commonwealth Shipping Company in 1955. With it came the small tramping fleet of King Line which was wholly owned by Union-Castle. King Line was created in 1889 by Owen Philipps, later Lord Kylsant, and chairman of the Royal Mail Group until his and the group's demise in 1931. In 1959 the all-

Last of the King Line tramps: *King Henry* (1958) unloading sulphur from South America at Irwell Park Wharf, Manchester, on tramp duties in June 1962. (Author)

Clan Macleod (1948) and her cargo of rhinoceros drew compassion from striking dockers at London who discharged the animals ready for transhipment to their respective zoos.

diesel tramp fleet of King Line forsook its yellow funnels with black tops to become owned and managed by Clan Line and repainted in Clan colours. The fleet included wartime-built vessels which were quickly sold, and six modern ships of the same hull form, starting with *King Malcolm*, which was delivered in 1952, and ending with *King Henry*, delivered in 1958. The *King Malcolm*-class continued in the tramp and charter market but were eventually integrated into the main liner fleet, and later sold during the early 1970s.

In 1972 *Clan Macleod*, one of the post-war Greenock built ships, did hit the headlines. She arrived in the Thames with twenty-six white rhinoceros loaded in wooden crates as deck cargo at Durban, and destined for various UK zoos and safari parks. The problem was that the London dockers were on strike and the ship was ordered to anchor off Southend. The animals weighed anything up to three tons and their disquiet at the Southend anchorage was quickly highlighted by the press. The dockers rallied to the 'humanitarian' cry and a gang was sent out to the ship by tug to load the crates into barges for immediate discharge ashore and onward transhipment to their destinations. The press had a field day and in the *Daily Express*, a cartoon by Giles portrayed *Clan Macleod* as a modern day Noah's Ark challenging the might of the dockers!

But, in due course, and like all the other British deep-sea liner companies, Clan Line suffered badly at the hands of the cheaper foreign flag fleets and failed to commit to the container era in time to save its position in the South African and more distant trades. By the early 1980s the merged interests of

Clan Macgregor (1962) was one of the last general cargo ships to serve Clan Line.

Clan Ranald (1965) arriving at Southampton on 26 June 1969. (Author)

Cayzer Irvine and Union-Castle Line under the British & Commonwealth banner operated just twelve ships, five of which were large bulk carriers owned by King Line. Of the others there were two general cargo ships, *Clan Macgillivray* and *Clan Macgregor* completed in 1962 for the Indian route, and five refrigerated cargo ships, including the sisters *Clan Ranald*, *Clan Ross* and *Clan Robertson* built in 1965 and 1966 for the South African service, but renamed firstly with Castle names and later by 'Universal' names. As the company's shipping interests declined, Cayzer Irvine/British & Commonwealth took to banking and insurance as well as aircraft, machine tool manufacture, making fork lift trucks, soft drinks and computers. This diversification was such that in the early 1980s a telephone caller enquiring about one of the company's former ships was told in no uncertain terms, 'British & Commonwealth has nothing to do with ships and has never had such a connection'!

14

Tramps, Bulkers, Other Specialists and the Jute Trade

OF ALL THE NUMEROUS Scottish tramp shipowners, large and small, Maclay & McIntyre of Glasgow and H Hogarth & Sons of Ardrossan, affectionately known as 'Hungry Hogarths' and not without reason, were undoubtedly the most successful. Smaller companies were also successful in their own right including, for example, Watson Brothers of Glasgow, whose sailing ship and steamer names all began with *Ben*, Crawford & Barr's Vale Steamship Company with the ship name suffix *-vale*, and Purdie, Glen & Company of Glasgow, formerly Purdie, Glen & Murray, whose steamers' names all began with the prefix *Auchen-*. Employed solely in tramping, one of the fleet, *Auchenblae*, built in 1902, was elevated to the liner trades when she was sold to Manchester Liners in the Great War and briefly carried the name *Manchester Trader* until she was sunk by gunfire in 1917. Several other small Scottish tramping companies are now all but forgotten. Who, for example, remembers the Glasgow based tramps of Clark & Service's Ardan Steamship Company, George Nisbet & Company's Clydesdale Navigation Company,

Typical of the Watson Brothers' fleet was *Ben Nevis* (1905) built by Russell & Company of Aberdeen. (John Clarkson)

Auchenblae (1902), typical of the Purdie, Glen & Murray fleet of tramp steamers was elevated to liner duties when sold in 1917 to Manchester Liners to become *Manchester Trader.*

Barrdale (1925) was a typical unit in the Barr Shipping Company managed by Barr Crombie.

The oldest ship lost during the Great War in the Gow Harrison fleet was *Venetia* (1898).

Vancouver (1905) was one of the last dry cargo tramp steamers to be operated by Gow Harrison, who increasingly focused on the tanker charter market.

Campbell & Son, Crawford Shipping Company, Glen & Company, David Alexander & Sons (Grove Line), Monro Brothers and even Barr Shipping, with its characteristic Barr names, *Barrdale, Barrhill, Barrwhin,* etc?

Gow Harrison & Company was created with the merger of Alan C Gow & Company and P H Dixon & Harrison in 1895. The Gow Harrison tramp fleet mostly had names beginning with 'V' but also owned tankers from 1913 for charter to the major oil companies. Six of the company's eighteen ships were lost in the Great War including *Venetia*, completed in 1898, and the oldest ship in a modern fleet. The tanker fleet was developed between the wars and the last tramp steamers were sold, *Vancouver* in 1932 and *Vestalia* in 1933. Gow Harrison ceased trading in 1951 but Harrisons (Clyde) Ltd was formed in 1956 to own and manage the three tramp ships in the Dornoch Shipping Company and the Nile Steamship Company. In 1960 the Monarch Steamship Company (formerly Raeburn & Verel) was taken over. A few years later Harrisons (Clyde) went into bulk carrier management and later into offshore oil support as the majority owner of the Stirling Shipping Company.

Raeburn & Verel started trading as Raeburn & Dunn in 1873 and in 1878 became Raeburn and Verel when William Raeburn adopted John Verel as his new partner on the retirement of Captain Dunn. Their first ships were *Galatea*, 2,000 tons gross and built in 1870, and *Marbella*, an 800-ton steamer of the same vintage. The company focused on trade with America and the Far East where its main income was opportunist tramping with occasional charter voyages to liner companies. The company thrived and owned fourteen ships

Caledonian Monarch (1928), built by Napier & Miller, Old Kilpatrick for Raeburn & Verel. On 14 January 1942, *Caledonian Monarch* (Master James Valentine Stewart) was reported missing after the convoy SC-63 was dispersed in position 51°N/62°W. The master and forty crew members were lost.

by 1890. It rebranded as the Monarch Steamship Company with delivery of *British Monarch* in 1902. Sir William Raeburn (1850–1934) was elected Unionist party MP for Dunbartonshire in 1918 and served two terms of office, standing down in 1923. Rebuilding in the 1920s, a new *British Monarch*-class (*British*, *Caledonian*, *Celtic* and *Imperial Monarch*) comprised two-deckers capable of 12 knots and able to burn either coal or oil. They were attractive-looking ships with distinctive cowl-topped funnels. The Monarch Steamship Company lost six ships in the Great War and thereafter only maintained a small fleet of six or eight ships. It rebuilt again in the 1950s when the motor ships *British Monarch*, *Celtic Monarch* and *Scottish Monarch* were delivered, and it was this modern fleet that was taken over by Harrisons (Clyde) in 1960, but allowed to retain the distinctive fleet nomenclature and red funnels with black tops. The final ship in the Monarch Steamship Company fleet was another *British Monarch*, a first generation bulk carrier (18,616 tons gross) completed in 1965 by Scotts Shipbuilding & Engineering at Greenock and leased by the builders to Harrisons. After a long working life and three further owners she was scrapped in China in 1998.

Another long-forgotten company is W S Miller & Company of Glasgow. Second-hand ships formed the nucleus of the fleet when trading started in 1892, and in 1903 Miller renamed his company the Ellaston Steam Ship Company. Eleven ships were lost in the Great War, leaving only three

Lornaston (1925), built by R Duncan & Co, Port Glasgow, for Glasgow tramp owners W S Miller & Co. She was sold in 1940 to Galbraith, Pembroke & Company. On 8 March 1945, *Lornaston* (Master David Cownie) was torpedoed and sunk by *U-275* northwest of Fécamp. The master, forty crew members and seven gunners were picked up by HMS *Holmes* and HMS *Palencia* and landed at Newhaven.

surviving vessels. One second-hand and four new ships were received in the 1920s, the last *Lornaston* in 1925, replacing older ships which were all sold in the 1920s. The owners of the company retired from shipowning in 1940 and the remaining fleet was disposed of.

There were many other companies – the Queen Line of Glasgow, for example, is typical. It was founded by Thomas Dunlop, provisions merchant of Glasgow, in 1868, and successfully evolved from a fleet of sailing barques to one of steamships. His first ship, *Wye*, was purchased in London for £2,800 but lost money on her first voyage for Dunlop and his partner John Neil, due to the master's liking for strong drink. Once Captain Joseph Stediford, an Isle of Wight man, was appointed, *Wye* turned profitable and was sold to raise cash for a new barque, *Marion Neil*, in 1871. Dunlop commissioned his first steamer, *Clan Davidson*, in 1883. The Clan nomenclature encompassed nine sailing ships, including the celebrated *Clan Mackenzie* which was known to outstrip even *Thermopylae*, herself the envy of *Cutty Sark*. Captain Harris, one-time master of *Clan Mackenzie* recalled: 'This vessel was the best I was ever in. You could do anything with her and she was always dependable with a good breeze to do 360 miles in 24 hours when deep loaded'. Dunlop operated several four-masted barques in the 1890s.

Dunlop abandoned the Clan Line nomenclature to avoid confusion with Cayzer Irvine and adopted that of Queen Line. In the late Victorian era, royal emissaries attended launches of three of a class of seven steamers built at Sunderland: *Queen Olga*, Queen of Greece, *Queen Louise*, Queen of Denmark and *Queen Cristina*, Queen Regent of Spain, while others such as *Queen Eleanor*, Queen of Aquitaine, had long since passed on.

Queen Elizabeth, built in 1907, was one of the first British ships to suffer at the hands of the trade union movement at an overseas port. Alongside at Bombay in June 1914, Boatswain Wilson challenged Captain Henry Munro to reduce the crew working hours or he would charge them to cease work. The Captain went ashore to see the shipping master and on his return found the ship silent, the crew on strike save for two boys, and Wilson nowhere to be seen. Captain Munro charged Wilson with disobeying lawful commands and the magistrate then ruled that the crew had not complained about the hours when they signed on, that Wilson had disobeyed orders, and had persuaded others to do likewise. He was jailed for three weeks. Boatswain Wilson, it later transpired, was brother to Havelock Wilson, the celebrated trade unionist pioneer.

The Queen Line steamers were mainly spar-deckers suitable for charter into the liner trades. By the start of the Great War the company operated ten steamers, and it bought three second-hand post-war, *Queen Eleanor*,

Queen Eleanor (1896) was the sixth in a class of seven steamers ordered from Bartram Haswell & Company at Sunderland

Queen Maud and *Queen Olga*, to compensate for war losses. In the 1930s the company received four new motor ships as part of the Government Scrap and Build Scheme. During World War II the company managed *Empire Freetown* for the Ministry of Transport, and the Liberty ship *Samaye*, which after the war was purchased and named *Queen Victoria* under Captain George Hyslop. Captain Hyslop took command of *Queen Anne* when his former command was sold. *Queen Anne* was formerly the newsprint carrier *Kelmscott*, built in 1943 for the Newsprint Supply Company, which was owned by the British newspaper industry to ensure newsprint imports could be maintained during the war. *Queen Anne* carried out a number of charters for the New Zealand Line, P&O and Elder Dempster. Dunlop's Queen Line continued to trade up to the mid 1950s when the last ship, another *Queen Eleanor*, built in 1943 as *Stanpark*, was sold and the company dissolved.

By way of contrast, Maclay & McIntyre was at one time the biggest shipowner in Britain, with a fleet of fifty vessels trading worldwide by the eve of the Great War, but greatly diminished after the war. Hogarth also was the largest tramp shipowner in Britain, when, at the eve of the Second World War, it held a fleet of thirty-nine ships. The tramping industry, by no means glamorous, was lucrative, provided owners could distribute their fleet across the Seven Seas, ready to move in on potential cargoes. The trick was always to minimise the prospect of light-ship voyages. It was also hard work for the crew as cargoes ranged from bulk minerals such as coal, a variety of ores or sulphur, other dense cargoes, timber and, of course, grain. At each loading port the deep holds had to be in a fit state to carry the next cargo. Malcolm Cooper sums up the trade in an article which first appeared in *Ships Monthly*, February 2009:

> Supply demand and prices of these [cargoes] were highly cyclical, and freight rates correspondingly volatile. This volatility was reflected in the prices of new and second-hand ships. The key to success was to build up a fleet relatively cheaply in slump conditions, earn high rewards from shipping freight in the following boom, and then reduce the fleet, reaping considerable capital gains in the process as prices peaked before the next slump set in.
>
> All this called for excellent market intelligence and timing, strong nerves, and a reputation for success which could attract shippers and investors at the right time in the cycle. Both Maclay and McIntyre possessed these attributes in abundance.

Joseph Maclay, a shipping clerk, and Walter McIntyre, an ironmonger, first set up in business in 1885. They successfully canvassed enough financial support to acquire the four-ship fleet of G Hood & Company of Glasgow, and buy a fifth second-hand vessel and the brand new *General Gordon* from Alexander Stephen, the latter against a soft mortgage. The pair cleverly used a variety of ownership companies, each company packaged specifically to attract investors in a particular sector of trade. This was common practice among the tramp shipowners in the late nineteenth and early twentieth century. Expansion was rapid so that by 1890 they had fourteen ships at sea and just five years later had increased their fleet to a massive thirty-five ships. The owners adopted an African nomenclature for their ships, no doubt reflecting keen personal support of various missionary expeditions.

Joseph Maclay, known to his crews as 'Holy Joe', was the driving force of the company and served as shipping controller for much of the Great War, a service for which he was later knighted. Maclay & McIntyre lost sixteen ships in that war, two to natural hazards and a third posted missing. The value of merchant ships rose as losses increased and several steamers were sold during and immediately after the war, leaving a fleet of just six. Rebuilding during the 1920s provided the company with nine brand new ships, all but one built on the Clyde. As the Depression hit, several were laid up and the pre-war steamers were taken out of lay-up one by one and scrapped. With the end of the Depression in sight, orders were placed at favourable prices with three separate builders on the Clyde for three 8,000-tons deadweight vessels, and these were given the new Loch names, *Loch Maddy*, *Loch Lomond* and *Loch Ranza*. Two further ships were built at Sunderland in 1937 and named *Loch Dee* and *Loch Don*.

Maclay & MacIntyre's *Loch Dee* (1937).

By September 1939, when war was again declared, Maclay & McIntyre had twelve ships in operation, two of which were just two years old. The company emerged from war with just four ships and peacetime trading resumed, of necessity on a greatly diminished scale. Lord Maclay died in 1951 and much of the impetus of old seemed to depart the company, although four former wartime standard ships were bought to replace older fleet members between 1951 and 1955. Declining freight rates in the latter half of the 1950s had the company returning a loss and the four remaining ships were laid up in 1959 and eventually sold.

The prospects of the tramp shipowners must have looked good in the late Victorian period, as a number of companies engaged in the home trade took to tramping. One of these was the Clyde Shipping Company, the directors of which decided to order a single large steamer in 1889, suitable for the tramp and charter market, from W B Thompson & Company at Dundee. This was *Ailsa Craig*, with a handy gross tonnage of 3,382, which served the company for the next thirty years, very occasionally taking coastal liner voyages from Glasgow. The experiment was obviously a success and in 1892 two more steamers were completed for the tramp trades, *Dungeness* from Gourlay Brothers at Dundee and *Longships* from W G Thompson. Two bigger ships, the sisters *Foreland* and *Goodwin*, joined the tramp fleet in 1894 and 1895 respectively, and a further pair, *Needles* and *Spithead*, in 1898 and 1899. *Kish* and *Nore* followed in 1902, the latter launched as *Kalibia* on charter to the Anchor Line, *Skerries* joined the fleet in 1906 and the sisters *Beachy* and *Hurst* in 1909 and 1910. All five of these ships were lost in the Great War, along with *Spithead*. Others were sold between 1910 and 1926, although the *Foreland* was lost at sea in 1901.

The Hogarth story is similar to that of Maclay & McIntyre and starts in 1862 when the young Hugh Hogarth, from Stevenston, went into partnership with Captain James Goodwin as ship chandlers at Ardrossan. Interest in the Canadian trade led them to buy a number of Canadian-built wooden brigantines and barques. However, the partnership was dissolved in 1878 when Hugh Hogarth found himself owner of six sailing ships. His first steamship, and first with the Scottish 'Baron' nomenclature, was *Baron Ardrossan*, built for him at Whitby and delivered in 1881. He then ordered a series of fast sailing ships starting with the famous *Machrihanish*. He commissioned a variety of sailing ships and steamships until 1892 when the last sailing ship, the three-masted steel ship *Colintraive*, was delivered by A Rodger & Company of Port Glasgow. Thereafter, a new steam *Baron* was delivered pretty much every year until the Great War although the building programme was supplemented by a few second-hand purchases.

As with Maclay & McIntyre, a web of separate one-ship companies was developed for ownership and provision of management services. But unlike Maclay & McIntyre, the Hogarth interests included a regular liner service from Glasgow to Portugal and Spain which was operated from 1919 by *Baron Forbes*, a relatively small ship that had been given to Hogarth as war reparations in 1919, and which had accommodation for a few passengers. The ship was always advertised as loading for Lisbon and Huelva. In the 1920s and 1930s, the company also had a share in another cargo liner service operated jointly with Isbrantsen Lines, connecting New York with various South African ports. These interests undoubtedly helped Hogarth through the hard times when Maclay & McIntyre were struggling.

Although the Hogarth head office had moved to Great Clyde Street in Glasgow in 1880, all the steamers retained Ardrossan as their port of registry throughout the history of the company. The Hogarth Shipping Company was created in 1898 and Hugh Hogarth's two eldest sons, Samuel Crawford and Hugh junior, became partners. Hugh Hogarth died unexpectedly at the Sunday church service in Ardrossan in April 1904 and Samuel Crawford Hogarth, then aged thirty, assumed the role of senior partner.

At the start of the Great War the various Hogarth companies owned twenty-three ships, but emerged in 1918 with just thirteen ships. A ship chartering agency was opened in London in 1919 to act on behalf of the Hogarth companies and others. A close liaison had been formed with an iron ore company in Huelva, Spain, and the new agency undertook all chartering work for them. While *Baron Forbes* maintained the liner service to Spain, others were sent for iron ore and sulphur export cargoes. A regular programme of rebuilding and upgrading was maintained throughout the Depression and not one ship had to be laid up, the essentially modern fleet remaining economical throughout the period of depressed freight rates in the early 1930s.

The Hogarth companies suffered grave losses in the Second World War during which twenty ships were lost. One of the worst losses was *Baron Kelvin*, torpedoed off Tarifa with the loss of twenty-six lives. A large number of 'Empire' ships were managed for the Ministry of War Transport. However, at the end of the war, Hogarth was able to purchase five of the managed ships, each of which emerged, after refit and upgrading, with the classic dull yellow funnels with black tops to become the *Barons Ailsa*, *Elcho*, *Elibank*, *Geddes* and *Murray*.

Two new and valuable trades emerged. *Baron Haig* brought the first ever bulk sugar cargo into the UK in 1949, a trade which became the mainstay of

Hungry Hogarth's tramp steamer *Baron Kelvin* (1924) was built by Charles Connell & Company and sunk by torpedo in October 1941.

the company until the late 1960s. The other new trade was export of cars to America and Canada in the late 1950s and early 1960s.

The only oil tanker was commissioned when the Caledon Shipbuilding & Engineering Company completed the *Baron Kilmarnock* at Dundee in 1953. She was the first motor ship in the fleet. Two major dry cargo building programmes followed, six 9,000-ton deadweight vessels of the *Baron Inverclyde*-class between 1954 and 1956 and a further eight slightly larger vessels of the *Baron Jedburgh*-class between 1958 and 1960. The first group was powered by the normal triple expansion engine but also had a low pressure exhaust turbine known as the Bauer-Wach system, while the *Baron Jedburgh* and her sisters were all motor ships. The hull colour for the fleet was changed from black to grey in 1960.

By the mid 1960s it was recognised that the engines and superstructure amidships single-decker was no longer in demand for many of the bulk cargoes on offer. The future lay in the engines aft bulk carrier and Hogarth commenced a building programme that would replace even its new motor ships. The first of the new big bulkers was *Baron Inverforth*, which was delivered from builders in Sunderland in 1965. The new ship was so successful that over the next seven years a series of nine big bulkers was built for the company, this time in Norway. The new ships had deadweight capacities of between 20,000 and 24,000 tons.

In collaboration with Scottish-based Lyle Shipping Company, a 50:50 partnership in Scottish Ship Management was commenced in 1968. Ships of both companies retained their own identity but came under common management. In 1980 Lyle bought Hogarth out of the partnership and continued to manage the former Hogarth vessels in the fleet. Despite considerable attempts to diversify, including developing the North Sea oil rig support company Seaforth Maritime, the management company was forced out of business by cheap foreign flag competition and ceased to trade in 1986. Interestingly, for much of the tenure of H Hogarth & Sons a Hogarth family member was present at senior management level – Alistair Crawford Hogarth was appointed chairman in 1974.

Lyle Shipping was of similar pedigree to Hogarth, although its roots extended back much longer to the mid nineteenth century in Greenock where Abram Lyle was both a sugar refiner and a sailing shipowner. The steam tramp ship business developed through the late nineteenth and early twentieth centuries, but by then the family were concentrating on the sugar refining business that grew into the world famous Tate & Lyle Group. Lyle Shipping had a greatly diminished fleet after the Second World War and relied heavily on purchase of wartime standard ships to rebuild its business. According to D M Taylor, writing in the company newsletter *Lyle Journal*, October 1967, Lyle Shipping relied in post-war years on cargoes of wheat, lumber and 'lead pulp' from Vancouver to the UK; nitrates from Chile to Spain and Egypt; Jarrah wood from western Australia to Ceylon and Suez; whisky, motor cars and generals of all descriptions from Glasgow to the west coast of the United States; salt from Aden to Calcutta; rice from India and China to Japan; wool from New Zealand to European and British ports; case oil from Mexico to India; and grains, hides and bones from Argentina. With time, the focus was solely on bulk mineral cargoes and specialist ships to carry them.

Lyle Shipping was one of the first tramp owners to recognise the potential of bulk carriers and took delivery of the engines aft accommodation amidships, motor ship *Cape Franklin* in 1959. She was followed by two steam turbine, engines aft, vessels in 1960 and three further motor ships during the next five years. Innovative though these vessels were, they were all succeeded by second-generation bulkers within a decade. Economy of scale meant that the bulkers inevitably had to become bigger. In the late 1960s Lyle Shipping, in company with the Donaldson Line, even invested in Caledonian Airways in acknowledgement of a new industry that could only expand. Government had earlier banned shipping companies from investing in aviation, but this strange ruling was overturned during the 1950s. Back on the high seas, expansion of Scottish Ship Management allowed the Temple-named ships of Lambert Brothers (Shipping) to come under its management, so that by 1975

Typical of Lyle's first-generation bulk carriers was *Cape Franklin* (1959).

it had eight ships owned by Hogarth, three by Lambert and eleven Lyle ships under its management.

A series of four so-called Cardiff-class bulkers were added to the fleets in 1976 and 1977, two for Lyle and two for Hogarth. They were built at Govan to a standard 26,000-ton deadweight design, the first, *Cape Ortegal*, going straight out to join the Australia and Far East services. Australian coal was respected as a relatively clean cargo, whereas loading and discharging the much hated Australian phosphate exports, which covered the entire ship in fine particulate dust and penetrated every nook and cranny, was the nightmare of every Lyle crew. Unlike the old tramp ship philosophy of limiting voyages in ballast to an absolute minimum, the bulkers tended to shuttle between relatively few ports returning light-ship to reload. An interesting sideline was the carriage of sheep from Australia to Jeddah in pens on the main deck and on the hatch covers, the bulker otherwise in ballast. All well and good, until the sheep disembarked and then came the problem of the clean-up. One master did remark that it brought his entire crew shoulder to shoulder, with the chief engineer scrubbing alongside the mess steward!

In 1981 four 27,000-ton deadweight ships were under completion at Brazilian yards, the first to be delivered being *Cape Arnhem*. The original order had been placed by Lloyd Brazileiro and taken over by Lyle and Hogarth at an early stage. Similar to other fleet members, she had five holds served by four 25-tonne deck cranes equipped with grabs. Innovative provision was made to carry containers, 365 TEUs in the holds and a further 148 on deck. The ships carried a crew of thirty-six. Some of these larger units were registered in Monrovia to attract tax concessions. But by 1986 Lyle Shipping had sold much of its fleet in the face of daunting trading conditions and severe competition in the bulk freight market. Its last ships were *Cape Hawke* and *Cape Otway* which were sold prior to the company being placed in the hands of the receiver in July 1987.

There was also one other important, Scottish-registered, bulk minerals carrier, J & J Denholm and its Denholm Line of Steamers. J & J Denholm was originally a shipping agency, founded in 1866, which became a shipowner with the purchase of the schooner *David Sinclair* in 1873. A substantial fleet of steamships was built up, largely on the tramping trades. But as with others, the Second World War proved catastrophic, J & J Denholm lost ships as new as *Wellpark*, completed only in 1938, and the company had only two ships

Wellpark (1938), built by Charles Connell & Co, Scotstoun for J & J Denholm. She was sunk by German raider *Thor* five hundred miles south-southwest of St Helena on 28 March 1942. (John Clarkson)

to its name when peace resumed. The business was reconstructed and the aim was to diversify, with a number of joint venture companies managed by Denholm. By 1960 Denholm managed the bulk ore and coal carriers in the fleets of Denholm Line of Steamers, Scottish Ore Carriers, H Clarkson & Company and St Andrew's Shipping Company. All the bulkers were of modest proportions and were capable of discharging at Glasgow's General Terminus and operating in the Manchester Ship Canal and at smaller port facilities such as Workington and Port Talbot. By the mid 1960s Denholm had added Advanport, Falkland Shipowners and Pacific & Atlantic to its management portfolio. It later became a member of the Seabridge Shipping consortium along with Bibby Line, Bowring Steamship Company, Furness Withy, Houlder Brothers, Hunting & Son and Silver Line.

Success in ship management and associated services led J & J Denholm to focus on port services. In 2003 the ship management business was merged into the Anglo-Eastern Management Group while Denholm Logistics is today one of the leading forwarding agents based in the UK. The group is also heavily involved in oilfield support work, provision of industrial services and owns Denholm Seafoods, a major fish catching and processing business. Denholm Ship Management, in association with Serco, has the contract for the management of marine services to support the Royal Navy and the privatised dockyards.

Fishing also became the mainstay of another Scottish company, Salvesen of Leith. The Salvesen story starts in Norway with Christian Salvesen, the youngest of six brothers who, with their three sisters, were brought up in the small port of Mandal. Christian came to Scotland to help one of the brothers to establish a shipping agency at Grangemouth, but who was also working alongside George Turnbull with an agency at Leith. Christian took over the Leith office in 1851. In due course the partnership was split and both Turnbull and Salvesen were able to use the assets to set up separate companies. Christian Salvesen & Company was formed in 1872 with offices in Bernard Street and, in company with his own sons Tom, Fred and Theodore, took delivery of the steamship *Marna*, which was bought from her builders at Sunderland when her original owners were unable to complete payment for the vessel. The agency business was maintained and was indeed more profitable than shipowning in those early days.

Salvesen established a service between east-coast Scottish ports and Norway that was to continue for just short of one hundred years. It adopted the red and white colours of Norway and the red funnels with a white band and a black top soon became commonplace in Leith. The black top was dropped

Typical of Salvesen's tramp fleet, and which also served as supply ship to the whalers, was *Culter* (1941), built by Caledon Shipbuilding & Engineering at Dundee as *Empire Rhodes* for the Ministry of War Transport.

in favour of blue in the Great War in order to distance the company from the German national colours. Salvesen developed a strong tramp fleet that also served its whalers as supply ships. The company survives today as the well-known refrigerated warehouse and distribution network whose lorries are a familiar sight on UK motorways.

Christian Salvesen successfully steered his company until his death in 1911 – he was 85. Although Christian had relinquished the operational running of the company to his sons, it was he who decided that the company could usefully turn to whaling. Salvesen had been the sole agent for imported whale oil for several Norwegian and Danish whale oil companies. He had invested quite heavily in the whale oil industry in order to secure the agencies. However, whale stocks had dwindled severely in the Arctic Ocean and Dundee-based whalers were finding it hard to satisfy the local jute and lino industries.

Whaling in the Southern Ocean had been pioneered by the Norwegian C A Larsen in 1904. Various exploratory expeditions had been made earlier, including a four-ship expedition from Dundee in 1892, accompanied by naturalist William Murdoch and artist William Burn Bruce. Salvesen opened new whaling stations in the Falkland Islands and later at South Georgia, and took delivery of his first group of Norwegian-built whale catchers, *Busta*, *Foula*, *Linga*, *Ramna*, *Vaila* and *Swona* between 1906 and 1908. The early factory processing ships were all second-hand, two of the larger being

Whale catcher *Ramna* (1908) on Admiralty duties at Scapa Flow, stranded on the German battlecruiser SMS *Moltke* (1910), two days after the surrendered German battle fleet was scuttled on orders from Admiral Scheer on 21 June 1919. *Ramna* was refloated on the next tide.

Salvesen's whale factory ship *Sourabaya* (1915) was completed as *Carmarthenshire* for the Royal Mail Steam Packet Company and converted to her new role in 1929.

the former Royal Mail Steam Packet Company's liners *Cardiganshire* and *Carmarthenshire*, which were bought and converted in 1929 and renamed *Salvestria* and *Sourabaya* respectively. Both ships were lost in the Second World War. The Norwegians were the main competitors and companies such as A/S Hektor, which in 1920 brought out the first purpose-built factory ship, *Ronald*, was typical. Associate Hector Whaling, formed in 1912, later became part of the Cayzer Irvine (Clan Line) empire.

It was Salvesen's whaling interests that made Edinburgh Zoo into a focus for penguins and other Antarctic species. Lord Salvesen was also the zoo's first chairman, alongside William Bruce who was the vice chairman.

In 1941 the Southern Whaling & Sealing Company was bought from Unilever, bringing the characteristic 'Southern' ship names into the fleet. Many vessels of the combined fleet were requisitioned for war service. Heavy losses required two new factory ships to be commissioned, the *Southern Venturer* and *Southern Harvester*, to allow post-war resumption of whaling activities in the Antarctic. The *Southern Venturer* and *Southern Harvester* were ice-strengthened twin screw triple expansion-engined ships, built in 1945 and 1946 respectively. Several support tankers were also bought post-war,

Southern Garden (1919) was bought by Salvesen in 1947 and converted for use as a supply ship for the Antarctic whaling fleet. She was withdrawn from service in 1957. (John Clarkson)

including the elderly *Southern Garden* and *Polar Maid*, which served Salvesen until scrapped in 1957 and 1960 respectively. The factory ships survived in Salvesen colours until 1962 and 1963 respectively after which they were sold, along with their whaling quotas, to Japanese owners for just under £2 million. The remaining thirty-eight catchers were either sold, scrapped or abandoned where they lay. Mr L M Harper Gow, chairman of Salvesen at the time, stated that the main reason for the company wanting to withdraw from the industry was the 'terrible reduction' in the number of whales in the Antarctic and that it was no longer certain that they could be caught in sufficient numbers to cover the costs of an expedition'. Little concern for conservation and biodiversity was evident in those days!

One of the Salvesen whale catchers, *Southern Actor*, is a museum ship preserved at the Sandefjord Whaling Museum in Norway, where she was taken for renovation in 1995. *Southern Actor* was one of the many catchers built in post-war years and was delivered, like so many of her class, by Smiths Dock at Middlesbrough. Delivered in 1950, she served *Southern Harvester* in her first eleven seasons, and ended her time with *Southern Venturer* after one season working from Leith Harbour land station in South Georgia. Like all the Salvesen whaler fleet, she was partially crewed by Norwegians (they were particularly fine gunners, apparently, and one of them, Ole Christensen served aboard her for eleven seasons).

Salvesen's *Fairtry II* (1959) was one of a series of freezer factory trawlers, successful at their trade but ahead of their time. *Fairtry II* was laid up in 1967 and sold four years later for use as a submersible mother ship.

Post-war it was also decided that experience with whaling might usefully be applied to factory fishing. The experimental freezer trawler *Fairfree* led the way, followed by the stern-loading factory ships *Fairtry, Fairtry II* and *Fairtry III*. In the 1960s Salvesen again diversified and bought into fish factories in Grimsby, so starting the company's current focus on cold storage and distribution.

Salvesen flirted with the offshore oil industry and also maintained a small interest in deep-sea work until 1982. It ran colliers on the North Sea coastal routes, culminating in the big bulk carriers *Barra Head* and *Rora Head*, which had a gross tonnage of 4,690. The present-day survival of the company, albeit no longer a shipping company, stems purely from its ability and willingness

End of the line: *Barra Head* (1980) was one of a pair of North Sea colliers which were the last ships to be ordered for Salvesen's short sea trade. They were built in Japan.

to diversify into new trades as opportunity arose. Directors have included sons, grandsons and great-grandsons of the company founder Christian Salvesen. Next time you see a Salvesen distribution lorry on the motorway, remember the Mediterranean ships, the whalers and the fine history of this proud Scottish company.

The focus of the whaling industry was not an accident. Dundee was also the centre of the Bengal jute trade, jute and whale oil being the key ingredients to jute milling and the manufacture of sacking, carpets and later also linoleum. The jute trade started in the 1830s. Typically, the journey took ships down the 120 miles of twists and turns in the Hooghly from Calcutta and then the 8,000 miles to Dundee via the Cape. The first direct cargo to Dundee was landed by the barque *Selma* in 1840 after a 156-day passage from Calcutta. The trade peaked in 1883, when over a million bales of jute were landed at Dundee.

Dundee shipowners played a major part in the trade. David Bruce & Company's Dundee Clipper Line, for example, had eleven sailing ships built for the jute trade between 1874 and 1878 alone and in 1881 its *Lochee* made the fastest passage ever from Calcutta in just ninety days. Captain Charles Barrie's Dundee–Calcutta Line, later also known as the Den Line, was another local shipowner. Barrie had come ashore in 1881 and quickly built up a fleet of sailing barques trading to Calcutta. He doubled his fleet in 1883 by buying four sailing ships at favourable prices from Donald Currie's Castle Mail Packets, Currie being keen to shed his sailing ships in favour of steamers.

Barrie's four-masted barques, *Lawhill* and *Juteopolis* (see chapter 6), were completed at the Caledon yard of W B Thompson & Company in 1891 and 1892, and were unique in having their topmasts fitted to the after side of the lower masts – a personal requirement of Captain Barrie. Although a moderate value and stable product such as jute was still suited to the typical hundred-day voyage of the sailing clippers, the opening of the Suez Canal began to allow steamers onto the route. Indeed, the world's very first Conference system was created in 1875 as the Calcutta Steam Traffic Conference, in order to regulate freight rates and operators, and assure a degree of protection for jute suppliers in Bengal and consumers in Britain.

Barrie sold his two crack barques at the turn of the century in order to build up his Den Line of Steamers. The first steamer was built for him locally by Gourlay Brothers in 1893 and given the name *Invertay*. She was of modest size and her capacity was considerably less than most of his barques – clearly, she was a trial with the new technology. However, times were changing and rather than bales of raw jute coming into Dundee, Bengal was now exporting manufactured gunnies, a higher value product that warranted passage via Suez aboard a steamship. Barrie realised that he too had to shed his sailing ships if he was going to keep pace with the trade, and he set about building up a fleet of steamships. These all had the prefix 'Den of'; the first, *Den of Arlie* delivered in 1895, was designed with a comfortable and economical cruising speed of 10½ knots. The steamers all carried Indian crews working under Scottish officers.

As time went on the Den Line diversified into liner charters and some of the *Dens* even had modest passenger facilities. By the Great War the charter work had become dominant although Den Line was still involved with the jute trade. It was during the war that the company foresaw the difficulties of a relatively small shipowner specialising in long-distance voyages. As prices had soared as the Great War progressed, the Barrie family took the opportunity to sell its fleet and withdraw from shipowning. An attempt to return to shipowning was made post-war, when the war reprisal *Santa Clara* was received and given the old name *Den of Airlie*. The venture was not a success and she was sold two years later. However, the company remained an important shipping and forwarding agent at Dundee for many years thereafter.

The other great Scottish company involved heavily with the carriage of jute was the Falls Line of Glasgow. A timber importing business was established in Glasgow during 1874 through the partnership of William Wright and Captain Michael Breakenridge, both originally from Irvine. In due course, like so many other timber importers, the company went into shipowning. Russell & Company was contracted to build the first ship, the Russell and Wright families being already acquainted. This was the iron-hulled full-rigged *Falls of Clyde*, launched in December 1878 and now in preservation in Hawaii, and which was followed three months later by *Falls of Bruar*. They were fast and large: *Falls of Bruar* made a passage in her early career from Calcutta to Dundee in ninety-six days. By the end of the 1890s the Falls Line owned a fleet of ship- and barque-rigged sailing vessels, each owned by a separate holding company, for example, the Ship Falls of Earn Company.

The first Wright and Breakenridge steamer was the *Falls of Inversnaid* delivered in 1888, and initially part-owned, by Russell & Company. Although one more barque, *Falls of Berwick*, was commissioned six years later, subsequent new builds were all steamships. In 1890 Malcom Breakenridge left the partnership, his gross dislike of steam being acknowledged, and William Graham, Wright's brother-in-law, was brought in as a partner to create Wright, Graham & Company. By the eve of the Great War the company had just two ships. Like all good tramp shipowners it had built in the bad times and sold in the good: one ship, *Falls of Lora* was sold on the stocks and launched for Liverpool owners as *Drumcruil*. Like the Den Line, they were sold at inflated wartime prices, and the company was wound up in December 1917.

Port facilities at Dundee had needed to be developed to accommodate the jute steamers. In 1875 the Victoria Dock opened to handle the barques and steamers alike. However, by the 1930s the steamships in the trade were too big for the dock entrance and moved to the riverside King George V Wharf which had 28ft of water at low tide. Ships belonging to all the Far Eastern traders could be seen: P&O, British India, Brocklebank, Clan Line and the Hall Line of Liverpool. Many of the ships were locally built and Gourlay were responsible for the construction of many of the Hall Line ships, including a group of three in the period 1881 to 1883. Fire was always a risk, and the P&O cargo liner *Galway* suffered a serious cargo fire while alongside in December 1975. But the jute trade was in decline, and shortly afterwards the former *Clan Macintyre*, then flying the Panamanian flag as *Eastern Princess*, took 1,000 tons of redundant equipment from the jute mills to Calcutta.

The fire risk of a jute cargo was accompanied by the problem of the cargo swelling should it get wet. This was amply illustrated by the sinking in the Lower Thames in January 1909 of the coastal steamer *Dundee*. She carried a transhipped cargo of jute from London Docks which was destined for Dundee. She had been built by Gourlay Brothers in 1888 with accommodation for 125 passengers in two berths and operated on the east-coast passenger and cargo liner service managed by the Dundee, Perth & London Shipping Company. *Dundee* had collided with the Carron Line steamer *Thames*, arriving from Grangemouth. The *Dundee* came off worst and, as she was making water, was run ashore near where the former Isle of Grain oil refinery once stood. It took five months before the ship could be floated off and only then was it realised that the jute had swelled to the extent that frames had been buckled and plates burst. The cargo was condemned and the ship was declared a constructive total loss.

The development of shipping semi-manufactured gunnies rather than raw jute allowed direct shipment to South America, where the meat industry's demand for sacking was intense. Clan Line and Andrew Weir in consortium with T & J Harrison and Ellerman maintained a regular gunny service from Calcutta to the River Plate from 1910 onwards. This only stopped in the late 1950s when the Indian Line interjected with lower freight rates.

Scottish shipowners were involved in many other specialist trades for various lengths of time. As opportunity arose, the shipowner put in his bid and consequent links were developed in a variety of trades; the jute trade was just one of them.

From Sheep discharging *by Captain I Michie,* Baron Napier
(as reported in Trident, *the house magazine of*
Scottish Ship Management, June 1977)

After an excellent run from Australia to the Red Sea we ended the passage at 0800 hours on 31 March, wove a tortured course through the myriad reefs and ships at anchor and picked up the pilot at 0853. Our first line was ashore at 0937 and we were all fast by 1000. Pratique was granted at 0930 before coming alongside, the doctor boarding shortly after the pilot and leaving again by boat.

Agents and Customs boarded on arrival and it was necessary to fill in piles of forms, among them one to guarantee that all the alcoholic beverages and all tobacco, surplus to immediate crew requirements, were under seal. Customs officials then sealed the bonded store and also the main and emergency radio transmitters as it is, of course, forbidden to transmit while alongside.

After completion of formalities the labour came aboard and commenced setting up a sheep discharging ramp from the starboard pilot ladder access gate. We were told that the sheep were to be run directly onto the quay and this we started to do at 1100 hours. The sheep were rather loathe to tackle the fairly steep ramp down onto the quay and there was much pulling and prodding of the animals amidst guttural Arabic curses before they started to run. The plan was to run off the starboard side first, then the sheep between the hatches, followed by the port side and lastly the sheep on top of the lids.

As we had already reduced the pen divisions greatly on passage there was little to do in this direction, but the local labour proved to be standing where the sheep were supposed to be going, with the result that they would stop running and bunch together until some more had been hauled to the top of the ramp and thrust down it, when they would again get the idea and another group would go romping off until thwarted once more by a misplaced stevedore.

After a couple of hours of this, we had managed to discharge nearly 1,600 sheep by our count and then the job collapsed. The receiver suddenly appeared on the scene, said that it was 13 miles to his holding pens, and that all the sheep that had been discharged must be reloaded. This we refused to do, after perhaps an hour of diplomacy by the stockman, the Chief Officer, the Port Administration Officers and myself, the receiver said that he had rented a holding yard a mile and a half away and proceeded to drive the sheep off. All the remainder were, however, to be loaded into trucks.

Eight large Mercedes trucks erupted onto the quay at this point and, with much blowing of horns and shouting, jockeyed for position to be first backed up to the ramp. Fifteen minutes of seething confusion later the first truck was in position and the stevedores again started trying to drive the sheep onto the trucks. This proved to be even more difficult than before as the truck tail gates protruded above the end of the ramp meaning that the sheep had a steeplechase course to negotiate in their final leap into the truck. Those not prepared to jump in this manner were unceremoniously bundled into the back of the vehicles.

The trucks held about 50 sheep each and, with no shortage of trucks, work continued until 2200 hours by which time nearly 4,500 sheep had been landed. The stevedores by this time developed a system consisting of flailing the sheep with bamboos and rubber hoses and dragging the reluctant ones by a leg or by the horns. All the sheep on deck had been cleared and the ramp had been erected to No. 5 hold lids and this area cleared also.

Work resumed on No. 4 hatch top at 0700 hours the morning of Friday 1 April and, again with sufficient trucks all the sheep were discharged by 1030 with the loss of only two sheep since our arrival. About four took off into the wide blue yonder after they were off loaded, but I think they were all recaptured. Tallies were compared and the shore tally gave a figure of 6,377, ours 6,409 which was not too big a discrepancy considering the confusion that had reigned. The shore tallyman was working on behalf of the shipper's insurance company. Shortly before the sheep were completed, work was started on discharging the bagged feed into the trucks, this work continuing until the early afternoon.

As Friday is the Moslem equivalent of our Sunday and a day of prayer, we were informed that there would be no labour from 1100 to 1530 hours as the stevedores insisted on going to pray. Nobody, however, had told the stevedores this and they continued to work throughout the day. When the bagged feed was completed, they started to land the fencing, wires, stanchions and ramps, our crew having dismantled the fencing, coiled the wires and piled the stanchions for them. All fittings were landed into trailers and this work was completed by 1810 hours. As pilotage ceases at 1800 hours and we had decided at about 1500 hours that it was very unlikely that we would finish in time, I requested the first available sailing on the morning of 2 April. Pilotage was consequently ordered for 0700 hours.

The agent arrived with clearance at 0645 hours and prepared to take our two stockmen ashore. Pilot arrived promptly at 0700 hours and after the stockmen had their bags checked by the Customs guard at the gangway and the Agent had made a couple of journeys to the Immigration Office, they finally went ashore at about 0725 hours.

We were finally all gone and clear with the anchor aweigh at 0800 hours and the pilot disembarked at 0830. I think that all sighed with relief at leaving, until they had a good look at the foredeck and hatch-tops, where a daunting quantity of sheep droppings was caked and matted.

15

A Heritage to be Proud of

It was the shipping industry which from the middle of the 16th century sought out, found and built up the entire fabric of our Empire. This it did unsupported in the hope of trade. The shipping industry is the mother of the old Navy, and in sober fact, the mainstay of our lives. It has ridden out storms of a thousand years, and will continue to do so if left to work out its own salvation ... It is the task of the industry to serve the community as a whole; history has shown how well it has fulfilled that role in peace and war.

Philip Runciman, from the chairman's address, Anchor Line AGM, 1943

So what became of it all? A proud seafaring heritage is manifested today by the ferries of CalMac and Northlink still flying the St Andrew's cross at the Jack and whose masters all nowadays carry foreign-going certificates. Ferries to Belfast tend to be registered to flags of convenience, and the ferry port of Stranraer has recently fallen into disuse as newer and larger ships moved to the new port facility further down Loch Ryan. There are also a number of offshore oil support ships, although the observer at Aberdeen will report that the majority have Scandinavian owners. Otherwise, Glasgow may be found on the stern of a few large container ships, bulkers and tankers operating for the mega-international companies, but then only to satisfy some operational requirement to qualify for crewing or tax benefits.

But there is still a great deal of evidence of the maritime heritage of Scotland. *Glenlee* was completed in 1896 and launched, with three masts stepped and rigging in place, by Anderson Rodger & Company at Port Glasgow. She was rigged as a barque and had a steel hull 245ft in length (282ft to the tip of the bowsprit) and 38ft in breadth. At 1,613 tons she was one of a number of large sailing ships built for shipowners Archibald Sterling & Company of Glasgow for the Australian grain run. Interestingly, she was built to an original Russell & Company design which continued to be built by both W T Lithgow and Anderson Rodger after the dissolution of the original Russell partnership. *Glenlee* was sold to Dundee owners, R Ferguson & Company in 1899, and given the name *Islamount*. She had several further owners and was extensively modernised in 1922 when she became the Italian-owned *Clarastella*. Two years later in March 1922 she was sold to the Spanish navy for use as a sail-training ship and renamed *Galatea* when twin Polar diesel engines were installed. She was dismasted in a storm off the Azores in October 1946, and later lost many of her sails in another storm in 1954, when a number of cadets suffered injuries.

During much of the 1960s she lay abandoned at Punte Verde, where many of her fittings were plundered and several fires were set by vandals. Looting only came to end when a copper valve was stolen from the bottom of the ship allowing her to sink. It was in this waterlogged condition that the Clyde Maritime Trust bought the hulk and arranged for it to be brought home to Scotland. That was only the beginning, and renovation of the ship, now at the new Riverside Museum at Glasgow, has cost many millions of pounds, including the re-stepping of masts and rigging and the carving of a figurehead similar to the original one, which is still in the possession of the Spanish navy. Again named *Glenlee*, she is a fine landmark and a worthy representative for Scottish maritime heritage. Of similar vintage, though of completely different provenance, is *Discovery* which is preserved at Dundee (see chapter 8).

Another significant landmark is the Burrell Collection housed in its new gallery at Pollok Country Park on the south side of Glasgow. In 1944 Sir William Burrell (1861–1958) gifted the City of Glasgow his collection of art. Burrell was a shipowner, Burrell & Son, also shipbuilders (the yard was at Dumbarton), managers and agents, ship brokers and insurance representatives. George Burrell set up business in 1856 as a shipping and forwarding agent in Port Dundas at the Glasgow end of the Forth & Clyde Canal. William, born 1832, joined his father the following year. The interests in barges and smacks on the canal continued until the Great War under the trading name Burrell & Haig, but the deep-sea interests were maintained by Burrell & Company. The first deep-sea investment was 32/64th of the new iron-hulled steamer *Fitzwilliam*. The first few ships in Burrell & Son ownership tended to focus on trade to the Mediterranean, but when the larger *Strathclyde* was delivered by Blackwood & Gordon in 1871, Burrell chartered her to Gellatly, Hankey & Sewell to trade to India via the Suez Canal. Five years later, and still on charter, she was sunk in collision in the English Channel.

The Mediterranean services went from strength to strength with a new ship delivered almost every year. In September 1877 *Fitzmaurice* was on passage to Valencia and came upon the floating and abandoned cylinder containing Cleopatra's Needle. The line to the tug *Olga* had broken and a boat and six men were lost in an abortive attempt to recover it. *Fitzmaurice* successfully got a line onto the cylinder and towed the salvage into Ferrol. William Burrell was awarded £2,000 salvage money which he offered to forgo if the obelisk were erected at Greenock. He got his £2,000, as Cleopatra's Needle, to this day, graces not the Esplanade at Greenock but the Embankment in London!

Burrell commissioned larger ships in the 1870s and commenced services to the Far East. *Strathleven* brought the first refrigerated meat cargo into London in 1880, the first refrigerated cargo being carried the previous year by Anchor Line's *Circassia* inbound from America. William Burrell's sons George and William came into the business at about this time and business links were developed with Hungary to develop a sea route to the Adriatic at Fiume, now Rijeka, to both Glasgow and Leith. This wing of the company was later sold to the Hungarian government with management retained by Burrell. William senior died in 1885 and sons George, who was just twenty-eight, and William, then twenty-four, assumed charge. Over the next thirty years the ships took up tramping, but maintained the Austro-Hungarian ties and new links that had been developed to the Caribbean.

The old trick of building in hard times when prices were low (twelve ships were ordered in the mini-recession in 1894 and twenty orders to the same design, all to Clyde shipbuilders asking just £6 per ton, were ordered in 1905) and selling ships in the subsequent boom (ten in 1906 to the newly formed Commonwealth Government Line of Australia) was a task carried out to the letter by Burrell & Company. Many of the fleet were owned by single-ship companies and some had Chinese and Lascar crews under British officers. During the Great War the value of shipping rose dramatically and Burrell sold twenty-three ships and lost seven others to enemy action. The company emerged into peacetime with a fleet of just two vessels, *Strathearn* and *Strathlorne*. Sale of *Strathearn* in 1919 left *Strathlorne* on the tramp market alone, until she too was sold in 1930. In the meantime, George Burrell had died in 1927, the surviving brother William was then approaching seventy, and as neither brother had a son following in the business, no further investment was ever made.

Since childhood the brothers were avid collectors of art works including the largest collection of the work of Joseph Crawhill (1861–1913). About eight thousand items were lodged in William's home, Hutton Castle in Berwickshire, and it is much of this collection that he bequeathed to Glasgow which is now housed in the new gallery at Pollok Country Park, an excellent reminder of an important merchant fleet.

There is also the sailing ship *Cutty Sark* sitting in her dry dock at Greenwich, near the National Maritime Museum. Although she was recently badly damaged by fire, she has now been fully restored in a most imaginative way and is again open to the public. Scott & Linton contracted to build *Cutty Sark* to a design by Hercules Linton for just £17 per ton, a low price that subsequently bankrupted the builders once the hull was launched. (A cutty sark – literally a short shirt or camisole – see Robert Burns' *Tam O'Shanter*.) When the hull was launched she was towed across the River Leven to William Denny and Brothers, and was completed and rigged ready to sail in just twelve weeks. She left London on her maiden voyage to Shanghai in February 1870 under the command of Captain George Moodie.

The Clyde-built four-masted barque *Pommern*, once of the famous German owned Flying P-Line, is also preserved. Frank Scott describes her in *Mariner's Mirror* (November 2012):

> She is now a museum ship at Mariehamn in the Åland Islands, but is quite unlike the other preserved sailing ships of that era in that her rig and layout is exactly the same as it was in her days as a sailing freight carrier. Indeed she is in virtually the same condition in which she was laid up at the conclusion of her last grain-carrying voyage for Gustaf Erikson in August 1939 ... She has none of the dainty elegance of the *Cutty Sark* ...

And Clyde-built, there are, of course, still the famous Cunarders *Queen Mary*, in the role of hotel and conference centre, preserved at Long Beach in California and, of course, *Queen Elizabeth 2* which remains mothballed at Dubai, but which might be on the move shortly to a new static role in China.

Queen Elizabeth 2 (1967) as built by John Brown & Company, Clydebank, with steam turbine engines, at the start of a liner voyage from Southampton to New York on 30 May 1969. (Author)

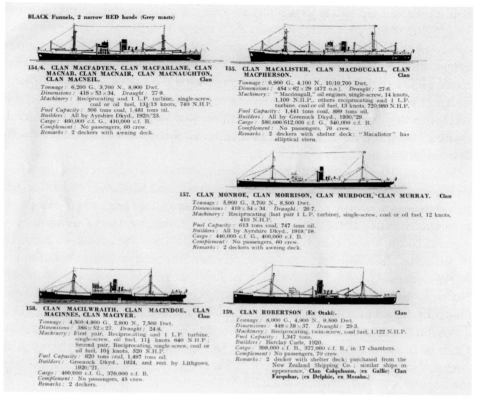

Part of the Clan Line entry in Paymaster-Lieutenant Commander E C Talbot Booth's *The British Merchant Navy 1937–8*.

So, now that all the Clan, Ben, Anchor and Henderson lines are no more, it seems that CalMac and Northlink are nowadays the biggest Scottish ship operators. The history of both is well-documented and fascinating, but it is not always realised that services go back before the days of steam. For example, the 'North Company' can trace its ancestry back to 1790 when the Leith & Clyde Shipping Company was formed to provide a service between Edinburgh and Glasgow via the Pentland Firth (the Caledonian Canal was only opened in 1822). Using a fleet of small sailing vessels, the company quickly established its reputation at numerous intermediate ports, and then amalgamated with the Aberdeen, Dundee & Leith Shipping Company in 1820 to become the Aberdeen, Leith, Clyde & Tay Shipping Company. The word Tay was dropped from the title in 1824. The company operations were centred on Aberdeen.

The Aberdeen, Leith & Clyde Shipping Company acquired its first steamer, *Velocity*, in 1821. She was a product of Denny at Dumbarton. The order was precipitated by competition from a rival company, the Leith & Aberdeen Steam Yacht Company which had put a steamer on the Leith to Aberdeen route earlier that year. This was the only time the North Company had any serious competition in its long existence, and that ceased in 1826 when the rival ship was sold when the respective owning partners' agreement ended. By that time the summer-only steamship services had been extended to Inverness, and finally as far as Wick.

In 1836 a new ship, the *Sovereign*, inaugurated a weekly service between Newhaven (adjacent to Leith), Aberdeen, Wick and Kirkwall, and extended to Lerwick initially on alternate weeks. Two years later the company won the prestigious mail contract to the islands. The company used the monarchy nomenclature for the next three decades, and the first screw steamer to be built for the company was *Queen* in 1861. The first to adopt the famous 'saint' nomenclature was the former paddle steamer *Waverley*, built for the North British Railway in 1864, and acquired by the Aberdeen, Leith & Clyde Shipping Company in 1867 when she became *St Magnus*.

In June 1875 the company was reconstituted as the North of Scotland, Orkney & Shetland Steam Navigation Company. The title was changed in 1953 to North of Scotland, Orkney & Shetland Shipping Company. In 1961 the company sold out to the Coast Lines Group for a surprisingly small price, it being said at the time that this reflected the North Company's reluctance to consider roll-on roll-off traffic. The identity of the North Company and its ships remained unchanged until the imposition of the corporate image of parent P&O defaced the appearance of the ships in 1975, after which the trading name became P&O Ferries (Orkney & Shetland Services) and the ships were re-liveried in P&O colours. The last historic sailings north from Leith to the islands were taken unceremoniously in 1985 by the small trailer ferry *ROF Beaver* carrying bagged fertiliser. P&O later withdrew from the Aberdeen and Scrabster services in 2002, having lost a competitive tender for government subsidies to a new company, Northlink, which was jointly owned by the Royal Bank of Scotland and Caledonian MacBrayne. They in turn have lost the contract by competitive tender to Serco. The simple, plain, dull yellow funnels and black hulls of the North Company, however, will long be remembered, especially by the islanders.

Steam arrived early on the Orkney inter-island services when Captain George Robertson of South Ronaldsay 'retired' to the islands with his steamer *Quarry Maid*. He bought her lying at Liverpool and sailed her to Leith with

The trailer ferry *ROF Beaver* (1971) leaving Leith on 27 February 1985 for Kirkwall with bagged fertiliser. (Author)

a cargo of grain. Renamed *Orcadia* she arrived at Kirkwall late in February 1864. Journeys that once took seven or eight hours in a lugger now took just two hours and this so revolutionised life on the islands that a new *Orcadia* was commissioned just four years later.

The history of Hutcheson/MacBrayne and associated companies is equally historic. Similarly, the story of the paddle steamer services on the Clyde and Forth are steeped in history with stories of minor collisions, thankfully few sinkings, and races between rival ships for the pier. The need for speed helped develop new technology, the steam turbine engine having its first commercial trials aboard *King Edward* on the longer Clyde routes, while the North British Railway needed to retain shallow-draught paddle steamers in order to access the shallow railhead pier at Craigendoran.

It is easy to forget that there were other operators vying for holiday passengers. The steamers of the Isle of Man Steam Packet Company, funnels adorned in Cunard-style crimson with black hoops and black top – a legacy to both companies from Robert Napier, were regular visitors to the Clyde until 1985. Indeed, they were as much a part of the Glasgow Fair week (later fortnight) and other Scottish holidays as they were of the various Lancashire Wakes weeks, when factory and office workers and their families set off in droves to cross the Irish Sea for a few days by the sea, Manx style.

The Manx boats maintained a seasonal service to Ardrossan, or Greenock in adverse weather, throughout much of the twentieth century. When service requirements allowed, the steamers were also deployed on excursions to and from the Isle of Man. The Clyde ports of Ayr and Rothesay received regular seasonal visits from the Manx boats, while services to the Isle of Man focused on the annual summer holiday weeks enjoyed by the various towns in Lowland Scotland. A letter received by the author from Geoffrey Hamer in 2004 reported an analysis he made on the final few years of calls made by the Isle of Man Steam Packet Company on the Clyde:

> Several ports had occasional visits, in addition to the regular summer service between Douglas and Ardrossan. In both 1967 and 1968, there were two excursions from Ayr to Belfast and one from Belfast to Ayr. The steamers also had occasional charters between Northern Ireland and Ardrossan. In 1969, there was a one day trip from Ayr to Belfast, and two trips to Rothesay – the *Manxman* with a party from Belfast on 16 July and the *Mona's Isle* from Larne on 22 July, which seems to have been the last Rothesay call by a Manx steamer. The steamers anchored in Rothesay Bay while their passengers were ashore.
>
> In 1970, the *Manxman* made an evening cruise from Troon, and on two occasions, the *Manx Maid* had to divert to Greenock because of bad weather. In 1971, the *Manxman* made another evening cruise from Troon and the *Mona's Isle* did a Larne–Ayr day trip. The *Manxman* did another Larne–Ayr day trip in 1973 and again on 15 July 1975, which seems to have been the last visit to Ayr by a Manx steamer.
>
> 1974 was the last year of the eight passenger ship Isle of Man fleet and the Ardrossan–Douglas route still carried good numbers: at the start of the Glasgow holiday, there were five sailings from Ardrossan on Friday 12 July – the *King Orry* at 1030, the *Manxman* at 1500, and the *King Orry*, *Manx Maid* and *Tynwald* at 2330. Many of these passengers spent the night sitting on wooden benches aboard ship, so it is hardly surprising traffic declined as people chose to take their holidays elsewhere. Traffic on the Ardrossan route dwindled quickly … until the service finally closed after the 1985 season.

Today, the trail to the Isle of Man requires a trek down the M74 and M6 motorways to Heysham to join the rather functional, and essentially basic, vehicle and passenger motor ferry *Ben-my-Chree* ('Girl of my Heart'). Girl of

The Isle of Man steamer *Tynwald* (1947) was an occasional visitor at Rothesay. (Author)

my heart, indeed, a cup of tea left on a table in the 'Quiet Lounge' creates a wave pattern that eventually pushes a spout of tea up from the centre of the cup in sympathy with the violent vibrations emanating from the machinery below. But the days of the steamers are remembered by many. And if only conversation could be made over the harmonic rattles of the Quiet Lounge, it would be reminiscences about a trip on the *Manxman* out of Ayr, or what a comfortable ship the old steamer *Tynwald* was in a beam sea …

We are left with many reminders and many memories of Scotland's proud maritime heritage. The heritage reflects a maritime community that was a driver of wealth creation through innovation, invention and entrepreneurship, engineering prowess, seamanship and business management. There are many memorials, including preserved vessels, the remnant docks and surviving shipyards, and memories of the sailors themselves.

Perhaps one of the oddest memorials is the Caledonian Canal where witch or wee folk must have walked up Neptune's Staircase to put a jinx on its waters. Designed by Thomas Telford, it was not, however, completed to his specification but was built to a shallower depth and of smaller bottom width. Telford's specification allowed for both warships and others to traverse from the east-coast route south to the English Channel to avoid marauding French vessels in the North Sea. But when in 1822 the canal was finally opened, eleven years later than planned and hugely over budget, the French had already become our trading partners. In 1840 the canal was rebuilt to a larger specification, but the rise of the steamship and adverse winds along the Great Glen discouraged use by sailing ships, and steamers tended to sail via Cape Wrath, regardless of the shortcut offered by the Caledonian Canal. By 1906 the canal was semi-moribund but open for business. It was used more in the wars, however, for supplying munitions and remained valuable to fishing boats wishing to pass east or west.

The canal passed from the Caledonian Canal Commissioners to the Ministry of Transport in 1920. In 1948 control was vested in the Transport Commission and in 1963 the British Waterways Board. All the locks were fully mechanised in the 1960s. The canal is now a vibrant tourist attraction – people come from far and wide to marvel at the eight-lock 90ft rise at Neptune's Staircase, between Corpach and Banavie – but its disappointment as a ship canal has never been overcome and now never will be.

A core of family names repeatedly came to the fore throughout the history of the Scottish Merchant Navy. Many families were intertwined through marriage, cross-investment and other business links. But lying beneath the mainstream history is a delightfully mischievous thread, with many a Scot ready to turn a penny for better or worse. Brian Watters provides one such example in his book *Carron, where iron runs like water*, of an incident that took place on 9 October 1826 at a quayside in Liverpool while loading the schooner *Latona*, bound for Grangemouth via the Forth and Clyde Canal:

Three casks had been taken down to the quay to be shipped on the *Latona*; they were addressed to Mr G Ironson, Edinburgh and were marked 'Bitter Salts'. These casks remained on the quay overnight, but on the following day when they were about to be loaded onto the ship, it was noticed that a horrible smell was emanating from them. Thomas Crosthwaite, the Carron Company agent, immediately contacted the Police who opened the casks. It was found that they did not contain bitter salts but instead held eleven dead bodies, salted and pickled. The carter who had delivered them led the Police to a cellar in Hope Street, situated below the schoolroom of one Dr D McGowan, a teacher of languages; it was there that a further 22 bodies were found. It transpired that McGowan's premises had been let to a man called Henderson from Greenock … He had fled, never to be called to account for his deeds. An accomplice, a man called James Donaldson, was caught, fined £50 and jailed for twelve months. The contents of the casks were presumed to have been destined for the Anatomy Classes at the University of Edinburgh!

That same core of family names even worked for the mischievous body-dealers Henderson and Donaldson!

But of the many once proud Scottish-owned ships and their owners, the speed with which the industry was overtaken was dramatic. Various factors combined to push the industry out of business and included the aeroplane, cheap foreign competition, and the container revolution which followed hard on the heels of the mini-recession of the early 1960s. By 1963 there were just twelve Scottish-registered deep-sea shipowning companies who between them managed or owned 195 ships (Table 1). By 1978 this had dwindled to just eight companies and eighty ships, although the total aggregate tonnage was almost the same. Although there were fewer ships the average size of the vessels had greatly increased during those fifteen year from 7,470 gross tons in 1973 to 18,400 gross tons in 1978, largely a reflection of the many new large bulk carriers that had been commissioned in the interim. The consequence was that more and more men came ashore while others took to new work in the offshore oil industry.

Orkney inter-island ferry *Earl Sigurd* (1931) was the last operational coal-fired steamship in the Merchant Navy. (Author)

The steamship that had dominated trade with Scotland for 150 years was no more, and with its passing a major Scottish industry and close-knit community was fading. The very last British coal-fired, saltwater commercial steamer was the Orkney inter-island ferry *Earl Sigurd*, completed in 1931 by Hall Russell at Aberdeen and sold for demolition at Bo'ness in 1969. Another steamer, the oil-fired Glasgow sewage sludge carrier *Shieldhall*, launched in July 1955 by specialist builder Lobnitz & Company, of Renfrew, remained in service a little longer. *Shieldhall* was built with accommodation for eighty passengers to allow elderly and deprived passengers to enjoy the trip to the sewage sludge dumping grounds in the lower Clyde estuary. She was withdrawn in 1976, although she saw further service working out of Southampton, and is now preserved and used for occasional excursions, based still at Southampton.

By 1982 deep-sea ownership was ebbing fast. Anchor Line had one ship, Ben Line seven, Clan Line had disappeared into British & Commonwealth Shipping alongside Union-Castle, Denholm Ship Management was still looking after fifteen big bulk carriers, Harrisons (Clyde) had four bulkers in the tramp market, although Harrisons also managed *Avon Forest* for the Burnett Steamship Company, Lyle and Hogarth as Scottish Ship Management still had sixteen bulk carriers in the tramp market, and Salvesen operated four large colliers on the North Sea coastal trade. In 1987 Scottish Ship Management conceded to cheap foreign competition in the bulk carrier tramp market and went into voluntary liquidation. Within a very short time there were just a handful of ships in specialist roles, most of which were managed by Denholm Ship Management, although Ben Line also met with some success with its container ships (see chapter 11) and four large chemical tankers.

Ben Line entered the offshore drilling arena in the mid 1970s in partnership with Ocean Drilling & Exploration Company of New Orleans (now Diamond Offshore). Similar developments were the creation of Star Offshore Services, 'SOS', of Aberdeen in 1974 to service the North Sea Oil platforms. Each of the Star ships was licensed to carry twelve passengers, while *Star Hercules* could accommodate forty-two, a useful facility when the weather grounded all helicopter services. Harrisons (Clyde) and Scotts of Greenock also recognised the potential in the North Sea work in 1974 and jointly formed the Stirling Shipping Company which, with its subsidiary companies, also provided diving support ships and safety vessels. Star is today a global company of high repute and Stirling, having concentrated on North Sea work, operates out of Peterhead, Aberdeen and Great Yarmouth with a fleet of twelve platform supply ships and three anchor handling vessels.

J & A Gardner's *Saint Angus* (1980) seen from the Kessock Bridge at Inverness on 14 June 1983. (Author)

A few Scottish-based coastal cargo-carrying companies survived into the 1980s. J & A Gardner's coal trade had ended and the company diversified into dry cargo coasters each fitted with a bow loading ramp, the youngest being *Saint Angus* and *Saint Oran*. Christian Salvesen (Shipping) still operated three colliers and managed others belonging to the Central Electricity Generating Board. George Gibson became an Anchor Line subsidiary and maintained a small fleet of liquid gas carriers. But those were all that were left.

Nowadays, thirty or so years later, the legacy of the great maritime industry that was once based in Scotland is fortunately still all around and there to be seen and enjoyed. There are specialist museums at Glasgow and Irvine, but there are also a variety of other reminders including the remnant docklands on the Clyde and Forth, and at Dundee and Aberdeen. Apart from the obvious wealth creation through development of trade and promotion of Scottish industry, the merchant marine also put Scotland onto the global stage. 'Clyde-built' was and is synonymous with excellence. Scotland needs to remember its maritime heritage and take pride in it and the men and women who contributed to that excellence. Although there are many memorials to the industry, of which CalMac and Northlink are perhaps the greatest reminders, it is the triumphs and failures, the achievements and disasters that make the heritage so lifelike. Indeed, it is names such as Henderson and Donaldson which conjure the triumphs and achievements, but it is also the many others, many of whom gave their lives prematurely for the sake of the Scottish mercantile marine.

And the memories live on. Sandy Ferguson fondly described one such memory from his service on the Henderson Line K-class cargo ships which were rostered onto the Elder Dempster Line's West Africa service in the 1950s and early 1960s:

> … followed by five years on various other K-boats running up the creeks of West Africa to uninteresting places – best forgotten – like Warri, Bruto, Sapele and Port Harcourt. Not only were these ports a long way up the creeks, but in one particular locality to turn the ship around, the bow had to be deliberately run into the mango swamps. When the most for'ad part of the vessel was grounded, steaming at slow speed ahead on the engine with the rudder hard over turned the hull enough for her to come astern on to the berth …
>
> When the stem entered the mango trees, the creepy crawlies that fell – not to mention the occasional monkey – onto the forecastle deck and down the backs of our shirts, doesn't bear thinking about. There were also mosquitoes, tsetse fly and mango flies in abundance in the West African creeks …
>
> During watches dressed in shorts on the bridge wing going up the creeks, the favourite ploy of the cadets was to creep up stealthily and gently touch the back of a shipmate's knee. This invariably resulted in a cry of horror and a leap that would do an Olympic high jumper credit!

Table 1: Scottish deep sea ships registered in 1963 and fifteen years later in 1978

Company	1963		1978	
	No of ships	Aggregate gross tonnage	No of ships	Aggregate gross tonnage
Anchor Line, Glasgow	6[1]	56,500	6	120,700
Ben Line Steamers, Leith	29	252,500	16	309,900
Clan Line Steamers, Glasgow	44	386,900	7	53,800
Currie Line, Leith	10	46,800		
J & J Denholm (Management)	21	160,800	20	420,700
Donaldson Line, Glasgow	8[2]	49,800		
Ellerman Lines, The City Line, Glasgow	8	60,300	Became part of Ellerman City Liners	
Glen & Company, Glasgow	5	9,000		
Harrisons (Clyde), Glasgow	3	26,200	8	207,000
P Henderson Company, Glasgow	17	99,200		
H Hogarth & Sons, Ardrossan	13	96,200	8	125,300
Lyle Shipping Company, Glasgow	11	108,200	12	187,200
Salvesen & Company, Leith	20[3]	104,700	3	47,400
TOTALS	195	1,457,100	80	1,472,000
Average size of ship gross tons	7,470		18,400	

[1]Includes passenger and cargo liners *Caledonia*, *Cilicia* and *Circassia*.
[2]Includes passenger and cargo liners *Laurentia* and *Lismoria*.
[3]Excludes whale catchers.

The Forth & Clyde, Caledonian and Crinan canals

Suez or Panama they might not be, but the main navigational canals of Scotland, although of more modest proportions, played a small role in developing Scottish industry by providing direct links to the markets. The oldest, the Forth & Clyde, provided a direct connection between industry in the west and the transport routes of the east, even promoting the burgeoning port of Grangemouth as a point of transhipment, which only later developed into an important focus of industry in its own right. The Caledonian was a short cut from east to west coasts following the line of the Great Glen and avoiding the rigours of the north coast of Scotland, while Crinan provided access to the north from the Clyde without the need to circumnavigate Kintyre.

The 35-mile long Forth & Clyde Canal was started in 1768 and eventually reached Port Dundas in 1777. The engineering foresight was that of John Smeaton, of Eddystone Lighthouse fame, and he was assisted in matters geological by James Hutton. The canal with its thirty-nine locks was only completed in 1790, opening up the valuable trade route between the west of Scotland, with its abundant primary resources and pool of skilled labour, with London and elsewhere via the North Sea. It also allowed the Carron Company, based at Falkirk, to ship its products in lighters directly to Port Dundas, situated on a spur of the canal. The spur was designed to allay the fears of Glasgow merchants who thought they should be bypassed once the canal was completed to meet the Clyde at Bowling. The main canal could accommodate vessels of 19ft breadth and 68ft in length. A special reservoir was constructed in the Kilsyth Hills to ensure that there was always sufficient water in the canal to allow constant use of the locks.

Before the Forth & Clyde Canal was operational, sailing ships from Port Glasgow destined for London had to travel down the Irish Sea and through the English Channel. But once the canal was opened, the sailing smacks could carry products from west to east, there to be reloaded aboard larger vessels for onward delivery to east-coast ports and London. The canal provided a valuable fillip to Scottish industrialists east and west and, once the benefits of the Industrial Revolution were realised, it became a busy waterway, with deeply-laden puffers and lighters traversing to and fro between the Forth and the Clyde. An interesting sideline developed on the canal at Doctor's Wood to the west of Bonnybridge. Here a local doctor brought corpses to the wood at night to sell to skippers on the canal, who in turn sold the cadavers on to anatomy teachers at the universities in both Glasgow and Edinburgh. But such enterprise was finally stamped on when it was exposed in the early 1830s.

In 1853 the management of the Forth & Clyde Canal fell to the Caledonian Railway, which was charged with integrating water and rail transport of goods. The canal stayed in railway ownership until it eventually became part of the newly formed British Waterways Board in 1962.

The Crinan Canal connects Loch Fyne with the Sound of Jura – from Ardrishaig to Crinan. It provides a valuable bypass to the arduous trip around the Mull of Kintyre for smaller vessels voyaging between the Clyde and the northwest. The Canal was constructed between 1793 and 1801, is nine miles long, 24–27ft broad and just 10ft deep, with fifteen locks. In the 1900s, the Royal Commission on Canals reported a scheme for its enlargement and deepening as a ship canal, a scheme that was never fulfilled because of the, by then, reduced emphasis on the sea journey for cargo between Glasgow and the West Highlands and Islands which was facing competition from the railways and, ultimately, from road transport.

The Caledonian Canal is partly natural, partly artificial, and traverses picturesque Great Glen or Glenmore, connecting Loch Linnhe with the Moray Firth. It provided a safe shortcut for coastal shipping that would otherwise have passed north-about Scotland via the treacherous Pentland Firth. It comprises lochs Lochy, Oich, Ness and Dochfour, joined by twenty-three miles of cuttings. In its heyday it was chiefly used by the fishing fleets, and by small steamers, some of which afforded tourists easy access to Loch Ness and all the attendant sights. However, it was never quite big enough to accommodate the merchant shipping traffic its designers envisaged.

James Watt made a survey in 1773 to assess the feasibility of the canal, but work was not begun until after Telford and Jessop made their first estimate of £474,551 in 1803. In 1822, when two-thirds finished, the canal was opened for navigation but it was only finally completed in 1847. The total length is sixty miles; depth at standard level 17ft; breadth at surface

100ft, at bottom 50ft. The eventual total construction cost was £1,311,270. However, the delay in construction meant that its dimensions were never enough to accommodate the shipping that would otherwise have used it.

As time went on, the steamers that serviced the transport of goods became larger, and many could no longer fit the confines of the canals. The ship canals became less important as land connections by rail and road improved, until by the mid twentieth century they were used only by small vessels in niche trades, as a means of deploying the fishing fleets between the North Sea and the Atlantic, and increasingly used as a leisure amenity. Needless to say, in the early days of steam virtually all the first-generation wooden paddle steamers could use the canals, but with the introduction of the screw propeller there was a determined effort to design ships that could carry the maximum cargo deadweight in a hull which took advantage of the limiting dimensions of the canal. The classic success of this approach was the Clyde 'Puffer' of Para Handy fame, which fitted the locks of the Forth & Clyde Canal with not an inch to spare, and could navigate throughout the canal fully loaded without grounding. Sadly, the Forth & Clyde Canal has been rudely truncated by road bridges for which money was apparently not available to allow other than a mean 9ft air draught. It is perhaps as well that the Carron Company puffers no longer run between Falkirk and Port Dundas!

References

Body, G, 1971. *British paddle steamers*. David & Charles, Newton Abbot.

Duckworth, C L D & Langmuir, G E, 1972. *Clyde river and other steamers*. Brown, Son & Ferguson, Glasgow.

Ferguson, S, 2008. *From Burma to Barra, the life and times of a Marine Superintendent*. Ardminish Press, Gigha.

Gibbs, V, 1952. *Western Ocean Passenger liners and liners 1934–1969*. Brown, Son & Ferguson, Glasgow.

Harvey, W J & Telford, P J, 2002. *The Clyde Shipping Company*. P J Telford.

Howarth, D & Howarth, S, 1986. *The story of P&O*. Weidenfeld & Nicolson, London.

Hurd, A, 1922. *The Triumph of the Tramp Ship*. Cassell & Company, London.

Hyde, F E, 1956. *Blue Funnel, a history of Alfred Holt & Company of Liverpool from 1856–1914*. Liverpool University Press, Liverpool.

Knox, W W, 2013. *A history of the Scottish people, Migration: Scotland's shifting population 1840–1940*.

Laird, D, 1961. *Paddy Henderson*. George Outram & Company, Glasgow.

Lawson, W, 1927. *Pacific steamers*. Brown, Son & Ferguson, Glasgow.

Leake, B E, 2011. *The life and work of Professor J W Gregory FRS (1864–1932), geologist, writer and explorer*. Geological Society, London.

McAlistair, A A, 1976. *A short history of H Hogarth & Sons Limited*. World Ship Society, Kendal.

MacLehose, J, 1886. *Memoirs and portraits of one hundred Glasgow men*. James MacLehose & Sons, Glasgow.

McLellan, R S, 1956. *Anchor Line 1856–1956*. Anchor Line Limited, Glasgow.

Mitchell, W H and Sawyer, L A, 1966. *Wartime Standard Ships 2, the Oceans, the Forts and the Parks*. The Journal of Commerce and Shipping Telegraph, Liverpool.

Moore, K L, 2009. 'Maritime Scotland 1800–1914' in K Veitch (ed), *Transport and Communications: Scottish Life and Society: A Compendium of Scottish Ethnology*, vol 8. John Donald, Edinburgh, pp 97–136.

Robins, N, 2006. *The Corporation that changed the world*. Pluto Press, London.

Scott, F, 2012. 'Technology and the four-masted commercial sailing ship, 1875–1950'. *The Mariner's Mirror*, 98, 4, 409–20.

Taylor, J, 1976. *Ellermans, a wealth of shipping*. Wilton House Gentry, London.

Walton, T, 1896. *Know your own ship: a simple explanation of stability, trim, construction, tonnage and freeboard of ships, together with a fully worked out set of the usual ship calculations (from drawings)*. Charles Griffin & Company, London.

Watters, B, 2010. *Carron, where iron runs like water*. Falkirk Local History Society, Falkirk.

Weyndling, W, 2005. *West coast tales, riveters, wrecks and ring-netters*. Birlinn, Edinburgh.

Index

General

Ships

(year of construction in brackets)